John N. Adams and
Roger Brownsword

UNDERSTANDING CONTRACT LAW

Fourth Edition

LONDON
SWEET & MAXWELL
2004

Fourth Edition published by Sweet & Maxwell Ltd
Of 100 Avenue Road, Swiss Cottage, London NW3 3PF
http://www.sweetandmaxwell.co.uk

Third Edition published by Sweet & Maxwell Ltd 2000

Second Edition published by Fontana Press 1994
Reprinted 1996

First Edition published in Great Britain by Fontana Press 1987

John N. Adams and Roger Brownsword assert the moral right to be
identified as the authors of this work

ISBN 0421 858 508

Typeset by J&L Composition, Filey, North Yorkshire

Printed in Great Britain by TJ International Ltd, Padstow, Cornwall

CONTRACT LAW

John N. Adams, Barrister at Law, is Professor of Intellectual
Property at the University of Sheffield (formerly Professor of
Commercial Law at the University of Kent at Canterbury).

Roger Brownsword is Professor of Law at King's College
London and Honorary Professor in Law at the University
of Sheffield.

AUSTRALIA
Law Book Co.
Sydney

Canada and USA
Carswell
Toronto

HONG KONG
Sweet & Maxwell Asia

NEW ZEALAND
Brookers
Wellington

SINGAPORE and MALAYSIA
Sweet & Maxwell Asia
Singapore and Kuala Lumpur

UNDERSTANDING LAW
Editor: Roger Brownsword

Understanding Law
John N. Adams and Roger Brownsword

Understanding Contract Law
John N. Adams and Roger Brownsword

Understanding Criminal Law
C.M.V. Clarkson

Understanding Public Law
Gabriele Ganz

Understanding Equity and Trusts
Jeffrey Hackney

Understanding Tort Law
Carol Harlow

Understanding Property Law
W.T. Murphy and Simon Roberts

CONTENTS

PART II: THE JUDGES AND THE RULE-BOOK

AUTHORS' PREFACE TO THE FIRST EDITION

There has probably been a greater consensus about the basic syllabus in the law of contract than in any of the other core law courses. This consensus is reflected in the high degree of homogeneity in the ground covered, and the style of the standard text books. Recently, however, this consensus has begun to break down, and students are being introduced to a wide variety of approaches drawn from the considerable amount of sociological and economic literature which has appeared over the last twenty years or more. Whilst some of the economic literature is relatively easy to match with the traditional approach, the sociological literature, selected on what is all too often a "pick-'n'-mix" basis, presents difficulties to students who find themselves confused by the apparent disjucture between the textbook approach and the approach adopted in the readings. One of the objects of this book is to provide students with a sort of map which will allow them to locate the traditional textbook material within a theoretical landscape. Given the vastness of the subject, we have only been able to provide, at best, a rough monitoring map, rather than a walking map. We hope, however, that by building from the traditional textbook approach, and its materials, we will enable students to find their bearings. Whilst we start with our feet very firmly on the ground, we end up heading for the epistemological stratosphere, as we have thought it necessary to provide a critique which will locate the theroies of change, as well as our own analysis, in the methodology of social science generally. The attempt to make this comprehensible may be ambitious, but we believe it to be absolutely necessary, because it is something about which lawyers who turn to social science are too often ignorant.

We would like to thank Professor John Griffith and Professor Brian Simpson for reading various parts of this book, and for their very helpful comments. Also, we would like to thank Margaret Keys and Shirley Peacock for their secretarial assitance. Needless to say, responsibility for the final text, and for errors and omissions, is entirely ours

John N. Adams
Roger Brownsword

PART I

GROUNDWORK

1

UNDERSTANDING CONTRACT:
FIRST STEPS

This book is an introduction to the law of contract, and to theories about the law of contract. The law of contract, roughly speaking, is about the legal rules regulating agreements that the courts will enforce. These rules determine whether a particular transaction, the purchase of this book for example, is contractual, and to this extent they specify the conditions under which agreements may be enforced, and prescribe the remedies available in the event of defective or non-performance.

In Part I we prepare the ground by introducing (though at this stage not expanding upon) some of the main themes, including aspects of the historical development of contract; in Part II we concentrate on the modern English law of contract as it is conventionally studied, and attempt to elicit one significant network of values and tensions underlying it; and, finally, in Part III we consider some theories about the transformation of contract. Our first step, however, is to indicate how our approach to contract relates to the traditional presentation of the subject. After that, we draw a thumbnail sketch of the ruling concept of contract.

1. STUDYING CONTRACT

The study of law has been dominated by a particular approach, pejoratively branded by its critics as the "black-letter" approach. Within the black-letter tradition, the study of law is equated with the narrow study of legal rules. The books containing these rules, traditional student texts such as those written by Atiyah (1989), Beatson (2002), Furmston (2001), and Treitel (2003), we parody by referring to them collectively as the "rule-book". The purpose of this device will become apparent in due course. At this stage, however, it should be pointed out that there are in fact significant differences between these texts, and students should not be misled, by the label "rule-book" being applied to them collectively, into thinking that there are not. Moreover, readers should not be misled into thinking that they are rule-books in the sense, for example, that the books laying down the rules of football or cricket are rule-books. They are books which set out to explain the scheme of concepts employed to categorize, analyse and resolve certain types of dispute. However, to the extent that traditionally to study contract is simply to familiarise oneself with the rules and principles contained in these textbooks, we feel justified in using the admittedly imperfect label "rule-book" as shorthand for them.

The principal objection to the traditional presentation is that it invites an uncritical approach to contract, at best discouraging enquiry, and at worst encouraging misunderstanding. Critics of the standard approach contend that, just as we would not think that someone who could recite British train timetables understood railways, we should not think that an ability to recite the rule-book indicates an understanding of contract.

Like the critics of the traditional approach, we seek to stimulate enquiry and to promote understanding. Given that our book is of an introductory nature, this means that we aspire simply to lay the foundations for a critical approach to the law of contract. However, this does not necessitate working with radically different materials from those to be found within the traditional presentation. On the contrary, our focus is largely the traditional contract materials themselves.

Now, in the light of our concession to the traditional materials, it may be thought that our talk of a critical approach is simply cosmetic. This, however, is not so. We challenge a number of key assumptions, which are taken for granted in the black-letter tradition. Some appreciation of the extent of our departure from the traditional approach can be gleaned from the following comments which will, we hope, clarify the thrust of our approach.

(i) *Identifying the law of contract*

An inspection of the standard contract textbooks will reveal that whilst these books gloss the law in different ways, they share a high degree of homogeneity both with regard to the body of doctrine that they take to represent as the law of contract, and with regard to the cases that they use to expound that doctrine. Within the traditional presentation, contract has crystallised into an agreed litany of rules, principles and cases, all organised in a somewhat similar way. The traditional approach does not much question the basis for selecting this catalogue of materials.

The materials for the contract rule-book have to be gathered together from a basic stock of legal materials, that is, from statutes and case-law (precedents). The contract rule-book is not self-selecting: statutes and precedents do not come ready-marked for inclusion in the rule-book. The materials traditionally selected for inclusion, however, are drawn almost entirely from case-law; statutes hardly feature at all. Indeed, contract is traditionally viewed as the case-law subject *par excellence*. Yet for many years there has been widespread statutory regulation of agreements (*e.g.* concerning agreements between employers and employees, and landlords and tenants). Accordingly, a simple objection to the traditional selection of materials is that its case-law bias unjustifiably ignores or marginalises many relevant statutory developments. These developments, it may be noted, however, in general presume the scheme of things set out in the rule-book. What we are saying, therefore, is not that the rule-book is redundant, but that the picture it presents is rather of the foundations than of the building. Moreover, just as you cannot lay the foundations of a building properly without knowing what kind of a structure is to be built on top of them, so the foundations laid down in the rule-book do not always support adequately the structures which need to be built on them.

The upshot of these reflections as far as students are concerned is that we have a choice. We can follow the traditional rule-book, or we can accept the critics' invitation to add to it various statutes and other materials which regulate agreements. Of course, this choice is immaterial to legal practitioners seeking to advise clients on their legal position, for here all relevant materials must be taken into account.

For our rather different purpose, the choice must be confronted. Where, as in Parts I and II, we are concerned to understand the origins of the rule-book as traditionally conceived, tensions *within* it, ideologies surrounding it, and its use in dispute settlement, then, necessarily, our focus is the contract rule-book itself. However, where, as in Part III, our enquiry is directed at understanding the transformation of the legal regulation of agreements, we are concerned with a broader concept of contract.

(ii) Compartmentalisation in the rule-book

As we have said, the traditional presentation of the contract rule-book follows a more or less standard pattern. One of the features of this pattern is that the materials are arranged in a compartmentalised fashion. First, there are the materials on "offer and acceptance", then on "consideration", "intention to create legal relations" and "certainty of terms". At a later stage, the materials on "misrepresentation", "mistake", "illegality" and "frustration" are expounded. Finally, the materials on "remedies" are dealt with. Rather like a ticket collector on a railway train, the student of contract moves from one carriage to the next, the materials in each compartment apparently having no closer connection with one another than the passengers in each carriage.

All expositions require some sort of formal structure, but the result of the traditional presentation often is that students do not see connections between different sections of the rule-book. Such connections can be made in a number of ways, but the connection we wish to make is that all sections of the rule-book exhibit symptoms of the tensions arising out of two competing general contractual philosophies. Thus in Part II we attempt to break away from the traditional presentation to the extent that we try to show that a variety of contract disputes are shot through with the same pattern of competing considerations, and that the rule-book materials are underpinned by competing philosophies which are indifferent to the traditional compartments.

(iii) Inconsistency in the rule-book

We can press the metaphor of the railway train a little further. According to the traditional presentation, the rule-book materials, like the passengers on a train, are all travelling in the same direction. The materials in the rule-book must be viewed, in principle, as harmonious. To some extent this makes life easy for the student as inconvenient decisions are dropped out of the rule-book, but, at some stage or another, every student of contract will be put through the exercise of attempting to reconcile certain notorious rule-book precedents which seem plainly to be at odds with one another. As an intellectual exercise, this has merits, but only so long as it does not lead students into believing that there is one seamless web of law.

The traditional rejection of inconsistency in the rule-book and the assumption of reconcilability are not presuppositions of our discussion. As we have hinted already, we see disputes centred on the traditional rule-book as exhibiting various tensions. Sometimes judges are guided by the rule-book, at others by desired results. Sometimes judges' decisions are underwritten by considerations of commercial convenience, at others by considerations of fairness and reasonableness. One key to understanding contract is to understand the complex interplay between these competing considerations or ideologies (which is not to say, of course, that they are the only ones). Inevitably, these conflicting ideologies inject inconsistent doctrines into the contract rulebook. Attempting to reconcile conflicting precedents, it may be argued, is misguided rather than heroic (which is not to say that careful characterisation of fact situations and the seeking out of *real* differences between cases is a pointless exercise: it is an essential part of the common law tradition—see Llewellyn (1960)).

In our view, it is a mistake to think of contract as a train-load of doctrine chugging along in one direction. Rather, it is carried on several trains, some bound on collision courses with one another.

(iv) Fidelity to the rule-book

The standard presentation usually carries the implication that judicial decisions are governed by the traditional rule-book materials. Whilst we would not deny that the rule-book materials are important, it will be clear from our earlier observations that we cannot accept that judicial decisions are necessarily, in the final analysis, governed by these materials. Our portrayal of contract in Part II presupposes a fundamental tension between a rule-book approach and a result-orientated approach.

Our assumption that judges on occasion deviate from the materials of the traditional rule-book is by no means novel. The central contention of the American legal realist tradition is that judicial decisions can only be understood if they are interpreted less in terms of the "paper rules" than in terms of the "real rules" (see, *e.g.* Llewellyn, 1960; Twining, 1973). Cast in the terminology of American legal realism, our presentation of contract disputes suggests that the paper rules are only sometimes decisive. Where the paper rules are not decisive, the real rules reside either in the facilitation of commerce, or in the promotion of fairness and reasonableness (which ends are different, and not always compatible).

(v) The significance of the rule-book in practice

By rejecting the assumption of judicial fidelity to a consistent rule-book, we have challenged the traditional presentation of contract. Yet, some critics of the traditional approach may complain that even our view of the rule-book fails to be sufficiently critical. In order to understand contract, such critics will argue, it is not enough to grasp how the traditional rule-book figures in judicial thinking, particularly in the practice of judges in the higher courts. We must grasp the general significance of the rule-book.

Such critics urge that we should study contract "in its social context", and that we should recognise the distinction between the law-in-the-books and the law-in-action. This is somewhat akin to emphasising the possibility of a gap between railway timetables and the actual running of the trains, between the paper timetable and the real timetable. The timetables say one thing, but, as we all know, the trains often run differently.

In the case of contract, the critics are quite right to caution against jumping to conclusions about the practical significance of the rule-book. For example, students tutored along traditional lines may form a view of a world in which victims of breaches of contract invariably litigate their rule-book remedies, and in which agreements are unfailingly drafted in the light of the rule-book. Such a world is, of course, imaginary.

Let us first consider the assumption that victims of breaches of contract litigate. Is this so? There are many kinds of victim of many kinds of breach of many kinds of contract. We can categorise contracts according to their trading context (shipping, building, engineering, commodities, etc.), their subject matter (sale of goods, sale of land, supply of services, etc.), degrees of formality (written or oral), mode (electronic or non-electronic) routineness (*i.e.* whether individual terms were negotiated), duration (*i.e.* whether the contract is to be performed over a period of time as opposed to simultaneous performance), the status of the parties (consumer individuals, companies, etc.), and so on. Out of the many variables around which a contextualising typology could be constructed, we will concentrate on the following three categories (for an extension of this typology, see Chapter 9):

(a) a "private" contract, *i.e.* where neither party makes the contract in the course of a business;

(b) a "consumer" contract, *i.e.* where one party makes the contract in the course of a business, but the other party (the consumer) does not; and,

(c) a "commercial" contract, *i.e.* where both parties make the contract in the course of a business.

Admittedly, the idea of someone making a contract "in the course of a business" is a bit vague (see *Stevenson v Rogers* (1999)), but this threefold categorisation of contracts at least enables us to structure our thinking about which victims of breaches of contract are likely to litigate their rights.

Starting with the parties to a private agreement, the rule-book in fact assumes that domestic and social agreements, as opposed to non-business dealings, are not normally intended to be legally binding. Consequently, private parties who seek legal advice may well abandon the idea of litigation as soon as they are warned that the courts will not lightly find that private agreements are intended to be contractually binding. This, however, makes the bold assumption that private parties are sufficiently litigious to contemplate taking legal advice in the first place. Ordinarily, one would expect the combination of cost, ignorance, and friendship to militate strongly against any such action.

Consumer contracts are a little more complex, for the parties, being of different standing, may each see litigation in a different light. From the point of view of the party who makes the contract in the course of a business, the need for litigation may be avoided by various routine safety devices (*e.g.* taking security for a debt, insisting upon cash on delivery or the use of card-guaranteed cheques, etc.). Beyond this, the policy one takes on pursuing bad debts, or on acceding to customer complaints, will be a matter for cost/benefit analysis and more general considerations concerning one's trading reputation. From the standpoint of the consumer, the inconvenience, uncertainty, mystery, and cost of litigation (actual and feared) all militate strongly against pursuing a contractual remedy through the courts. Consider, for example, what one might do if having purchased a copy of this book one found several pages missing. Suppose one telephoned the bookshop, only to be told politely but firmly:

(i) "It is not the policy of the bookshop to exchange books or to refund money";
(ii) "Complaints cannot be considered without proof of purchase";
(iii) "Complaints should be addressed to the publishers";
(iv) "All books are checked and deemed to leave the shop in perfect condition"; or,
(v) "Books are sold on the basis that the shop accepts no responsibility for their quality or condition. Sorry!"

Can the bookshop duck out of responsibility like this? Is the rule-book on the side of the purchaser or the bookshop in this sort of dispute? Most consumers simply do not know. So what do they do? Put it down to experience, and avoid that particular bookshop in the future? Contact their local Trading Standards Department, or Consumer Advice Centre? Write an outraged letter to a consumer complaints column of a newspaper? Or consult a lawyer? For self-evident reasons, the last option is the least likely to be taken up. Accordingly, consumers litigate this type of dispute only exceptionally.

Finally, we come to commercial agreements. Now, here (as in the case of consumer contracts), the rule-book assumes that the parties intend to enter into legally binding relations. Nevertheless, it would be a mistake to assume that commercial contractors are fond of litigation. Indeed, one of the truisms of the "law in context" school is that businessmen do not normally litigate their disputes. As Stewart Macaulay (1977), the doyen of this school, has put it:

> "In all of these societies [where the relevant research has been conducted, namely, Poland, the USA, Great Britain, Indonesia, Japan, Korea, and Ethiopia]—which differ so greatly in social structure, culture, and political and economic ideology—the picture looks much the same. Industrial managers and merchants seldom litigate to solve their disputes about contract, preferring to use other techniques of dispute avoidance and settlement." (see further, p.507)

But, how does one account for this international commercial aversion to litigation? Clearly, one reason is simply the cost of litigation (and, remember, in English law the general rule is that the loser pays the winner's costs). Another, equally important, reason, as confirmed by a number of well-known studies (see, *e.g.* Macaulay, 1963; Beale and Dugdale, 1975), is that commercial enterprises locked into a mutually beneficial network of economic relationships cannot afford to damage these relationships by litigating their disputes—indeed, in longer-term contractual relationships of this type, one would expect longer-term calculations to discourage short-term opportunism of any kind (whether in the form of litigation or otherwise) in favour of a culture of more co-operative relationships with one's fellow contractors (see Campbell and Harris, 1993). Moreover, it must be remembered that litigation remits the issue to the contract rule-book, a rule-book largely devised in the nineteenth century and often ill-suited to resolving the kinds of disputes presented by commercial contractors nowadays (see, *e.g.* Williamson, 1979). Accordingly, a plausible hypothesis is that the probability of commercial litigation is a function of: (a) the present value of continuing economic relationships; and (b) the level of the anticipated return from litigation—in short, the higher the value of continuing economic relationships and the lower the anticipated return, the less likely it is that commercial contractors will resort to litigation (*cf.* Trubek, 1975). In such a context, the economically rational response to a dispute is to settle by means other than litigation. Conversely, of course, where the value of continuing relationships is low and the anticipated return is high, we can expect more frequent recourse to litigation. In line with this view, research into an apparent increase in commercial litigation in the United States, has detected a growth of "one-shot" dealing (where the value of continuing relationships is low) as one of the explanatory factors (see, *e.g.* Galanter and Rogers, 1988).

Although the weight of the law in context research confirms that litigation is the exception rather than the rule in the commercial community, it does not follow that the rule-book has no bearing on dispute-settlement (it might, for example, play a background role in the informal compromise of commercial disputes) or on the nature of the relationship between the contractors (there is evidence, for example, that the rule-book can contribute in various ways to the creation of a relationship of trust, confidence and co-operation between the parties, see Deakin and Michie, 1997). Nor does it follow that commercial disputes are never litigated. As we have just remarked, where commercial contracting becomes more one-shot and less relational (less economically inter-dependent and less long-term), litigation may become more attractive to disputants. Moreover, although managers and merchants may generally prefer to avoid litigation, it cannot be assumed that these contractors always have an entirely free hand in deciding whether or not to litigate (*cf.* Blegvad, 1990). For example, within large organisations, in-house lawyers might encourage a more formal (legalistic) approach to disputes. Similarly, it should be borne in mind that quite a lot of commercial disputes are really about the apportionment of insurance risks, and the real disputants are insurance companies standing behind their clients. Thus, international carriage contracts, for example, tend to be characterised by a relatively high level of litigation.

Just as we must avoid assuming that the possibility in principle of exercising one's rule-book remedies is automatically converted, in practice, into litigation, we must avoid too the assumption that the rule-book *necessarily* shapes the drafting of agreements, or that where it does shape the drafting of agreements it does so in a direct way. We can comment briefly on this aspect of the rule-book's practical significance, once again taking our bearings from our threefold categorisation of contracts.

Private contractors will rarely draft the *minutiae* of their agreements, let alone draft them in the light of the rule-book. Quite apart from any other inhibiting factors, lay ignorance of the rule-book must militate against conscious rule-book planning.

Consumer contracts present a rather different picture. As readers will be aware, it is common nowadays for consumers to be offered goods or services on a dealer's or supplier's non-negotiable standard terms. Predictably, such terms tend to be weighted in favour of the dealer or supplier, and, over the years, there has been quite a "game" as draftsmen have endeavoured to make their standard forms "judge proof". In this sense, standard form consumer contracts have certainly been drafted with the rule-book in view. More recently, however, the legislature has intervened in this game by enacting a range of statutes aimed at consumer protection. The upshot of this legislation is that many hitherto typical contractual terms are now unenforceable; and many standard form provisions in consumer contracts have been revised or deleted (see below, p.223).

If drafters of consumer contracts do not necessarily apply the spirit of the rule-book, there is evidence that the rule-book may be openly flouted by the drafters of commercial contracts. The context which most invites such defiance of the rule-book is where a commercial relationship rests on gross disparity of bargaining power. Commercial giants can effectively lay down the law to commercial pygmies, and there is little that the latter can do about it. For example, a multi-national motor manufacturer may be able to dictate terms to both its dealers and component suppliers. The fact that the terms may be of dubious legal effect when tested against the rule-book is irrelevant, for dealers and suppliers cannot afford to step out of line and be terminated (see, *e.g.* Macaulay, 1966—which study also shows how the dealers were able to organise themselves politically to redress the imbalance).

Our sketchy comments on the practical significance of the rule-book should not be misunderstood. We have not attempted to provide full answers to our questions about litigation and drafting, merely to draw attention to some of the problems associated with the operation of the rule-book in practice. An understanding of the operation of the rule-book in practice, however, would require investigation—both theoretical and empirical—on a scale far beyond anything so far attempted (*cf.* Vincent-Jones, 1989). This, of course, does not imply that we regard such enquiries as irrelevant or unprofitable. On the contrary, our critical approach assumes that such enquiries can make an important contribution to the understanding of contract. As we said before, there is more to understanding railways than reading the timetable.

2. THE RULING CONCEPT OF CONTRACT

According to the standard view, the field of contract comprises "formal contracts" (promises made formally in a deed—the formalities are set out in s.1 of the Law of Property (Miscellaneous Provisions) Act 1989) and "simple contracts" ("agreements" or "bargains" not made in a deed). In both cases, contract is concerned with the enforcement of expectation-based obligations. To this, the rule-book adds some important light and shade.

First, formal contracts are marginalised. Whatever their historical significance, and, as we will see, it was considerable, formal contracts are no longer conceived to be a central concern of contract. Secondly, agreement and bargain are viewed as the focal aspects of contract. Contract may have its roots in promises, but the conventional starting point tends to be the idea of a contract as an enforceable agreement. Thirdly, "bilateral contracts" (agreements constituted by an exchange of promises) are taken to be paradigmatic.

To come to terms with the rule-book concept of contract we must do a little groundwork with respect to promises and agreement. Consider, first, the following three categories of promise:

(i) A strictly unilateral (gratuitous) promise, *e.g.* Jack (of "Jack and the Beanstalk") promises to give away his mother's last cow to the butcher whom he meets on the way to the market, Jack (contrary to the story) asking for nothing in return for the cow.

(ii) A promise-in-return-for-an-act, *e.g.* Jack (again contrary to the story) promises to give the butcher the cow if the butcher can grow a beanstalk, climb up it, kill the giant

who lives in the land at the top of the beanstalk, and
return safely with the giant's riches.

(iii)   A promise-in-return-for-a-promise, *e.g.* Jack (this time
more or less as in the story) promises to give the butcher
the cow if the butcher promises to give him some magic
beans in return.

Promise (i) *requires* no reciprocal act (as in (ii)). Nor does it
require any reciprocal promise of performance by the promisee (as
in (iii)). It could be straightforwardly unconditional, as in our
example, or it could be conditional, but not in a way that makes a
return demand on the promisee (*e.g.* where Jack promises to give
the cow to the butcher if it rains the following day). What really
matters about promise (i) is not so much whether it is unconditional or conditional, but that it requires no return act or promise
of performance from the promisee. Promises (ii) and (iii), by
contrast, are "reciprocal-conditional" precisely because they do
stipulate some return act or promise of performance.

Next, we can distinguish between the following three senses of
agreement:

(i)   Agreement-as-acceptance, meaning a promisee's willingness to stand in the position of promisee with respect to a
particular promise (*e.g.* the butcher indicates that he
agrees to accept Jack's gratuitous promise to give him his
brown cow—maybe the butcher would not have so
accepted a gratuitous promise to give him a white
elephant).

(ii)   Agreement-as-bargain-form, meaning a form of reciprocal arrangement (*e.g.* Jack proposes to give his cow to the
butcher in return for some reciprocal act or promise
of performance).

(iii)   Agreement-as-commitment, meaning a promisee's indication of his commitment to an agreement-as-bargain-
form, where the promisor has stipulated the making of a
reciprocal promise.

To what extent can these three senses of agreement be found
where we are dealing with each of the three categories of promise
previously identified?

First, if Jack gratuitously promises to give away his cow to
the butcher, the butcher can either accept or not accept.
Assuming that the butcher accepts Jack's gift, there is agreement-

as-acceptance. However, there can never be agreement in either of the other two senses, for both these senses presuppose a return condition for the promisee, and this is missing in the gratuitous promise. Next, if Jack promises to give the butcher his cow only if the butcher grows a beanstalk, climbs up it, kills the giant who lives in the land at the top of the beanstalk and returns safely with the giant's riches, then Jack's proposal is an agreement-as-bargain-form, and this stands irrespective of whether the butcher accepts Jack's challenge. If the butcher accepts the challenge, then there is also agreement-as-acceptance. What there cannot be, however, is agreement-as-commitment, since this presupposes a promise-in-return-for-a-promise. Finally, if Jack promises to give his cow to the butcher if the butcher promises to give Jack some magic beans, then, regardless of whether the butcher so promises, Jack's proposal constitutes an agreement-as-bargain-form. Assuming that the butcher makes the return promise, there is also agreement-as-acceptance and agreement-as-commitment. The promise-in-return-for-a-promise alone has the potential to yield agreement in all three senses.

These abstract distinctions are reflected in the doctrinal watershed between enforceable and unenforceable promises. English law, as we will see, exhibits a tension between the policy: (a) to enforce only promises which form part of an agreed exchange; (b) to enforce promises which induce reliance and change of position; and (c) to enforce a restricted number of gift and other gratuitous promises.

Now, it may seem obvious why English law should refuse, as it does, to enforce gift and other gratuitous promises, except in certain specific cases such as (viewed realistically) gratuitous promises made in contemplation of marriage, or gratuitous promises to answer for the debt or default of another if properly evidenced in writing (guarantees). English law views simple contracts as agreements in the form of a bargain (agreement-as-bargain-form), and this is just what is lacking in the case of promises of gifts. This, however, begs the question: it does not explain why agreement-as-bargain-form rather than promise is taken to be focal. Why enforce informal reciprocal-conditional promises, but not generally informal gratuitous promises? A tempting suggestion is that gratuitous promisees are getting something for nothing, unlike reciprocal-conditional promisees, and so there is no pressing reason to assist them. This, however, is at odds with the courts' willingness to enforce gratuitous promises, provided that they are made in a deed, or in specific cases, some of which were mentioned above. Two other reasons might be advanced in support of the general policy of non-enforcement of informal gratuitous promises. First, it might be argued that it is right to protect gratuitous promisors against the consequences of impulsive promises which they later regret. Certainly, if Jack had promised to give away the cow to the butcher he would have had cause for regret, for his mother, it will be recalled, was furious with him for having traded the family's last asset for the beans. Secondly, one might defend the policy as a strategy to discourage mischievous claims. After all, it would not do to have the courts swamped with rogue butchers fraudulently claiming that cattle owners had informally promised to give away their livestock to them. Neither explanation is entirely convincing. As we shall see, mainstream contract doctrine hardly encourages the protection of impulsive promisors, and, even if the law were paternalistic, to refuse to enforce all informal gratuitous promises would be too sweeping unless one supposed that judges were incapable of distinguishing serious promises, made with due deliberation (possibly even in writing), from impulsive (possibly even joking) promises. Moreover, given the deterrents to litigation, the second argument does not really seem to stand close examination. A more convincing (albeit less simple) explanation can be found in the development of the rule-book itself, which we discuss in the next chapter (*cf.* Gordley, 2001).

We can close this introduction by reflecting on the relationship between the idea of agreement, and the pattern of the ruling concept of contract as set out in the rule-book. When it is a matter of drawing the line between those informal promises which are enforceable and those which are not, agreement-as-bargain-form is crucial. This, as we have seen, generally shuts out gratuitous promises not in a deed, and restricts enforcement to unilateral (promise-in-return-for-an-act) and bilateral (promise-in-return-for-a-promise) contracts. This implies that unilateral and bilateral contracts are effectively on a par with one another. In terms of enforceability this is true, but it ignores our earlier point that the ruling framework takes the bilateral contract as its model. The centrality of the bilateral contract ties in closely with the structure of the idea of agreement, for, as we have seen, it is only in the bilateral contract that agreement in each of its senses is instantiated. Once contract is associated with the idea of agreement, it is natural to treat the bilateral contract as the paradigm, the unilateral contract as a slightly deviant case, and the gratuitous promise as an extremely marginal case, and this, on the whole, is the ruling concept of contract (*cf.* Atiyah, 1978a).

2
THE RULE-BOOK IN HISTORICAL PERSPECTIVE

What we attempt to provide in this chapter is not a history of the law of contract (excellent accounts of this can be found in the standard works, see, *e.g.* Furmston, 2001: 1 *et seq.*). What we try to focus on are those historical developments which are relevant for the purposes of the present exposition. We also attempt to place the rule-book in the tradition to which it belongs, which today is an academic tradition: the rule-book today is above all an academic product. It has an uneasy relationship with many types of mercantile transaction, which it might reasonably be supposed would fall within its scope. It is quite useful to be disabused at the outset, however, of the view that the law of contract as expounded in the rule-book is necessarily of central importance to commerce. There are, of course, good reasons why business-men do not need to bother with the rule-book at all in many situations (see pp.10–12). However, more unexpectedly, there are quite a number of well-developed branches of commercial *law* which simply do not square easily with the ruling concept of contract as expounded in the rule-book, and there are situations where the rule-book gives an answer much at variance with commercial convenience (or with common sense). We will give some illustrations.

Bankers' documentary credits are the principal mechanism of payment in international sales, but the beneficiary under them gives no "consideration." (*i.e.* pays nothing) to the issuing or confirming bank (see pp.74 *et seq.*). No one doubts, however, that if the beneficiary presents the correct documents, he is entitled to be paid by the bank, and that in the case of a confirmed irrevocable credit, the bank cannot withdraw its offer before such presentation. This exception to the general rules falls within an area of mercantile law, which includes negotiable instruments, where (as explained below) the general rules have never really applied in their full rigour. Other exceptions have had to be created by statute. For example, a car is insured by its owner. Persons injured by the insured therefore have no claim in contract against the insurers because they are third parties to the contract of insurance. This rule is now modified in some instances by statute, but it still gives rise to anomalies in other situations. A statutory modification had also to be introduced in the case of bills of lading which are the documents which govern the terms under which goods are carried by sea. For good commercial reasons (partly in order to obviate double insurance) these limit the carrier's liability. This limitation is now regulated by international conventions. Obviously, the exemptions are binding between the original parties to the contract of carriage, but frequently the goods are sold whilst they are still at sea, and the bill of lading transferred to the buyer who of course is not a party to the original contract of carriage. Without the statutory modification contained in the Carriage of Goods by Sea Act 1992 (replacing the Bills of Lading Act 1855), the indorsee (usually the buyer) would not be affected by these limitations, nor incidentally would he be able to sue the carrier on the contract of carriage (see *The Aliakmon*, 1986). A more homely example of a similar problem is the manufacturer's guarantee you find in the box when you buy new goods. The contract of sale is made with the shop where you bought the goods, and even if you post off the "guarantee" card to the manufacturer it is difficult to see what consideration you give in return for it. Such a "guarantee" looks more like a promise by the manufacturer than a bargain with you, the customer (see pp.13–14 and 89–91). Once again, legislation has come to the rescue of the common law rule-book, reg. 15(1) of the Sale and Supply of Goods to Consumers Regulations (SI 2002/3045) providing that, where goods are sold or supplied to consumers with guarantees of this kind, then the guarantee "takes effect at the time the goods are delivered *as a contractual obligation* owed by the guarantor under the conditions set out in the guarantee and the associated advertising" (our emphasis).

How it comes about that so many commercial transactions do not fit comfortably into the rule-book requires some explanation. In the remainder of this chapter we attempt to provide an explanation, and to explain some other features of the rule-book which may puzzle the student.

1. THE EMERGENCE OF THE MODERN LAW OF CONTRACT

(i) The law merchant

As we have just pointed out, the law relating to negotiable instruments provides important exceptions to the rules set out in the rule-book, *e.g.* exceptionally, third parties can benefit, and "past consideration" (*i.e.* past performance) is good consideration. Historically speaking, the rules relating to bills of exchange, which are an important type of negotiable instrument, were not part of the common law at all, but part of a separate body of rules, the "law merchant". The way in which this law evolved, and was absorbed into the common law, makes an instructive comparison with the way in which some of the less commercial rule-book rules seem to have arisen.

An important part of international trade in the Middle Ages was carried on through the system of fairs which existed throughout Europe and North Africa (remnants of this system existed in North Africa down to recent times). Merchants would travel from fair to fair with their wares. Like other sections of the contemporary population, merchants had their personal law (a very different concept from our concept of national law), so that when they needed to resort to a tribunal they resorted to their own tribunals, *e.g.* fair (*i.e.* market) courts (the growth of national tribunals in any modern sense occurs fairly late). The English fair courts tended to deal with smaller internal transactions (V HEL 113). There were many other courts dealing with mercantile disputes, however. Important towns would have their courts, *e.g.* London had the "hustings" in the Guildhall, and in the fourteenth century a system of royal courts was set up in the Staple towns, competing with the older courts. In the later fifteenth century, partly because of changing patterns of trade, partly because of the advantages it offered as a tribunal, merchants began to litigate their suits in the Court of Admiralty. One advantage this court offered was that its procedures were based upon the ideas of the civil law, which would have been more familiar, to foreign merchants at any rate, than those of the common law.

We must again set aside our modern notions of a single national law, for Admiralty was in the main a civil law, *i.e.* a Roman law-based, tribunal—as were the Court of Requests and Star Chamber, both in the sixteenth century operating side by side with the common law courts. Indeed, these tribunals were serviced by separate professions trained in the civil law. Whereas the common law barristers would join one of the four Inns of Court, and had no need of a university degree, the civil lawyers were university educated, and the court lawyers joined an institution known as Doctors' Commons. By and large, the professions tended to come from different back-grounds, the common lawyers from the gentry, and the civil lawyers from more humble origins. The civil lawyers were both ideologically and from the point of view of patronage more dependent on the Crown (see Levack, 1973). It was their misfortune therefore that they found themselves on the losing side in the political turmoil which culminated in the civil war. An effect of the successful attacks of the common lawyers on the civil law tribunals was to ensure that when a national law of contract developed, it was not civilian, and that merchant custom became part of the common law. Ironically, as we will see, however, the rule-book, when it emerged, owed a great deal to a civilian tradition.

The two branches of the Law Merchant, commercial law and maritime law, were developed and applied in similar special tribunals throughout Europe. The Law Merchant was a cosmopolitan body of law, though not an entirely homogeneous one (V HEL 60 *et seq.*). Thus northern maritime customs differed from those of the Mediterranean towns, and there were local variations in commercial customs. Some of the most important branches of English commercial law were derived from the Law Merchant, for example the law governing contracts of marine insurance, and, as mentioned above, the rules governing negotiable instruments, also the rules governing contracts of carriage by sea, and many other branches of our modern commercial law (VIII HEL 99 *et seq.*).

A general characteristic of this body of law, and of the tribunals which administered it, was its aptness to the needs of merchants. After the decline of Admiralty and the civilian legal profession, the common lawyers who had coveted mercantile work found themselves ill-equipped to deal with it. Partly this was because of the technical procedures of the common law, in particular difficulties in accommodating rules of the Law Merchant within the common law scheme of forms of action (on the "forms of action" in contract disputes see below). A further problem was that even if a case could be got to trial (and the procedures were slower than those of Admiralty), juries were ill-equipped to adjudicate on such technical matters. Many of the problems were surmounted in the course of the seventeenth and eighteenth centuries, Holt C.J. and Lord Mansfield being prominent in this regard (see Simpson, 1984). The result was, however, a peculiarity compared with Continental Europe: one group of courts, the royal courts, administering both common law rules and a body of rules deriving from the Law Merchant. On the Continent, by contrast, the Law Merchant continued in general to be administered by specialist courts. A consequence was that English commercial law developed more slowly than that on the Continent, partly through lack of specialist knowledge on the part of the legal profession, and partly (as noted above) because of the existence of inconvenient common law rules. Notwithstanding that we were burdened with one of the most backward bodies of commercial law in Europe, the fact that we could in the course of the eighteenth century advance along the road to becoming the first industrial nation is a salutary reminder that the relationship between legal rules and economic development may not be as direct as some people suppose. However, what requires explanation is that in the nineteenth century, when many inconveniences of the old substantive and procedural rules were swept away, and when we would expect mercantile law to occupy a central role in shaping the rule-book (which is essentially a nineteenth-century product), it remained largely in the wings.

(ii) The marginalisation of the formal contract

Students of contract quickly learn that there are two sorts of contract: simple contracts, and formal contracts contained in a deed. Of the latter, they will learn little more until they come to study land law. However, at an early period in the development of the common law, the formal contract was the dominant form of contract litigated in the courts. In this section we seek to explain why it came to be used, and how it came to be eclipsed by the simple contract.

A problem which confronts all tribunals, ancient or modern, is to determine which version of the facts to believe, for it is likely that the parties involved in a suit will tell very different stories. A modern court deals with this problem by hearing the testimony of the parties, hearing the witnesses each party has brought to court, and considering any written or other evidence they may be able to adduce. This process would have been quite alien to either the local courts or the royal courts at an early period. In the local courts, trial by compurgation or wager of law was used. This procedure was also used to adjudicate the disputes of the parties suing out writs of debt and covenant (which were the earliest "contractual" actions) in the royal courts. Under this procedure, the defendant swore, for example, that he did not owe the plaintiff money, and produced eleven oath helpers to swear to his credibility. In a small, closely knit community, with little geographical mobility, where everyone knows everyone else and belief in divine retribution is strong, this system of trial has something to be said for it. Indeed, in some respects it is not far removed from the reality of what often went on in trials of felony at Assizes up to the nineteenth century. The defendant accused of felony was not himself permitted to give evidence. How then could he acquit himself in the absence of other witnesses? The answer, which appears from the judges' notebooks which survive from the period, is that he would adduce evidence as to his character from such worthies as the local clergyman, and other trustworthy people who knew him. In practice, this system may have worked as well to protect the innocent as our modern system, for at the end of many criminal trials today it is impossible to be absolutely certain of the guilt of the defendant simply because it is impossible at the end of hearing the testimony to know what the truth was (even if all witnesses believed they were testifying to the truth). (*cf.* Adams and Brownsword, 2003, Chapter 6). Our system, or something based on similar principles, is simply more rational in a society in which people do not live in tightly knit communities and have not much fear of divine retribution.

At all events, up to the end of the thirteenth century or perhaps the beginning of the fourteenth century the mode of proof in actions of covenant was the same in the royal courts as it was in the local courts. Provided that the plaintiff could produce the witnesses to the transaction and the requisite number of oath helpers, he would succeed. However, sometime between 1290 and 1320 the royal courts began to require proof of the promise by a deed. The effect of this momentous decision is with us to the present day. The word "covenant" now possesses the meaning of an agreement contained in a deed, and such formal contracts are used in rather special circumstances, of which the one most familiar to the man in the street is the conveyance of land. Why did the royal courts take this step? The reason possibly was one familiar enough to us at the present day, to reduce pressure of work by ensuring that informal agreements were litigated in the local courts. It is not clear, however, that covenant was ever a particularly popular action. Moreover, the use of a deed in conjunction with the writ of debt was a commonly used mechanism for the enforcement of obligations until quite a late period. The obligor would bind himself by a deed to pay a certain sum of money on a certain day unless he had performed some act before that day, *e.g.* repaid a loan to the obligee. If he repaid on time, the bond would be returned to him; if he did not, he became liable for the greater sum and it could be recovered in debt. This device could be used as a mechanism to compel obligees to perform many kinds of obligation (Simpson, 1966). In an action to enforce such a bond, "debt on an obligation", there was no wager of law. However, in ordinary actions of debt, where there was no deed, wager of law was used.

From the later fourteenth century, a new action had begun to emerge, which was to confine the role of the formal contract to something like that which it enjoys at the present day. This new action was assumpsit which, from a tortious origin, had developed by the sixteenth century into an action for breach of promise. Specific sums of money owed, *e.g.* for the price of goods sold, or money lent, still had to be recovered under a writ of debt, however, and the mode of trial in that action in the absence of a deed was still wager of law, whereas in the newer action of assumpsit it was trial by jury. Although the requirement that particular forms of writ should be used for particular situations may seem at first sight strange, it is not so very different from the requirement that in order to get a grant or whatever from modern bureaucracies such as local authorities, the correct form has to be used. The early common law courts, in fact, exhibit features of modern "bureaucracies" in the non-pejorative sense in which sociologists use that term (see Weber, 1978, pp.958 *et seq.*). At all events, plaintiffs preferred trial by jury, and attempts were therefore made to use the writ of *assumpsit* in circumstances where the rules required debt. In 1602, in *Slades* case the King's Bench (one of the common law courts) decided that plaintiffs might do so (the Common Pleas had decided the same way some thirty years earlier). This case is usually regarded as one of the watersheds in the history of the common law of contract. After it, *assumpsit* became the general remedy for breaches of informal contracts, whether the plaintiff was complaining about a failure to pay a definite sum of money, or a failure to do something else. Havighurst (1961) sees *Slades* case and the eclipse of wager of law (which helped the powerful because they could afford to buy oath helpers) as part of a trend towards the development of modern contract law as a mechanism for redressing the balance between the weak and the strong. (Other views on the development of modern contract law are discussed in Chapter 9.)

(iii) The view of contracts as unilateral

Today, as we have seen, contracts are viewed as bilateral transactions, in which each of the parties exchanges obligations. However, this view grew up only in the nineteenth century. Originally a promise made on sufficient consideration was enforceable, but consideration did not imply a bilateral exchange. It was, rather, a question of having regard to the circumstances in which the promise was made (see Simpson, 1975). Thus, given the evidentiary value attached to writing, it is scarcely surprising that Lord Mansfield held in *Pillans v van Mierop* (1765) that a promise in written form was enforceable. Unfortunately, possibly because of fears that unsigned writings might take the place of deeds upon which stamp duty was levied, this development was nipped in the bud by the decision in *Rann v Hughes* (1778). The result of that decision was that a promise not in a deed had to be supported by consideration to be enforceable. But, what was consideration? Although Victorian lawyers answered along the lines that it was either "some right, interest, profit or benefit accruing to one party, or some forbearance, detriment, loss or responsibility given, suffered or undertaken by the other" (*Currie v Misa*, 1875), this was almost certainly not the view in the sixteenth century, seventeenth century or eighteenth century. Probably the doctrine originally had close affinities to the canonist doctrine of *causa* (see Barton, 1969; Simpson, 1975), and was concerned with the determination as to whether or not a promise was meant seriously by reference to the circumstances in which it was made. Thus it appears that a moral obligation was a good consideration. In *Lampleigh v Braithwait* (1615), for example, where the plaintiff had obtained a pardon for homicide for a condemned man at his request, and in gratitude been promised £100, it was held that the defendant was bound to pay this sum. Victorian attempts to rationalise this decision on the basis of an implied understanding on the plaintiff's part that he would be paid when he set out to obtain the pardon (see *Kennedy v Broun*, 1863), are an anachronism. The crucial point at the time seems to have been that the plaintiff had acted at the request of the defendant. Consequently, the subsequent promise of £100 was made on a good consideration. Under the older view, the bargained-for exchange of promises was only one kind of consideration. Moreover, the idea of a contract entailed in this older doctrine is essentially unilateral. It would have no difficulty in comprehending a whole range of important commercial transactions which, as mentioned above, at the present day fit uneasily into the law of contract. How did it come about then that the general law of contract which emerged in the nineteenth century was unable easily to comprehend these important situations?

The fact of the matter is that in 1800 there were very few detailed rules of contract. The preconditions for the emergence of detailed rules existed by that time, in particular the judge and jury had clearly defined functions, but the range of issues left to the jury was much greater than would have been considered acceptable by the mid-nineteenth century. One reason for the increasing redefinition of questions (formerly left to the jury) as questions of law was very probably the increasing numbers of contract cases coming before the courts. Judges, whatever people may think, do try to promote justice. One important principle of justice is that like cases be treated alike. A judge sitting through a number of similar cases is likely to feel uneasy about the fact that different juries are returning different verdicts. Given that any common law judge of 1800 must have been sitting through a much larger number of similar contract cases than his predecessor of 1700, it is scarcely surprising that he should wish to limit the jury's discretion. There may also have been pressure from the commercial classes for greater certainty, but given that the law of contract which did emerge was in so many ways uncommercial (and remains so to this day), it is doubtful if this was a very strong element. Indeed, it is the highly artificial academic nature of the rule-book which is its most curious feature. This is not to say that it does not cover many commercial situations. It is simply that what had emerged was surprisingly out of touch with the world of commerce whose tool it might have been supposed to be.

2. THE ORIGINS OF THE RULE-BOOK

The rule-book as we know it today is essentially a nineteenth-century creation. It is the creation largely of textbook writers. It may surprise the reader to learn that there were no English textbooks on contract before 1790, and that the ancestors of modern student textbooks (such as Anson; Atiyah; Cheshire, Fifoot and Furmston; and Treitel) only appeared in mid-Victorian times. The earlier literature of the common law tended to be written by practitioners for practitioners. They sought primarily to help the reader to answer the question "What was done in such a case before?" By contrast, the writers of the great Victorian textbooks, such as Sir William Anson and Sir Frederick Pollock, were attempting to identify underlying principles, which would be illustrated by their application in particular cases. In trying to build an orderly and symmetrical edifice upon the foundations of a few basic propositions, *e.g.* that a contract must be supported by consideration in the sense of "An act or forbearance of one party, or the promise thereof, [which] is the price for which the promise of the other is bought . . ." (Pollock), these writers were at the same time both trying to assert a distinctively common law tradition, and paradoxically doing this in a way which owed more to Continental tradition than to the common law tradition. It is necessary at this point to examine this tradition.

(i) Continental influences

Roman law influenced the development of the common law at various stages, and the revival of the study of Roman law is of great importance to our story. Up to the eleventh century, the Church had a virtual monopoly on learning in all fields. In that century, however, an event which was to contribute greatly to the destruction of this monopoly occurred. A dispute arose between the Holy Roman Emperor and the Pope over the right of a lay prince to invest a prelate with the symbols of his office (the "Investiture Dispute"). The intellectual upheaval to which this dispute gave rise is one of the watersheds of Western intellectual history. For our purposes, the rise of the universities, and in particular the impetus this gave to the study of Roman law (especially at Bologna) were the most important consequences of it. A reason for this development was that the Church, itself a product of the Roman Empire, was legalistic. Roman law appeared to provide weapons with which laymen could attack the legal arguments of the Pope. With the emergence of more "universities" (the term is somewhat problematic at this early period), the study of Roman law spread, and the jurisprudential techniques to which it gave rise were to influence the development of the Church's own law, canon law (see Ullmann, 1975), which in turn is a possible source of some common law doctrines, notably consideration (see Barton, 1969). The important thing to note for our purposes is that Roman law scholarship lay at the heart of university scholarship, and as more universities were founded, so the study of Roman law spread. This development of a university tradition of legal scholarship was to be crucial at a later period in the development of the rule-book.

An unusual feature of the law of England, as opposed to Continental countries, was the rapid growth of a centralised system of courts which imposed itself over the length and breadth of the country (we will ignore the existence of special jurisdictions). On the Continent, jurisdictions tended to remain decentralised, and administered a chaotic system of customary rules which had been derived from various sources. The Continental country of the greatest importance for our purposes is France. The need to try to do something to rationalise the legal system had become pressing there by the end of the seventeenth century, especially having regard to the success of the monarchy in centralising government by that time. Given that the universities were the repositories of legal learning, albeit in Roman law, it was scarcely surprising that the systematisers of the customary law should emerge from that quarter. One of the most influential of these was the jurist Pothier, who wrote treatises on, amongst other things, the law of obligations and the law of sales. A mark of these treatises is their systematic approach.

The common law was not systematic. It had developed largely as an ad hoc response to the problems presented to judges by particular cases (and even more haphazardly reported). The judges and counsel who developed the system formed a tightly knit community, which even to this day bears many of the characteristics of a medieval guild. By the end of the eighteenth century, the common law was contained in a huge literature, consisting of a mass of privately produced law reports, treatises which essentially simply listed precedents under convenient heads, digests and the like. Before Blackstone's Commentaries, which were published between 1765 and 1769, there existed no readily accessible comprehensive account of English common law. Contract got rather slight treatment in Blackstone, partly no doubt because there was not much law, and partly because he derived his organising scheme from an earlier writer, Hale, and that scheme simply did not leave much space for a treatment of contract (the problem of organising schemes is endemic in large-scale works, and results even at the present day in works with surprising omissions).

When Pothier's works began to be read in England they must have appeared a revelation of clarity of exposition. There simply was no equivalent. Pothier started from a theory about the underlying justification for obligation and built his system on that theory. Thus, a basic proposition was that every contract involved a loss of freedom of action, a kind of limited slavery, and consequently the only justification for obliging parties to limit their freedom by making them keep their promise was the reciprocal obligation given in return by the other party. From this followed the proposition that the minds of the parties had to be completely *ad idem*. It also followed that absolute mutuality of obligation was at the very heart of the matter. This underpinning of *consensus ad idem* and mutuality of obligation generated a number of subordinate propositions. In the first place there had to be a point in time at which the minds of the parties could be said to have met, and this was represented by the offer and acceptance model. It followed too that only the intended offeree could accept the offer, thereby generating a doctrine of mistake of identity. If the parties were mistaken as to the subject matter (A intending to sell green widgets, B to buy blue ones), the contract was void because they were not *ad idem*. It also entailed the requirement that the parties should have intended to enter into legal relations.

This view, in its concentration on the moment of formation, in effect entails total presentiation, *i.e.* bringing the future into the present (by anticipating future events and therefore risks)—see Macneil (1974). It is unable to comprehend many aspects of a whole cluster of everyday situations, nowadays generally referred to as "relational contracts". These situations are characteristically of significant duration (*e.g.* franchising contracts); close whole personal relations form part of them (*e.g.* contracts of employment); the object of exchange typically includes both easily measured quantities (*e.g.* wages), and quantities not easily measured (*e.g.* the projection of personality by an airline hostess); and future co-operative behaviour is anticipated (*e.g.* as between the players and management of a football team)—see Macneil (1978). This characterisation of relational contracts is an "ideal type" (see pp.236 *et seq.*). An important category of commercial contract with many features of the relational contract as above characterised is the manufacturer's "requirements contract", where a component manufacturer is bound to supply the manufacturer up to a certain number of units in a given period, but the manufacturer is not bound to buy—so that if demand falls, the manufacturer does not have capital unnecessarily tied up in unsold inventory. Such a one-sided contract is completely lacking in mutuality of obligation (see Adams, 1978a).

Pothier also dealt with many other aspects of contract, such as causation and remoteness of damage, which had received slight treatment at common law, largely because they fell within the matter it was the jury's province to determine. Pothier's marriage of law and philosophy must have seemed very exciting, and in the Age of Reason particularly attractive. At all events, eighteenth-century gentlemen were as concerned to have the right books on their coffee tables as people are today, and Pothier rapidly featured in cultured households.

The cultural ambience of the lawyers who administer a legal system is important, but especially so in a system such as the common law where judges are given considerable freedom in developing the law. There are obvious constraints on this free-dom, but in a situation such as existed in the law of contract in 1800 where the law consisted of a framework only, and develop-ment could take the form of filling in the details, and particularly in redefining the respective roles of judge and jury, the scope for creativity was considerable. In such a situation, it was inevitable that the educational background of the judges would play a part in influencing the development of the law. Not only were the works of Pothier and other Continental jurists to be influential, but also, as we will see, those of some English writers, notably the moral philosopher Paley, and the political economist Adam Smith. It is important to note however that this influence took place at first very much within the common law's case-by-case "problem orientated" approach, which was nearer in some ways to our realist paradigm (see pp.187 *et seq.*), whereas in the later nineteenth century, formalism (see pp.185 *et seq.*) had become an identifiable approach (which is not to say of course that at either end of the nineteenth century the judiciary displayed a homo-geneity of outlook—see pp.36 *et seq.* and Chapter 8. It is impor-tant to note also that formalism as we have characterised it is different from either conservatism or antiquarianism, being a concomitant of the rule-book (see pp.3–4).

An illustration of the use of Pothier in the problem-solving approach is the famous case of *Adams v Lindsell* (1818). The defendants in this case were wool dealers of St Ives, Cornwall. On September 2 they wrote to the plaintiffs who were woollen manufacturers in Bromsgrove, Worcestershire, offering to sell a quantity of wool and requesting an answer "in course of post". The defendants misdirected the letter to Bromsgrove, Leicestershire, and in consequence it did not reach the plaintiffs until 7 pm on September 5. That same evening, the plaintiffs posted a letter of acceptance which was delivered to the defen-dants on September 9. Had the original letter been properly addressed, the defendants could have expected a reply on

September 7. Having received no reply, and not of course realising their mistake in addressing the letter, they sold the wool on September 8. The plaintiffs sued for breach of contract arguing that a contract had been formed on the evening of September 5. The defendants argued that there could be no binding contract until the plaintiffs' answer was actually received. An earlier decision, *Cooke v Oxley* (1790), supported the defendants' proposition, for the offer to sell the cloth was a bare promise when made, unsupported by consideration, and had been withdrawn by the time they received the acceptance. A promise for a promise had to be exchanged simultaneously. The effect of such a doctrine would be, however, that no contract could ever be completed by post. If the defendants were not bound by their offer when accepted by the plaintiffs until the answer was received, then the plaintiffs ought not to be bound till after they had received notification that the defendants had received their answer and assented to it. And so it might go on *ad infinitum*. The answer was that the defendants must be considered in law as making, during every instant of the time their letter was travelling, the same identical offer to the plaintiffs so that the contract was completed by the acceptance of it by the latter. This solution to an obviously inconvenient problem was straight out of Pothier: the minds of the parties met when the letter of acceptance was posted (for possible application to e-mail acceptances, see Murray, 2000; and for e-commerce generally, see p.59).

A number of other useful rules were introduced into the law from the same source, including the rule laid down in *Hadley v Baxendale* (see p.182).

(ii) The rise of the textbook and of contract as an academic study

The systematisation of contract law, and the development of the rule-book, *i.e.* the textbook, we have suggested is closely related to the development of formalism (as we define it—pp.37 *et seq.* and Chapter 8) as an identifiable trait. This in turn is closely related to the growth in England of law as an academic study, which, following in the footsteps of its Continental models, accorded a central place to contract, as understood through textbooks such as those of Anson and of Pollock.

In the field of contract, the first treatise of the new type appeared in 1790; this was John Joseph Powell's "Essay upon the Law of Contracts". Although this work seems in many ways to have been ahead of its time, it was the shape of things to come. In the course of the century this type of work was to have increasing influence.

Almost certainly part of the explanation for this change in the style of literature can be found in the growth in the study of law as an academic discipline, rather than purely as a practical discipline. Law was not an academic study in England before the nineteenth century. Blackstone's lectures which formed the basis of his Commentaries were not given as part of a degree course, although the Vinerian Chair at Oxford which he held was founded as a common law chair. The Downing Chair in Cambridge, founded in 1800, was similarly not part of any school of law. The law taught in either of the universities was Roman law. When University College London was founded in 1826 it did teach law, but numbers were small. When the Royal Commission on Legal Education reported in 1846, this was virtually the only law teaching occurring in any university in the country (the Committee's recommendations, by the way, are uncannily similar to those of the Ormerod Committee reporting on legal education in 1970 and were similarly ignored). In fact the taking of a degree in law as a preliminary to practice in either branch of the profession was unusual until after the Second World War. However, notwithstanding the lack of undergraduates, law degrees and law schools were founded in many English universities between 1855 (the establishment of the Cambridge LL.B) and the beginning of the present century, and there was an academic legal profession. Although the law schools remained small and had few students, this profession was to have a major role in establishing and in perpetuating the rule-book tradition. The fact that this tradition could remain pretty well unbroken right down to the present day is a reflection both of academic conservatism and of the disjuncture between the academic profession and the practising profession, which is much greater here than in the United States, and is probably greater today than it was in the nineteenth century. But it is also a reflection, perhaps, of something more fundamental. A possible explanation of the way in which contract drifted apart from commercial law (see, *e.g.* the comments of Scrutton L.J. in *Hillas v Arcos* (1932) quoted at p.97), it may be suggested, was that at the crucial period in the nineteenth century the English middle classes themselves began to lose touch with commerce. In this regard, we may gain some insights from Wiener's thesis on English culture and the decline of the industrial spirit (Wiener, 1985—for a contrary view see Rubinstein 1993). In England, so far from the values of the rising class (in the Marxist sense) bursting through and destroying the values of the old, at an important level the values of the gentry and aristocracy tended to burst through and significantly destroy the values of the new class. Thus, mill owners turned country gentlemen, and their children became lawyers (including academic lawyers), soldiers and colonial administrators rather than industrialists. Neither judges nor academics were immune to the low esteem in which commerce was regarded. Moreover, the Continental tradition offered a well worked out scheme of contract, which was a perfectly proper study for a gentleman, and obviated the need actually to bother too much about what went on in the real world.

Why then did the judges, who as we have said were responsible for the wholesale creation of doctrine in the earlier nineteenth century, not display the same creativity in abandoning or altering inconvenient rules at a later date? One obvious reason was the weight of received doctrine: as we have pointed out, in 1800 there was not much in the way of a law of contract. Another reason was the development of the doctrine of precedent in the course of the nineteenth century (see Cross, 1991, pp.24 *et seq.*). However, perhaps a further factor, as suggested above, was that judges in the later nineteenth century had become alienated from the commercial world in a way their predecessors were not. Whilst it may be objected that many members of the Bar who were eventually elevated to the Bench had considerable experience of commercial work, it is to be remembered how specific and limited that experience would have been. Inevitably, it would have been, for the most part, in the course of contentious business, and we have already pointed to some factors which limit the type of case which gets litigated (pp.7 *et seq.*). Moreover, litigation tends, for obvious reasons, to require a rather specialised view. It certainly does not entail having to know a great deal about the world of commerce. At all events, we do no more than suggest this as being a possibility.

(iii) The rule-book at the present day

In the present century, as a repository of a body of received doctrine, the rule-book continues to be of importance, but it is not very much referred to in everyday practice. It is primarily regarded as a teaching tool, providing students with the rules they need to answer examination problems drafted with it in mind. The practitioner, by contrast, is seldom concerned with contract in a general sense, but with *contracts*. The books practitioners consult tend to organise material according to a functional, *i.e.* transactional, rather than an abstract scheme. As noted above, one way of regarding law is that it is simply part of the bureaucracy of society (see p.23). As bureaucrats become ever more specialised, so lawyers become ever more specialised. Practitioners needing to advise on frustration of a charterparty, for example, do not go to books giving general expositions of frustration in the first place, they go to the expositions of frustration in relation to charterparties to be found in specialist works such as Scrutton on Charterparties (1996). Moreover, other bodies of law loom larger in everyday importance, even in the drafting of contracts, than the general rules of contract. Practitioners drafting contracts are usually more concerned with, for example, tax laws, competition laws and other such things than with the general rules of contract. To the extent that the general law figures, it is because it has some inconvenient rules, *e.g.* the rules, only recently revised, regulating whether third parties can take the benefit from, or be burdened by, a contract (see pp.86 *et seq.*), and these have to be borne in mind, for example when restructuring a group of companies for tax purposes. In the everyday world of commerce and legal practice, the rule-book, although it may not very often provide answers, at least probably does little harm either. Some of its rules are a bit of a nuisance; that is about it. If it has done any harm, it is perhaps in its influence on academic thinking about law. This, we hope, may become apparent to the student in the course of reading Part III.

Up to now, we have focused on the development of the rule-book. We must now consider the rule-book in the context of the reported cases it contains. These, as noted above, are its lifeblood, and the tensions they exhibit are revealing.

3

CONTRACTUAL DISPUTES

As we saw in Chapter 1, litigation is comparatively rare in contract disputes, and, indeed, in those cases where proceedings are begun litigants will often settle their dispute before the case reaches court. This means that only a fraction of contractual disputes are resolved by judges. Moreover, where a case is tried before a judge, it will often hinge on a disputed issue of fact (about who said, or did, what). Only occasionally will judges have to give a ruling on a disputed interpretation or application of the rule-book. It follows, therefore, that only a tiny fraction of contract disputes directly turn on what judges make of the rule-book materials. The second part of this book is devoted to a critical examination of this tiny portion of the totality of contract dispute settlement, and the even smaller portion of such decided cases which actually find their way into the rule-book.

By taking such a narrow focus, we are not forgetting that an understanding of contract implies an appreciation of all forms of contract dispute settlement, nor are we being perverse. The point is that the narrow focus is the traditional focus, and our intention is to put students on critical alert in relation to the materials with which they will be dealing. In the present chapter, we take two preparatory steps. First, we consider the scope for judicial disagreement in contract disputes. Secondly, we sketch a theoretical framework, which, we think, promotes our understanding of judicial employment of the contract rule-book (as traditionally conceived).

1. CONTRACT AND JUDICIAL DISAGREEMENT

Contract cases can present three different types of questions for a court:

(i) Questions of fact: *e.g.* whether or not the butcher said to Jack that the beans were "magic";
(ii) Questions of law: *e.g.* if the butcher and Jack both mistakenly assumed that the beans were magic (when they

were not), as a matter of law would such a mistake ever permit Jack to withdraw from the contract?

(iii)   Questions of law-application: *e.g.* if Jack and the butcher mistakenly assumed that the beans were magic, and if the law provided that Jack could withdraw only if the mistake was "fundamental", then on the particular facts was this a fundamental mistake? Jack did, after all, get the same beans he bargained for; they simply lacked the quality of being "magic".

Questions of fact are resolved by the judge of the trial court (County Court or High Court), or by the arbitrator (if the case is processed by way of arbitration). Appeals to the appeal courts are essentially on the grounds that the lower court acted on the wrong legal principle (*i.e.* erred on a question of law) or misapplied the correct legal principle (*i.e.* went wrong on a question of law-application). In principle, judges might disagree with one another on any of the three types of question. In practice, however, it is questions of law and of law-application (*i.e.* appeal court questions) which are the focus of judicial disagreement.

Such disagreements do not necessarily involve obscure or difficult points of law. For example, in *Esso Petroleum Co Ltd v Customs and Excise Commissioners* (1976), the question was whether Esso were liable to pay purchase tax on some promotional World Cup coins (advertised as "free" at Esso garages at the rate of one coin to every four gallons of petrol purchased). For reasons which need not detain us, this question hinged on whether the coins were sold to the motorist. To this apparently simple question three different answers were offered. One view (taken by the trial judge, Pennycuick V.C., and by Lord Fraser who dissented in the House of Lords) was that the motorist had a straightforward contract for the coins as part of the undisputed contract for the purchase of petrol. A second view (supported by the three members of the Court of Appeal, and by Viscount Dilhorne and Lord Russell in the House of Lords) was that the motorist had no contract for the coins, the coins being a gift. According to this interpretation, the promise to deliver the coins was not binding on Esso. The third view (relied upon by Lords Wilberforce and Simon in the House of Lords, and given as an alternative interpretation by Lord Denning M.R. in the Court of Appeal and by Viscount Dilhorne and Lord Russell in the House of Lords) was that there were two contracts involved in the transaction: one a straightforward contract for the purchase of the petrol, and the other a so-called "collateral contract" concerning the coins. The terms of the suggested "collateral contract" concerning the coins were to the effect that the garage promised to give the motorist a coin in return for the motorist entering into a contract to buy four gallons of petrol, not, it should be noted, in return for the motorist promising to pay money for the coins as such. Although this collateral contract analysis treated the coins as the subject matter of a contract, it was agreed that under the definition of a "contract of sale of goods" in the (then applicable) Sale of Goods Act 1893, this was not a contract of sale since the consideration for the coins under the contract was not money. The upshot of this confusing saga was that the coins could be seen as the subject matter of a contract of sale (the first view above), or as a gift (the second view above), or as the subject matter of a contract which was not a contract of sale (the third view above). On the first view, Esso lost, but on either of the other two views, which were the views which prevailed, Esso won.

The disagreements in *Esso* are doubly instructive. They point to the possibility of judicial disagreement not only on "simple" questions of law, but equally on questions of law-application (*i.e.* where, as in *Esso*, judges understand the relevant principles in the same way, but apply the principles differently on the facts). In contract, where many of the relevant principles turn on the concept of contractual intention, or on what is reasonable in the circumstances, it is important to realise that opportunities for disagreement on questions of law-application are legion.

It has often been remarked, of course, that the common law is more akin to a maze than to a motorway, with judges finding their own particular routes to converge eventually at a shared destination. Certainly, contract cases can be like this. However, disagreements on questions of law and of law-application are liable to generate disagreements as to the results of cases. If the common law is a maze, it is not one from which judges always emerge by the same exit.

2. JUDGES AND THE RULE-BOOK: AN INTERPRETIVE FRAMEWORK

In this section we introduce a theoretical framework which we will employ in Part II as a tool for analysis of material in the contract rule-book. Our purpose at this point is merely to develop this framework sufficiently for readers to be able to follow our discussion in Part II. As that discussion proceeds, the theoretical framework and its implications should move more clearly into focus. We therefore postpone a more comprehensive analysis until Chapter 8.

Our first step in constructing the theoretical framework is to think about how judges might proceed where they are called upon to interpret and apply the rule-book. In principle, we suggest, judges may approach their task from two different starting points. According to one approach, let us call it the "formalist" approach, judges will see their role in terms of unpacking the materials in the rule-book. Crucially, the rule-book will be treated as decisive even where the results are for some reason hard on one party. By contrast, according to the alternative approach, which we can call the "realist" approach, judges will proceed in a result-orientated fashion, irrespective of the dictates of the rule-book.

We can indicate the significance of these rival approaches if we imagine that a second case had arisen out of Esso's World Cup coins promotion, but with the following facts (which, incidentally, are far removed from the actual facts, which we will recall raised an issue of revenue law). Suppose that Alf, having chased half-way across London, found an Esso garage having a coin showing the head of his favourite England player, and suppose that, having purchased the required amount of petrol, Alf was told that he could not have the coin. Now, suppose that Alf sued Esso for breach of contract, arguing that he had a single contract for the sale of the petrol plus the coin. Guided by the *Esso* decision (where it will be recalled the single contract analysis was rejected by the majority of the Law Lords), a judge following the formalist approach would reject Alf's claim—irrespective of the hardship worked on Alf. By contrast, a judge following the realist approach, sensitive to the result of Alf's case, might well reason that Esso should not be able to get away with such sharp practice, and that Alf must win. This being so, Alf would be allowed to succeed either on his single contract analysis or on a collateral contract analysis (this being easy to square with *Esso* itself).

Now, before we continue, we must enter two clarifying reservations against our distinction between the formalist and realist approaches. First, the distinction is exceedingly stark. The implication of our presentation is that any judge who nods in the direction of the rule-book must be categorised as adopting a formalist approach whilst any judge who shows an interest in results must be pigeonholed as following a realist approach. Plainly, however, this suffers from the sort of distortion which we would instantly recognise if we were to describe everyone living in Britain as "northerners" or "southerners". To do justice to the complexity of judicial reasoning, we would have to construct categories lying between the formalist and realist poles (allowing, for example, for a result-orientated approach which holds only where some degree of fit with the rule-book is possible, or a rule-book approach which becomes result-orientated where the materials in the rule-book fail to settle the point *cf.* Adams and Brownsword, 2003). For our purposes, however, which are a matter of roughly getting our bearings, our crude distinction between formalist and realist approaches will suffice.

Secondly, judicial reasoning has been the focus of a wealth of jurisprudential writing (most recently see Dworkin, 1986). The terms "formalism" and "realism" enjoy some currency in this literature; indeed, some would argue that they are so overworked that they are no longer useful labels. The point, however, is that they are labels in common employment and it is difficult to think of satisfactory alternatives. The reader must however be aware of the particular way in which we use these labels. When we use "formalism" and "realism" (and similarly when, later on in this chapter, we use the labels "market-individualism", "consumer-welfarism" and "ideology") we use these terms *stipulatively*: that is, they mean in this book what we say they mean, not what anyone else says they mean. We use these approaches as *descriptive* models of how judges *do* decide cases, not as *prescriptive* models recommending how judges *ought* to decide cases. To be sure, the models could be used either descriptively or prescriptively, but in this book, at least, they are employed primarily as a descriptive resource (see further Chapter 10, especially pp.250–251).

The formalist and realist approaches are "ideal-typical" in the sense that we can conceive of them without either inspecting judicial practice or supposing that they will be fully instantiated therein (*cf.* Chapter 10). If we focus on the realist approach, however, it will be appreciated that we could conceive, in principle, of any number of criteria to serve as the measure of fitness of particular results. In our contention, however, two realist philosophies dominate contractual thinking in practice. These are what we shall term "market-individualism" and "consumer-welfarism".

Market-individualism has two limbs, a market philosophy and an individualistic philosophy. The market philosophy sees the function of the law of contract as the facilitation of competitive exchange. This demands clear contractual ground rules, transactional security, and the accommodation of commercial practice.

The individualistic side of market-individualism enshrines the landmark principles of "freedom of contract" and "sanctity of contract", the essential thrust of which is to give the parties the maximum licence in setting their own terms, and to hold parties to their freely made bargains. One particularly important entailment of market-individualism is that judges should offer no succour to parties who are simply trying to escape from a bad bargain, for the sum total of freely negotiated bargains is the good of society as a whole in that it results in an economically efficient use of resources.

The tenets of consumer-welfarism cannot be stated so crisply. In the most abstract terms, consumer-welfarism stands for reasonableness and fairness in contracting. More concretely, this is reflected in a policy of consumer-protection and a pot-pourri of specific principles. For example, consumer-welfarism holds that contracting parties should not mislead one another, that they should act in good faith, that a stronger party should not exploit the weakness of another's bargaining position, that no party should profit from his own wrong or be unjustly enriched, that remedies should be proportionate to the breach, that contracting parties who are at fault should not be able to dodge their responsibilities, and so on. Crucially, consumer-welfarism subscribes to the paternalistic principle that contractors who enter into bad bargains may be relieved from their obligations where justice so requires. To this extent, and at the price of some oversimplification, consumer-welfarism may be said to treat justice as more important than freedom (and vice versa for market-individualism). We can illustrate the potential opposition between the market-individualist and consumer-welfarist philosophies by considering a much debated modern case—*L. Schuler AG v Wickman Machine Tool Sales Ltd* (1974).

In *Schuler*, the parties had a distributorship agreement under which Wickman had sole selling rights in respect of panel presses manufactured by Schuler. Clause 7(b) of the agreement (specifically designated as a "condition" of the contract) placed Wickman under an obligation to send one of its representatives to visit the six largest UK motor manufacturers at least once a week to solicit orders. Wickman being guilty of a number of failures under cl. 7(b), the question was whether Schuler were entitled to terminate the agreement. The nub of Schuler's argument was that, by designating cl. 7(b) a "condition", they had indicated that any breach of the visiting obligation—even a single breach, and even a breach occasioning no apparent loss—entitled them to withdraw from the contract if they so wished.

The arbitrator, the majority of the Court of Appeal, and the majority of the House of Lords found in favour of Wickman; but Mocatta J. (hearing the appeal from the arbitrator's decision), Stephenson L.J. (dissenting in the Court of Appeal), and Lord Wilberforce (dissenting in the House of Lords) ruled in favour of Schuler. Superficially, the case was all about the technical meaning of the label "condition", but the policy considerations underlying this debate surfaced dramatically in the House of Lords. The majority of their Lordships could not accept the proposition that Schuler should, in principle, be able to put an end to the contract as soon as Wickman, in breach of cl. 7(b), failed to make one visit. This was, for them, altogether too much, and they condemned such a suggestion as "unreasonable" (Lord Reid at p.251), and "utterly fantastic" (Lord Morris at pp.255–6), and as "productive of absurd results" (Lord Simon at p.265), and "grotesque consequences" (Lord Kilbrandon at p.272). By contrast, Lord Wilberforce delivered a forceful dissent saying:

> ". . . to call the clause arbitrary, capricious or fantastic, or to introduce as a test of its validity the ubiquitous reasonable man (I do not know whether he is English or German) is to assume, contrary to the evidence, that both parties to this contract adopted a standard of easygoing tolerance rather than one of aggressive, insistent punctuality and efficiency. This is not an assumption I am prepared to make, nor do I think myself entitled to impose the former standard upon the parties if their words indicate, as they plainly do, the latter." (p.263)

Therefore, Wickman won, but not without Lord Wilberforce's strong dissent. What are we to make of such a sharp difference of judicial opinion?

Pretty clearly, Lord Wilberforce thought it right to defer to the commercial standards and expectations of the parties as plainly expressed in their contract. For him, the intentions of the contracting parties were paramount, at least within the bounds of public policy. It simply was not for judges to rewrite commercial agreements. Freedom of contract (*cf.* Chapter 8, p.192) was the ruling principle, market-individualism the underlying philosophy.

Ranged against Lord Wilberforce's position were the views of the four majority members of the House. One interpretation of the majority position is that their Lordships actually shared Lord Wilberforce's principle of freedom of contract but thought that, on the evidence, the parties had not intended to give Schuler the right to terminate the contract simply on the strength of a single breach of the visiting obligation. A more plausible interpretation, however, is that the majority acted on a different principle. Central to their thinking was the idea that it is appropriate for judges to relieve parties from contracts the effects of which as things have turned out are particularly oppressive. Seen from this perspective, it is perfectly legitimate for judges to impose their standards upon the contracting parties where this is necessary to preserve reasonableness in contracting. Such, of course, is the philosophy of consumer-welfarism.

Our two ideal-typical judicial approaches (formalism and realism) can be combined with our two contractual philosophies (market-individualism and consumer-welfarism) to yield the interpretive framework shown opposite.

Although each of the four elements contributing to this theoretical framework represents an essential ideological thread, it is important to underline the distinction between, on the one hand, formalism and realism as *general* ideologies of adjudication and, on the other hand, market-individualism and consumer-welfarism as area-*specific* ideologies. As general ideologies, formalism and realism constitute distinctive views about (or attitudes towards) the judicial role—views about how adjudication ought to be, and is, approached. Such ideologies are not specifically concerned with the judicial role in contract cases; in principle, they represent approaches to adjudication in any area of law, whether statute-based or case-based (see further Adams and Brownsword, 2003). Market-individualism and consumer-welfarism, however, are concerned specifically with contract law—not with criminal law, or property law, or family law, or any other branch of law. At one level, these are the ideologies that underlie much of contract doctrine; at another level, these are the ideologies that feed specifically into the adjudication of contract cases. Once we put together the general ideologies of adjudication with the specific ideologies of contract, we produce the more complex interpretive framework (as shown below) in which there is a synthesis of the general and the contract-specific ideologies. Moreover, each synthesis represents a new ideology, a distinctive cluster of ideas, values, and attitudes capable of shaping and directing the judicial approach to particular contract cases (*cf.* Chapter 10).

	Formalism	Realism
Market-Individualism	Rule-book approach (rules in rule-book reflecting market-individualism)	Result-orientated approach (guided by market-individualism)
Consumer-Welfarism	Rule-book approach (rules in rule-book reflecting consumer-welfarism)	Result-orientated approach (guided by consumer-welfarism)

Once again we must pause to avoid misunderstanding. Our theoretical framework is constituted by the concepts of "formalism", "realism", "market-individualism", and "consumer-welfarism", each of which is presented as an "ideology". Readers who have previously encountered some of these terms may be thinking that a framework so constituted is an eclectic mess. For instance, it may be thought that we mismatch formalism and realism because American writers tend to use the former term prescriptively and the latter descriptively; that our sketch of market-individualism is a perverse distortion of welfare-maximising economic theory, or of utilitarianism, to which neither Adam Smith nor Jeremy Bentham would ever have subscribed; and that our brief description of the concept of ideology betrays a breath-taking ignorance of Marxism. Should we not, therefore, go back to the drawing board? On the contrary, as we pointed out above, we are employing this terminology *stipulatively*. The correct usage of these terms is not written in tablets of stone (far from it), and it is simply irrelevant how anyone else, even Great Men, would employ them. For the purposes of this book, the terms mean what we stipulatively say they mean—and we say what we mean at an introductory level in this chapter, and comprehensively in Chapter 8.

Our discussion in the next part of the book is guided by our theoretical framework. The implications of this are twofold. First, we relate the materials in the rule-book to the ideologies of market-individualism and consumer-welfarism, our thesis being that these two philosophies constitute important ideological underpinnings of substantive contract doctrine, though they are not necessarily the only underpinnings. Secondly, we relate particular judicial decisions to the ideologies within our framework.

Our thesis here is that our theoretical framework yields three basic approaches in contract cases, represented by the formalist, market-individualist-realist (hereafter "market-individualist"), and consumer-welfarist-realist (hereafter "consumer-welfarist") ideologies. It is our contention that judicial decisions in contract would be better understood if they were described against the backcloth of this triangular ideological contest (*i.e.* formalist v market-individualist v consumer-welfarist). The overall pattern of our thinking is represented in the figure below.

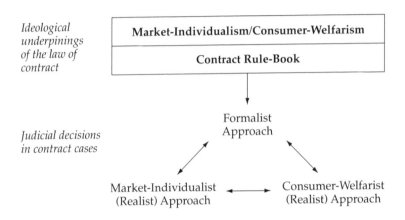

Ideological underpinings of the law of contract

Market-Individualism/Consumer-Welfarism

Contract Rule-Book

Judicial decisions in contract cases

Formalist Approach

Market-Individualist (Realist) Approach

Consumer-Welfarist (Realist) Approach

Some final cautions are in order. First, and very importantly, the triangular ideological contest represents a field of tensions within which judges operate. In any particular case, the tensions will be resolved in favour of one of the approaches. Now, it is sometimes convenient to talk about "formalist", "market-individualist" or "consumer-welfarist" in relation to the predilections of judges, rather than in relation to approaches they may adopt in particular cases. Our intention should not be misunderstood, however. We do not imply that all judges can be rigidly categorised as belonging to one or other ideological school bearing these labels. No doubt some judges are more consistent than others in following a particular approach, but the extent to which judges are consistent in this respect is a matter for investigation. Thus, whenever we use locutions such as "formalist judge(s)" or simply "formalist(s)", this important reservation should be recalled. Secondly, it would be a mistake to suppose that the market-individualist and consumer-welfarist approaches are irrelevant to the rule-book. Although judges adopting a realist approach of either sort by definition (ours) do not rely on the rule-book, their decisions nevertheless feed back into the rule-book. Thirdly, we have so far given only an outline specification of the ideologies within our theoretical framework. If it is not already evident, readers will see in due course that each of the ideologies embraces a cluster of ideas. Therefore, when we state that a judge in a particular case has followed, say, the formalist approach, we do not necessarily mean that he has followed all aspects of that particular ideology, merely some part or parts of it. Finally, by drawing our stark distinction between formalism and realism, by reducing judicial reasoning in contract cases to three basic approaches, and by packing into each ideology a whole cluster of ideas, we invite the charge that we caricature the judicial process. Our intention certainly is not to lampoon the judiciary. On the contrary, our thesis is that judges are inescapably caught in a web of tensions, of which we highlight three, and which they in good faith endeavour to resolve according to their own lights. If this involves simplification on our part, it is simplification which we hope is justified in the interests of stimulating the reader's thought and gaining some appreciation of the larger picture of contract.

PART II

THE JUDGES
AND THE RULE-BOOK

4
AGREEMENT

According to the standard view, to form a contract is to enter into an enforceable agreement. This invites two questions. First, how does the law conceive of an "agreement"? Secondly, what are the conditions of enforceability? In this chapter, we tackle the first question, leaving the second question for the next chapter.

1. *SMITH V HUGHES* AND THE FOUNDATIONS OF AGREEMENT

In the famous case of *Smith v Hughes* (1871), the defendant, a racehorse trainer, having "agreed" to buy some oats from the plaintiff farmer, refused either to pay for the oats when they were delivered or to accept further deliveries. The defendant maintained that he understood the agreement to be for old oats, not "green" oats (*i.e.* that season's oats) as actually delivered by the farmer. This type of situation poses the following general question: to what extent should the law found "agreement" on a person's inner intention, to what extent on outward appearance?

If the law adopted a "subjective" approach it would be guided by what a person really had in mind. In *Smith v Hughes*, for example, there would be no agreement unless the racehorse trainer subjectively intended to accept the offer which the farmer subjectively intended to make. The obvious difficulty with such an approach, however, is that subjective intentions simply are not open for inspection. As the American judge, Oliver Wendell Holmes (1899), observed:

> "I do not suppose that you could prove ... that words in a dispositive instrument making sense as they stand should have a different meaning from the common one; for instance, that the parties to a contract orally agreed that when they wrote five hundred feet it should mean one hundred inches, or that Bunker Hill Monument should signify the Old South Church." (p.420)

This point is associated with a number of further problems. Precisely because we cannot inspect one another's private intentions, we have to rely generally on what people appear to mean. If someone offers us "Bunker Hill Monument", we normally assume that this, not "the Old South Church", is what is on offer. To found contract on a subjective approach, therefore, would impede commerce, invite fraud, and unfairly defeat good faith reliance on the natural meaning of a promise.

Faced with such objections, an obvious move is to propose instead an "objective" approach. Thus:

> "In contracts you do not look into the actual intent in a man's mind. You look at what he said and did. A contract is formed when there is, to all outward appearances, a contract." (*per* Lord Denning M.R., in *Storer v Manchester City Council*, 1974, at p.828)

In fact English law makes the obvious move by adopting as its general position an objective approach to contract. By protecting good faith reliance on another's apparent meaning, the objective approach promotes both commerce and fairness, and it appeals, therefore, to market-individualists and consumer-welfarists alike.

This, however, is not quite the end of the matter, for, in *Smith v Hughes* itself, the judges of the Queen's Bench employed neither the subjective nor the objective approach. Hannen J., for instance, addressed the issue in the following terms:

> If ... the plaintiff knew that the defendant, in dealing with him for oats, did so on the assumption that the plaintiff was contracting to sell him old oats, he was aware that the defendant apprehended the contract in a different sense to that in which he meant it, and he is thereby deprived of the right to insist that the defendant shall be bound by that which was only the apparent, and not the real bargain." (p.610)

The key to this "modified subjective" approach, as we may term it, is not what a person subjectively means, nor what he objectively means. Rather, it rests on inter-subjective understandings and thereby militates against one party exploiting another's known misunderstanding. Thus, the moral philosopher, Paley (see Paley, 1809, p.126 *et seq.*—this book was first published in 1785), from whom the judges in *Smith v Hughes* were drawing their inspiration, cites the analogous case of the tyrant Temores who, having promised that no blood would be shed if the inhabitants of Sebastia surrendered to him, buried them alive (p.127).

For the moment, the important point is simply that the general strategy of English law has been on the whole to adopt the objective approach. It has not, however, been consistent. Modified subjectivism appears in some cases (increasingly, it may be argued, in sale of goods when the question arises what qualities the seller might have expected the buyer to have relied on him to provide), and pure subjectivism underlies some of the mistake cases considered later in this chapter.

2. THE "OFFER AND ACCEPTANCE" MODEL OF AGREEMENT

Students of contract learn that in order to form a simple contract, the parties must be in agreement, and that agreement is constituted by "offer and acceptance". An offer is the offeror's promise, an acceptance the offeree's assent to the offeror's terms. No agreement will arise, therefore, if the offeree rejects the offeror's terms, or purports to accept them subject to qualification, or purports to accept terms not on offer. Neither, of course, will agreement arise if no offer is made, or if the offer is withdrawn before acceptance.

In many ways, this early lesson in contract resembles an introduction to the rules of chess. The pieces can be moved in certain ways, certain combinations of moves and certain arrangements of the pieces have certain consequences, and so on. To understand how the offer and acceptance game is played, however, we must look rather more carefully at its salient aspects. This will reveal that, despite a strong pull towards formalism, not all judges play the game according to formalist rules.

(i) When is an offer not an offer?

In *Carlill v Carbolic Smoke Ball Co Ltd* (1893), the defendant company advertised an "offer" to pay £100 to anyone who contracted influenza after using one of their "smoke balls" as prescribed. Moreover, the advertisement said that £1,000 had been lodged with the Alliance Bank in Regent Street to show the company's sincerity in the matter. Mrs Carlill, having purchased a smoke ball from a chemist on the strength of the advertisement, and having used it as prescribed, caught influenza. The company refused to meet her claim for £100, arguing *inter alia* that the advertisement was intended only as a sales gimmick, not as an offer. In rejecting this argument, the court leant heavily on the objective approach (backed up by modified subjectivism), saying that it was natural to read the advertisement as an offer. The company, therefore, could not escape liability by appealing to its private intentions.

Although *Carlill* suggests that courts will generally hold that an apparent offer is an offer (in the strict contractual sense), matters are not so simple. For example, in the leading case of *Pharmaceutical Society of Great Britain v Boots Cash Chemists (Southern) Ltd* (1953), the Court of Appeal ruled that goods apparently "on offer" at a Boots' self-service store were merely displayed as a so-called "invitation to treat". It followed that the customer made the offer by presenting the selected goods at the cash desk, and that the shop had the option at that stage of accepting or rejecting the customer's offer. By contrast with *Carlill*, the reasoning in *Boots* had less to do with contractual intention than with the commercial convenience of various suggested contractual analyses of the shop layout, because the issue which the court was really deciding was whether or not Boots had infringed the Pharmacy and Poisons Act 1933 by their layout (*i.e.* as in the *Esso World Cup Coins* case, pp.35–36, a contractual analysis was being used to resolve what was really a question of public law).

In a line of decisions from *Boots* onwards, the courts have in fact analysed a number of general trading situations as invitations to treat rather than as offers (*e.g.* the display of priced goods in a shop window—see *Fisher v Bell*, 1961). Given that in none of these cases were the litigants private persons suing on a contract, these contractual interpretations have to be defended more as a matter of general policy than of specific contractual intention. By resolving such matters of policy obliquely, by reference to the law of contract, the courts were adopting a somewhat rigid approach, for the decisions are actually quite difficult to justify in straight contractual terms. Thus, a favourite argument with regard to the *Fisher v Bell* analysis is that shopkeepers with limited stocks might be inconvenienced if their displays or adverts were to be read as offers, for they might be met with more acceptances than they could satisfy. Although the underlying policy objective is plausible enough, this argument is unconvincing. Shopkeepers could equally well be protected by construing their displays or advertisements as offers subject to the condition that stocks be available. Another popular argument is that offeror shopkeepers would "be forced to contract with [their] worst enemy, [their] greatest trade rival, a reeling drunkard, or a ragged and verminous tramp" (Winfield, 1939, p.518). But this too is unconvincing, for offers need not be open to the whole world. Thus, enemies, drunks and the like could be rendered ineligible quite simply by the strategy of holding that they were impliedly excluded from the terms of the offer, and ought as reasonable people to have known this. This response applies equally to the "public safety" argument, that shopkeepers must have a discretion to refuse to sell matches, glue, solvents, etc., to young persons. Shopkeepers may need some protection, but the invitation to treat analysis is not the only way, and perhaps not the best way, of handling the matter, as it clouds the real issues.

Still, the invitation to treat analysis is only a general presumption: if the particular facts are strong enough the courts might switch the analysis. Thus, in the well-known American case of *Lefkowitz v Great Minneapolis Surplus Store* (1957), the Supreme Court of Minnesota held that the store issued an offer when it placed a newspaper advert in the following terms: "Saturday 9 am sharp; 3 Brand new fur coats, worth to $100; First come first served, $1 each." The case for treating this advert as an offer was, however, particularly strong. Not only did the specification of the number of coats weaken the limited stocks argument, and the "first come first served" the choice of customer point, but also this was akin to *Carlill* in that the plaintiff was a specific identifiable disappointed customer, who on two separate occasions was the first to present himself, only to be refused by the store. Similarly, in the more recent English case of *Bowerman v ABTA* (1995), where a disappointed consumer customer was directly involved in the litigation, the majority of the Court of Appeal applied *Carlill* in treating promotional material displayed at a travel agency as contractually binding.

The pattern of these cases, therefore, is that general rules are set for general situations in the light of general policy (particularly commercial) considerations, but as *Carlill* and *Lefkowitz* indicate, general rules (*e.g.* advertisements are not offers) may yield in special circumstances. Even this, however, is not the full story, for judges do not respond in a uniform manner to particular situations. Some judges stick to the general rules, others make allowances for the special circumstances. This is well illustrated by *Storer v Manchester City Council* (1974) and *Gibson v Manchester City Council* (1978, CA; 1979, HL), two test cases which arose when the Labour council in Manchester reversed the policy of the predecessor Conservative council to sell council houses to council tenants who wished to purchase their homes. The Labour council resolved to complete only those sales which were already legally binding on them.

Storer represented the position of about 120 tenants who had signed and completed the formal agreement to purchase. The council argued that it was not legally bound to complete such agreements because it had not signed and exchanged the formal contracts. The Court of Appeal unanimously rejected the council's defence and ordered specific performance. In particular, the court was unimpressed by the council's contention that, notwithstanding the simplified purchasing procedure employed, it still had no intention to be legally bound prior to exchange.

The second case, *Gibson*, was representative of the position of some 250 tenants who had applied to purchase their houses, but who had not advanced as far as the *Storer* group in the purchasing process. Although the Court of Appeal (by a majority) found in the tenant's favour, the House of Lords in *Gibson* reversed this on appeal, holding that the purchasing applications were still at the stage of negotiation.

Generally, interest in these cases focuses on squaring *Storer* (Court of Appeal) with *Gibson* (House of Lords). But *Storer* is consistent with *Gibson* in the Court of Appeal, and the significant contrast, we would suggest, is between the different approaches employed in the Court of Appeal and in the House of Lords. The House of Lords in *Gibson* approved of what it termed the "conventional approach" (also followed by Geoffrey Lane L.J. dissenting in the Court of Appeal in *Gibson*). Thus, Lord Diplock said:

> "My Lords, there may be certain types of contract, though I think they are exceptional, which do not fit easily into the normal analysis of a contract as being constituted by offer and acceptance; but a contract alleged to have been made by an exchange of correspondence between the parties in which the successive communications other than the first are in reply to one another is not one of these. I can see no reason in the instant case for departing from the conventional approach . . ." (see *Gibson*, 1979: 974)

These observations were aimed at the unconventional approach adopted by the majority in the Court of Appeal, and outlined by Lord Denning M.R. as follows:

> "To my mind it is a mistake to think that all contracts can be analysed into the form of offer and acceptance . . . there is no need to look for a strict offer and acceptance. You should look

at the correspondence as a whole and at the conduct of the parties and see therefrom whether the parties have come to an agreement on everything that was material." (see *Gibson*, 1978: 586)

Support for the conventional approach was derived from both formalist and market-individualist considerations. Their Lordships' insistence that "hard cases" must not be allowed to make bad law was classically formalist, and their concern not to disturb the settled understanding of the legal status of various moves made in a house purchase was distinctively market-individualist. Support for the unconventional approach was drawn from consumer-welfarism. This was very apparent in the emphasis placed upon the context of the dispute (this was a council selling houses to its own tenants, not a private sector sale), and in the desire to protect would-be purchasers against the disappointment of having their purchases unfairly snatched away from them (good law or not). Therefore, whereas in *Storer* the consumer-welfarist willingness to yield to the special case prevailed, in *Gibson* the consumer-welfarists were outvoted by formalists and market-individualists who refused to derogate from the general rule.

(ii) Withdrawal and acceptance

The general rules concerning withdrawal and acceptance of offers are as follows: (i) an offeror cannot withdraw his offer once it has been accepted; (ii) withdrawal of an offer is not effective until communicated to the offeree; and (iii) acceptance of an offer is not effective until communicated to the offeror. We shall consider withdrawal and acceptance relative to two special cases, namely, unilateral contracts and postal communications.

(a) Unilateral contracts and the challenge of the beanstalk

Many a student of contract has been teased by the problem of the withdrawal of an offer within a unilateral contract framework. Suppose, for example, that Jack promised to give the butcher the cow if the butcher succeeded in growing a beanstalk, climbing it, slaying the giant living at the top of the beanstalk, and returning safely with the giant's riches. The butcher, remember, is not being asked to *promise* to do any of this. Jack is simply saying that if the butcher beats the beanstalk challenge, then the cow will be his. Given Jack's unilateral contract proposal, when does Jack lose the right to withdraw his offer?

Two answers are generally assumed to be possible responses to
this question:

(X) The offeror can withdraw his offer at any time before the
offeree completes the performance.

(Y) The offeror can withdraw his offer at any time before the
offeree starts the performance, but not once the offeree has
started to perform.

The argument in favour of (X) is sometimes presented as a matter of the logic of offer and acceptance; the argument in support
of (Y) is seen as a matter of fairness. Accordingly, whereas (X)
appeals to formalists, (Y) appeals to consumer-welfarists.

The formalist argument builds on the general withdrawal principle (as it stands in a bilateral contractual framework), *viz.* that the
offeror cannot withdraw the offer once the offeree has accepted. It
is thought to follow from this that the cut-off point for withdrawal
of an offer in a unilateral contractual framework must likewise be
the moment of acceptance. Since it is commonly assumed that
acceptance only takes place within a unilateral contractual framework when the performance is completed, this points to (X). The
problem with this argument is that the analogy with the bilateral
contract is imperfect; moreover there is a subtle ambiguity in the
idea of bilateral contractual "acceptance". When the offeree under
a bilateral contract "accepts" the offer, his return promise is both
agreement-as-acceptance and agreement-as-commitment. But,
which aspect is crucial for the purposes of blocking withdrawal of
the offer? If it is agreement-as-acceptance, there seems no reason to
identify this in the unilateral contract with the *completion* of performance. If it is agreement-as-commitment, the analogy with
bilateral contracts breaks down since, *ex hypothesi*, there is no
agreement-as-commitment in a unilateral contract. It might be
thought that formalists can get round these difficulties by saying
that the common cut-off point, in both bilateral and unilateral
contractual frameworks, is not when the offeree "accepts", but
when the offeror "gets what he bargained for" (the return promise and the return act respectively). However, this simply begs the
question. The formalist cannot duck out of the difficulties just by
cosmetic word-play. Accordingly, the formalist argument points
less decisively to (X) than is generally supposed.

The fairness argument, which supposedly supports (Y), relies
on the intuition that it is harsh to allow an offeror to spring a last-
minute withdrawal on an offeree who is about to complete his

performance. In our example, the butcher perhaps would not be too upset about Jack withdrawing his promise of the cow if, at the time, he was about to step down from the beanstalk laden with his newly acquired riches. Nevertheless, there is plenty of support for the general principle that offerors should not be able to withdraw their offers once offerees have begun to perform. Certainly, the English courts seem to be coming round to answer (Y) (see, *e.g. Errington v Errington*, 1952); and many would settle for this as the triumph of fairness over formalism.

Nevertheless, it may be objected that answer (Y) is not, in fact, wholly fair. For instance, is it fair that the offeror, Jack, should be stuck with his offer when the butcher can abandon the challenge of the beanstalk with impunity? Equally, it can be argued that answer (Y) may be unfair to the offeree who incurs pre-performance expenses (*e.g.* if Jack withdraws when the butcher, without actually beginning to perform, has searched high and low for some magic beanstalk beans). There is no simple answer to these objections. There does not seem to be anything unfair about preventing the offeror making a bad faith withdrawal to cheat the offeree of some hard-earned reward; this, after all, was just the consideration which prompted the argument for answer (Y). But, of course, answer (Y) goes beyond this by blocking even a good faith withdrawal by the offeror once performance has commenced. This implies that it might be fairer to qualify answer (Y) by adding a proviso reserving to the offeror the right to make a good faith withdrawal, notwithstanding that the offeree has begun to perform. As for the alleged unfairness to the offeree who incurs pre-performance expenses, there seems nothing wrong with a good faith withdrawal by the offeror unless he has encouraged the offeree to believe that the offer will not be withdrawn (or has agreed to indemnify the offeree against his expenses in the event of a withdrawal). Once again, there may be a case for adding a proviso to answer (Y) dealing with special understandings between the parties. Answer (Y) is getting more complex by the minute! This is only to be expected, however, for fair rules are not easy to devise. The move from formalism to fairness is not necessarily a move from conceptual complexity to common-sense simplicity.

(b) Postal communications

In the leading case of *Byrne & Co v Leon van Tienhoven & Co* (1880), the defendants (in Cardiff) wrote to the plaintiffs (in New York) offering to sell them 1,000 boxes of tinplates. A week later, the defendants posted a letter withdrawing their offer. Before the letter of withdrawal arrived, however, the plaintiffs telegraphed (and confirmed by post) their acceptance. By applying the already established principle that a postal *acceptance* is effective on posting (see pp.29–30) together with the new principle that a posted *withdrawal* of an offer is effective only on *arrival*, it was held that the plaintiffs had a contract for the tinplates. Students are likely to be puzzled by the adoption of one rule for acceptances (effective on posting), but a different rule for withdrawals (effective only on arrival).

The key to understanding this resides in three points: (i) that the acceptance and withdrawal rules are part and parcel of a package of formation rules; (ii) that the courts are seeking out the package of rules which most expedites contracting at a distance; and (iii) that the offeror can always stipulate the particular mode of acceptance.

Suppose that we were legislating the *Byrne* postal rules afresh. Which of these combinations would we select?

(a) Withdrawal of offer effective on posting; acceptance of offer effective on posting.
(b) Withdrawal of offer effective on posting; acceptance of offer effective on arrival.
(c) Withdrawal of offer effective on arrival; acceptance of offer effective on posting.
(d) Withdrawal of offer effective on arrival; acceptance of offer effective on arrival.

Option (a) facilitates trading for neither party. The offeree cannot rely on his posted acceptance for fear that an effective posted withdrawal is already on the way, and the offeror cannot rely on his posted withdrawal for fear that the offeree has already posted an acceptance. Option (d) suffers from similar defects, the rules cancelling each other out. The choice, therefore, lies between options (b) and (c), both of which are coherent. By the time that *Byrne* fell for decision, given that it was already settled law that postal acceptances were effective on posting, option (c) was the only available coherent package. But, assuming a clean slate, should option (c) be adopted?

The principal objection to option (c) is that it puts the offeror unfairly at risk (see *e.g.* Bramwell L.J.'s famous dissenting judgment in *Household Fire and Carriage Accident Insurance Co Ltd v Grant*, 1879). Against this, defenders of option (c) can point to two things. First, it offers the earliest possible opportunity for reliance, secure in the knowledge that there is a contract. As it happens, it is the offeree who can so rely, but it could not be otherwise without delaying reliance. Secondly, it must always be remembered that the offeror is, so to speak, the "master of the offer", which means that he sets the terms of the agreement including, if he wishes, the manner of acceptance. Accordingly, the offeror can always hedge against any risk by stipulating that acceptance, whether by post or otherwise, will not be effective until it reaches him.

Even though a decent argument can be made out in favour of option (c), there is always the danger that formalists will apply the rules mechanically, blind to the fact that they are being unfairly manipulated by one side. In the modern case of *Holwell Securities Ltd v Hughes* (1974), however, Lawton L.J. suggested that the posting rule probably would not hold where "its application would produce manifest inconvenience and absurdity" (p.166). The significance of this proviso is twofold: first, it strengthens the appeal of option (c), and, secondly and more importantly, it is further evidence of judicial unwillingness to do obeisance at the temple of formalism.

(iii) The battle of the forms

At the heart of the offer and acceptance model of agreement lies the "mirror image" principle, namely that the acceptance should be an unqualified assent to the offer. However, what is the force of this principle where, as often happens in practice, commercial enterprises purport to contract with one another on their own conflicting standard terms?

The leading English case on the so-called "battle of the forms" is *Butler Machine Tool Co Ltd v Ex-Cell-O Corporation (England) Ltd* (1979), the salient facts of which were as follows:

(a) The plaintiff sellers, in response to an enquiry by the defendant buyers, quoted a price of £75,535 for a machine tool, delivery to be in ten months' time. The sellers' quotation was stated to be subject to the sellers' standard terms which included a price variation clause. The sellers also stipulated that their standard terms should "prevail over any terms and conditions in the buyer's order".

(b) The buyers duly placed an order for a machine, but the order was on the buyers' own standard terms which did not include a price variation clause. At the bottom of the buyers' order there was a tear-off acknowledgment slip saying, "We accept your order on the Terms and Conditions stated thereon".

(c) The sellers signed and returned the acknowledgment slip to the buyers, together with a covering letter saying that the order was accepted in accordance with the original quotation.

(d) When the sellers came to deliver the machine they relied on the price variation clause in their standard terms to claim a price increase of £2,892. The buyers argued that their own standard terms applied, thereby precluding any price increase.

Relying on the "conventional approach" (as applied by the House of Lords in *Gibson*), the Court of Appeal held that the sellers' quotation was an offer, the buyers' order a counter-offer, and the return of the acknowledgment slip an acceptance of the counter-offer. Therefore, the contract was on *Ex-Cell-O*'s terms.

Such a formalist approach is open to a number of objections. It is arbitrary (after all, why not regard the sellers' return of the acknowledgment slip, subject to the original quotation, as a counter-counter-offer?); it could threaten commercial convenience (would there have been no contract if the sellers had not returned the acknowledgment slip?); and it is wasteful, serving only to encourage lawyers to draft ever more ingenious provisions purporting to ensure that their client's standard terms prevail. The Uniform Commercial Code, which is in force in all but one United States' jurisdiction, has an express provision dealing with the battle of the forms (Art. 2–207). Under this, Butler arguably should have won. The buyers' placing of their order was arguably a "definite and seasonable" expression of acceptance (Art. 2–207(1)), and the offer expressly seemed to limit acceptance to the terms of the offer (Art. 2–207(2)—both parties being "merchants"). However, Art. 2–207, by focusing on one problem, that an acceptance which does not exactly match the offer amounts to a rejection of the offer (see *Hyde v Wrench*, 1840), creates as many problems as it solves (it has been likened to an amphibious tank originally designed for swamps sent to fight in the desert—White and Summers, 1995, p.6). There is simply no production line solution to these production line contracts (see Adams, 1983). Even realists may be driven to a formalist solution for want of any other more satisfactory way of resolving the matter (see Lord Denning M.R. in *Butler*).

(iv) E-Commerce

In Autumn 1999, it was widely reported in England that the well-known retailer Argos was in dispute with a number of its customers. Apparently, Argos had mistakenly advertised a particular line of television sets as being for sale at £3 when the intended price was £300. Although this was a spectacular mistake (which may or may not have given Argos a defence against its customers' claims, see *Hartog v Colin and Shields* (1939) below at p.64), the reason that this case was headline news was because the mistake was made, not in Argos' High Street stores, but on its on-line electronic shopping site. As readers will be aware, it was in the late 1990s that the possibility of using the internet to purchase products (particularly books, CDs, toys, electrical goods and so on) became a reality for many consumers. What is commonly styled "e-commerce" had arrived in the mass consumer marketplace and, with it, came a number of contractual conundrums (as the Argos case highlighted) (see Brownsword and Howells, 1999).

Just as alterations to traditional shopping environments have posed questions about the application of the basic building blocks of contract (see, *e.g.* the *Boots* case above p.50, which tested the legal position when Boots changed the layout of their stores from across-the-counter purchasing to self-service), so too the development of electronic shopping environments raises similar questions. When a customer visits an electronic shopping mall, are the goods that are displayed for sale to be treated merely as invitations to treat; do customers make the offer; and is it for the shop to accept or reject the offer? In other words, for formation purposes, is e-commerce to be treated in the same way as commerce in traditional environments (*cf.* Murray, 2000)? Certainly, many web sites are set up to resemble ordinary stores, where the purchaser makes the offer by taking selected products to a till at which point the seller accepts the offer (and the customer makes the required payment). This suggests that the formation rules are intended to apply in the standard way. If so, in an electronic contracting environment, one would expect that the contract would be formed at the point in time, and place, at which the message of acceptance was received (see *Entores v Miles Far Eastern Corporation* (1955), and *Brinkibon v Stahag Stahl* (1983)). However, for reasons that we will explain shortly, such a set-up might be unsatisfactory for sellers who are dealing with buyers in many different countries. An alternative set-up, therefore, is one where the buyer, having selected the required products, submits particulars of the products, together with his or her identity and credit card details to the seller. The seller then signifies order confirmation to the buyer by e-mail, and asks the buyer to click the purchase button, which when done completes the formation of the contract. In other words, the intention is to present the order to the customer (as an offer made by the seller) for the buyer to accept; and, crucially, if the buyer accepts, then the contract is formed at the seller's place of business, this being where the message of acceptance is received.

Yet, why should the seller be concerned whether the contract is formed at his end of the electronic connection or at the buyer's end? Provided that the seller and the buyer are situated within the same jurisdiction (as where we do our weekly food shopping electronically to avoid having physically to trundle a trolley around the local supermarket, or where an English consumer buys books from Amazon UK rather than Amazon US), there is no cause for concern. However, the outstanding feature of the internet is that it opens up the possibility of routinely contracting with parties situated in legal jurisdictions other than one's own. Where this happens, the parties have a direct interest in trying to ensure that their own local courts have jurisdiction to settle any contractual dispute that might arise and that their local law will apply to the case—hence the seller's strategy of setting up the site so as to make the seller's jurisdiction the place of formation (at least under English law relating to formation of contracts).

It is beyond the scope of this book to enter into detailed consideration of the difficult questions as to which courts have jurisdiction and which law should govern cross-border contracting. Suffice it to say that the puzzle as to whether it is the seller's or the buyer's rules of formation which apply might well hinge on which court is first seised of the matter. And, of course, the seller may have tried to pre-empt such matters by ensuring that the buyer accepts its standard form conditions, such conditions including a choice of law and jurisdiction clause designed to give jurisdiction to the seller's home courts and to make the seller's local law the governing law. However, consumer-welfarist thinking crosses borders, too, and the validity of such a clause may be problematic if its effect is to deprive the consumer of mandatory consumer protection measures (generally on the validity of standard form provisions, see the second part of Chapter 6).

3. THE REALITY OF AGREEMENT

Agreement presupposes free and genuine assent. In this section we consider the extent to which the law allows ignorance, mistake, and duress to be set against the reality of agreement.

(i) *Ignorance*

The law generally is not very keen to allow ignorance as an excuse, and the law of contract is no exception. For example, if a person signs a contract without reading it, there will normally be no getting out of it on the grounds of ignorance of its terms. Of course, it can rightly be argued that the law anyway has no business excusing someone who is so careless with his signature. This argument, however, cannot be applied to pleas of ignorance which are made in respect of terms incorporated by notice (*e.g.* as where a ticket says "For conditions, see back", and then the back may direct the condition-seeker on to a timetable or the like).

The practice of limiting liability by notice had established itself by 1800. However, after a number of pendulum swings for and against the practice, which echo the saga of exemption clauses in the twentieth century, the courts eventually settled for the principle that, provided "reasonable notice" had been given, such terms were binding (see *e.g. Parker v South Eastern Railway*, 1877). In the most important ticket case of more recent times, *Thornton v Shoe Lane Parking Ltd* (1971), Lord Denning M.R. highlighted the fictitious nature of "agreement" where the reasonable notice doctrine applied:

> "In those cases the issue of the ticket was regarded as an offer by the company. If the customer took it and retained it without objection, his act was regarded as an acceptance of the offer ... These cases were based on the theory that the customer, on being handed the ticket, could refuse it and decline to enter into a contract on those terms. He could ask for his money back. That theory was, of course, a fiction. No customer in a thousand ever read the conditions. If he had stopped to do so, he would have missed the train or the boat." (p.169)

In practice, the courts in modern times have applied double standards to the plea of ignorance in cases of this kind. Where the question of incorporation arises in a commercial contract, the courts will rarely accede to arguments based on ignorance. By contrast, in consumer contracts, prior to the passing of the Unfair Contract Terms Act 1977, the tendency was to treat ignorance as an excuse as the courts stepped up their efforts at consumer protection. For example, in the *commercial* setting of *British Crane Hire Corporation Ltd v Ipswich Plant Hire Ltd* (1975), the Court of Appeal held that the defendant hirers were bound by the plaintiffs' standard plant-hire conditions on the strength alone of a general understanding that the hire of a crane would be subject to the plaintiffs' usual conditions. Yet, in *Thornton*, a *consumer* case the Court of Appeal (including two of the same judges) refused to accept that a ticket, which was issued automatically on entry to a car park, constituted reasonable notice of the car parking conditions as displayed inside the premises. There is no mystery about this. Commercial contractors may actually be ignorant of the standard terms, but they are in a position, and can reasonably be expected, to look after their own interests. With consumers, however, the situation is different. Their relative ignorance and helplessness presents a compelling reason for consumer-welfarist intervention.

(ii) Mistake

The standard view (although terminologies may differ) is that there are three categories of mistake: *common* (where both parties contract on the basis of a shared mistaken assumption, *e.g.* Jack and the butcher mistakenly believe that the beans are magical); *mutual* (where the parties, without either realizing it, are at cross-purposes, *e.g.* the butcher offers Jack runner beans, but Jack thinks he is being offered magic beans); and *unilateral* (where the parties are at cross-purposes, and one party realises it, *e.g.* the butcher realises that Jack has misunderstood his offer to sell runner beans). Our present concern is with mutual and unilateral mistake (for common mistake see p.129).

It will be noticed that our examples of unilateral and mutual mistake concern mistake as to the subject-matter of the agreement. Some of the best known cases on unilateral mistake, however, are cases of mistaken identity. Accordingly, we will discuss some of the leading subject-matter cases, suggest the guiding principles, and then employ these principles in a brief discussion of the identity cases.

(a) The subject-matter cases

(i) *Mutual mistake: ships and the Ship*

For some unfathomable reason, the standard example of mutual mistake is *Raffles v Wichelhaus* (1864), where the plaintiff sued the defendant for failure to accept delivery of cotton pursuant to an agreement between the parties to sell cotton to arrive "ex *Peerless*" from Bombay. According to the "vulgar" account of this case, the court decided that there was no contract between the parties, because the plaintiff was referring to a ship called *Peerless* which sailed from Bombay in December, whereas the defendants were referring to a ship, also called *Peerless*, but which sailed from Bombay in October. In fact, this is gilding the lily somewhat (see Simpson, 1975). The court did decide for the defendants, but only to the extent of allowing them to present evidence of intention once the latent ambiguity in the reference to the *Peerless* was disclosed. Nevertheless, it is generally supposed that if the facts had revealed a mutual mistake, then there would have been no contract.

A direct indicator of the courts' approach is *Tamplin v James* (1880). Here, the defendant bought the Ship Inn, and an adjoining saddler's shop, at an auction. In bidding for the property, the defendant assumed that he was buying two pieces of garden which lay behind the buildings and which, for many years, had been occupied with the inn and shop. In fact, the gardens, which were not included on the plans, or in the particulars relating to the sale, were not intended by the vendors to form part of the sale—indeed, the gardens did not actually belong to the vendors. It was held that the vendors were entitled to specific performance. In rejecting the defendant's undoubtedly genuine mistake, the court took two arguments to be decisive. First, there was the general policy argument (analogous to the *Carlill* argument) against allowing unscrupulous contractors to escape from their obligations by pleading subjective misunderstanding. This would open the door to fraud. Secondly, even if the defendant had made a good faith mistake, he had acted recklessly, and the vendors needed to be protected against such an unreasonable mistake by the other party. The effect of this restrictive line of thinking is to prevent one party from springing a subjective mistake on the (unsuspecting) other side unless it is genuine and reasonable, and, of course, this promotes the market-individualist ideal of security of transaction.

(ii) Unilateral mistake: oats and skins

Suppose that in *Smith v Hughes* (1871), which we encountered earlier on in this chapter, the facts were found as follows. The farmer subjectively intended to offer green oats for sale, the buyer subjectively intended to accept an offer to sell old oats, and the seller realised that the buyer had mistaken the terms of the offer. This is where the modified subjective factor comes into play. Accordingly, the seller will not be allowed to take advantage of the buyer's (known) misunderstanding, and this means either that there is no contract or (as some consumer-welfarists might argue) that there is a contract in the terms intended by the buyer (at least, if the buyer so wishes).

What if we have a *Smith v Hughes* set-up in reverse (*i.e.* it is the offeree who realises that there is a misunderstanding)? This situation can occur where the offeror makes a slip in presenting his offer and the offeree, appreciating the slip, tries to take advantage of it. For example, in *Hartog v Colin and Shields* (1939), the defendant sellers slipped up in offering the plaintiffs a quantity of Argentinian hare skins at a certain price per pound, rather than the customary price per piece. This was a material difference as it meant that the skins were being offered at about one-third of their normal price. In line with modified subjectivism it was held that the plaintiffs must have realised that a mistake had been made in the offer, and that the defendants were, therefore, not bound to deliver at the quoted price. (*cf.* the *Argos* case, above, at p.59).

One crucial limiting principle must be noted. Mutual and unilateral mistakes are operative only if they are "offer and acceptance" types of mistake, not simply mistakes "collateral" to the terms of the agreement. Thus in *Smith v Hughes*, the judges of the Queen's Bench held that the trial judge had misdirected the jury by indicating that they should find for the racehorse trainer if they were of the opinion that the farmer realised that the trainer was under the impression that he was "contracting" for old oats. What this failed to make clear was the distinction between the trainer mistaking the age of the oats (*i.e.* a collateral mistake) and misunderstanding the terms of the offer (*i.e.* an offer and acceptance mistake). The importance of this subtle distinction was that collateral mistakes of the former type would not prevent an agreement being formed, and it would not matter that the farmer did nothing to correct the trainer's known mistake. As Cockburn C.J. said:

"The question is not what a man of scrupulous morality or nice honour would do under such circumstances. The case put of the purchase of an estate, in which there is a mine under the surface, but the fact is unknown to the seller, is one in which a man of tender conscience or high honour would be unwilling to take advantage of the ignorance of the seller; but there can be no doubt that the contract for the sale of the estate would be binding." (See further at 603–4)

This states a market-individualist axiom: contractors who enter into bad bargains cannot deny that a contract has been formed on the grounds that the other side did not warn them away from their "mistaken" bargain.

Summing up, where one party, A, pleads that there was no subjective correspondence of offer and acceptance underlying an apparent agreement, market-individualist considerations dictate that A will be able to defeat the agreement only in the restricted circumstances where:

(i) his mistaken offer or acceptance was in good faith;
(ii) the mistake was an offer and acceptance type of mistake, not simply a collateral mistake (*i.e.* the *Smith v Hughes* limitation); and
(iii) either the other party, B, realised that there was no subjective correspondence of offer and acceptance (*i.e.* the "modified subjective" approach);

or, A's mistake was reasonable in the circumstances.

(b) The identity cases

In a perplexing set of cases, the courts have addressed the significance of a unilateral mistake of identity where it arises in the following circumstances. Typically, a rogue (R) misrepresents his identity as X in order to deceive some innocent person (IP). As a result of the deception, IP allows R to take goods on credit. R fails to pay for the goods and sells them to an innocent third party (IT) who buys the goods unaware of R's original deception. On the face of it, this should not give rise to great legal agonising, because IP has a remedy against R for fraudulent misrepresentation, or for damages for breach of contract. In practice, however, R has a habit of disappearing without trace, or appearing without funds, and IP is left attempting to recover the goods from IT. One line of argument for IP is that his apparent agreement with R was illusory because it was founded on a mistake of identity. In consequence property in the goods did not pass to R and R could not pass property to IT.

If we lift the mistake of identity point out of this context and state it in terms of no correspondence of offer and acceptance, the situation must fit one of two patterns depending upon whether the rogue is the offeror or the offeree:

(i) Where R is the offeror: R, posing as X, makes an offer to IP; IP appears to accept R's offer; but IP believes that the acceptance relates to an offer made by X, and R knows this.
(ii) Where R is the offeree: IP makes an offer apparently to R, posing as X; R accepts; subjectively IP has addressed the offer to X, and R realises this.

It may seem not unreasonable to propose that in either case IP could defeat the apparent agreement. Once we return the mistake of identity point to its typical context, however, we find that there is a complication. It is all very well allowing IP to plead no agreement against R, but this generally means that IT will have to return the goods (or their value) which he has in good faith acquired.

In a celebrated trio of decisions, *Phillips v Brooks* (1919), *Ingram v Little* (1961), and *Lewis v Averay* (1972), the agonising of the courts is plain to see. In *Phillips*, a rogue posing as Sir George Bullough of St James's Square induced the plaintiff jeweller to let him take away a ring before his (subsequently dishonoured) cheque was cleared; similarly, in *Ingram*, three ladies from Bournemouth allowed a rogue posing as one P.G.M. Hutchinson of Caterham to take away a car against a (subsequently dishonoured) cheque; and, in *Lewis*, a postgraduate chemist from Bristol followed the example of the Bournemouth ladies by allowing a rogue, posing as Richard Greene (of "Robin Hood" television fame), to take away a car against yet another subsequently dishonoured cheque. The rogues, in each of these cases, disposed of the goods to innocent third-party purchasers. In *Phillips* the court ruled in favour of a pawnbroker IT as against the jeweller IP; the majority of the Court of Appeal in *Ingram* went the other way, ruling in favour of the Bournemouth ladies (IPs) as against a Blackpool car dealer IT; while in *Lewis*, the Court of Appeal unanimously reverted to the *Phillips* line by ruling in favour of the purchaser IT, a music student from Bromley, as against the postgraduate chemist IP.

The thrust of these decisions is that there is a presumption of a contract where IP and R appear to come to terms, and that IP will not generally be allowed to displace this presumption by appealing to a subjective mistake of identity. This tough line parallels the restrictive view governing the subject-matter cases, and for precisely the same market-individualist reasons. First, so-called mistakes of identity often turn out to be no more than "collateral" errors of judgment, particularly concerning the creditworthiness of the other party. Secondly, if the agreement between IP and R is unscrambled, so that IT must return the goods (or their value), this undermines the policy of protecting security of transactions.

In this light, market-individualists must regard the decision in *Ingram* as suspect. Even allowing that the little old ladies really did care about who was purchasing their little old car, it is unclear why IT should lose out. The only plausible answer is that the majority judges in *Ingram* operated within a consumer-welfarist framework, and thought that IT (being a dealer) was a better loss-bearer than IP (*cf. Phillips* and *Lewis* where IP and IT were of equal standing as loss-bearers).

This celebrated trio of cases now seems destined to become a quartet. For, recently, in *Shogun Finance Ltd v Hudson* (2002 CA; 2003 HL), the Appeal Courts have had occasion to revisit the mistake of identity puzzle. In *Shogun*, a rogue, having unlawfully obtained the driving licence of one Mr Patel who lived in Leicester, passed himself off as Mr Patel when purporting to enter into a hire-purchase agreement for a Mitsubishi Shogun motor car. At the motor dealer's premises where the transaction took place, the rogue produced this (authentic) driving licence as evidence of his identity and, before the hire-purchase agreement was signed off, the finance company ran the usual credit-rating checks against the name of Mr Patel. The checks came through as clean and the rogue, having paid a deposit and completed the paperwork, left with the car. Following the standard pattern of these cases, the rogue, before making his exit, then sold the car to an innocent third party who purchased it in good faith. The question was whether the finance company (IP) was entitled to recover the car or its value from the innocent third party (IT).

This question turned on the interpretation and application of s.27 of the Hire Purchase Act 1964. Stated shortly, the crucial point was whether the rogue was "the debtor" in possession of the vehicle within the meaning of s.27. If the rogue was "the debtor", then he could pass title to the innocent third party (and IT would win); if not, then no title could be passed by the rogue (and IP would win). By a majority, the Court of Appeal held that the rogue could not be identified as "the debtor" and ruled in favour of the finance company (IP).

The reasoning of the majority (Brooke and Dyson L.JJ.) is distinctly formalistic, appealing to two rule-book principles. First, because the rogue was not named in the agreement as the hirer (Mr Patel, of course, was so named), it was self-evident that the rogue could not be identified as the debtor party. Secondly, given the checks made by the finance company against the name and address of Mr Patel, the rogue must have known that his offer (or acceptance as the case may be) simply did not engage with the acceptance (or offer) made by the finance company. Dissenting in favour of the IT, Sedley L.J. viewed the prior case-law, as well as the instant case, in the very different result-orientated spirit of realism:

> "[T]he case is governed for better or for worse by the face-to-face principle. It may be that this test is only one of a group of differential rules of thumb for distributing loss among innocent parties; but it seems to be the one that fits the facts of this case. While this outcome happens to meet what seems to me to be the justice of the case, it gives little pleasure to arrive at it on such a jurisprudentially unsatisfactory basis." (583–584)

Why should the justice of the case indicate a ruling in favour of IT? Quite simply, applying the canons of consumer-welfarism, Sedley L.J. was not impressed by the precautions taken by the finance company before extending a credit line in excess of £20,000. As he saw it: "If there was ever a seller who ought to be treated as having assumed the risk of loss, it was . . . the present claimants" (580); and, whilst the IT was not as careful as he might have been and was in the motor trade (though not as a car dealer), he bought as a "private purchaser" for the purposes of s.27 and he was clearly neither the better loss-avoider nor the better loss-bearer. From this perspective, there is a certain irony in the majority's denial that title passed to the rogue. As in *Ingram v Little*, this denial in *Shogun* results in the interests of IP being prioritised. However, the blind formalism of the majority disables them from drawing a distinction between a finance company IP and vulnerable private sellers who stand as the IP.

What would the House of Lords make of this tangled web of doctrine and the conflicting policy considerations that underlie it? As events proved, the House made much the same of the muddle as the Court of Appeal, dividing three to two in support of the court's decision. The leading majority opinion is given by Lord Hobhouse. Taking a formalist approach, his Lordship contends that the answer lies in settled principles of English law, which are "clear and sound and need no revision" (para. 55). According to Lord Hobhouse, it is incorrect to characterise *Shogun* as a dispute concerning a mistake of identity arising in face-to-face dealings; rather, it is a relatively straightforward case concerning the construction of a written document—a document, moreover, that includes an explicit offer and acceptance clause. When the document expressly identifies Mr Patel as "the customer", and when the offer and acceptance clause states "You ["the customer named overleaf"] are offering to make a legal agreement by signing this document", there is no room for the argument that the rogue was the debtor. Lord Walker concurs; and Lord Phillips, despite being "strongly attracted" (para. 170) to the resolution proposed by the minority, delivers the crucial swing vote in favour of upholding the Court of Appeal's decision. For the minority, Lords Nicholls and Millett take a realist approach that strongly echoes the policy considerations rehearsed by Sedley L.J. As Lord Nicholls puts it, where a choice has to be made between two innocent persons, "the loss is more appropriately borne by the person who takes the risks inherent in parting with his goods without receiving payment" (para. 35); and, expressing the same prioritisation of the interests of the IT, Lord Millett suggests that "it is surely fairer that the party who was actually swindled and who had an opportunity to uncover the fraud should bear the loss rather than a party who entered the picture only after the swindle had been carried out" (para. 82).

In passing, Lord Hobhouse observes that the rogue "stole the car from the possession of the dealer just as surely as if he was a thief stealing it from the forecourt" (para. 52). If the rogue had simply hot-wired the car and stolen it from the forecourt, the usual rule would be that he obtained no title thereby (otherwise possession would be not nine, but all ten points, in law). This usual rule means that, in such a case, the owner (IP) will prevail against an innocent third party (IT) who has purchased the car from the thief. Why should it make a difference if the rogue obtains the car by a deception of the kind practised by the rogue in *Shogun*, or some variation thereof (the opinions in the House show some concern, for example, about "identity theft" and credit card fraud)? The short answer is that, on the one side, the owner (IP) has an opportunity to nip the fraud in the bud—and, in the case of a business owner, a calculated business judgment is made about the credit risk that will be run; while, on the other side, the innocent party is less likely to be suspicious about a (rogue) vendor who presents himself with both vehicle and supporting documentation.

At the beginning of his judgment, Lord Millett remarks that "[g]enerations of law students have struggled with this problem" and that "[t]hey may be forgiven for thinking that it is contrived by their tutors to test their mettle" (para. 57). After *Shogun*, law students seem certain to continue to struggle with the mistake of identity case-law; but it should at least be clearer that the source of the difficulty is not so much in the minds of their tutors as in the competing ideologies of contract law.

(iii) Duress

Somewhat obviously, the courts do not treat an agreement as genuine where it is made under threat to life or limb (see, *e.g. Barton v Armstrong*, 1976). The position with regard to weaker forms of duress is, however, less clear. The better modern view is that duress to goods will, in principle, render an apparent agreement voidable (see, *e.g. The Siboen and The Sibotre*, 1976). Significantly, in *North Ocean Shipping Co v Hyundai Construction, The Atlantic Baron* (1979), Mocatta J. accepted that economic duress might render an apparent agreement voidable.

In *The Atlantic Baron* the defendant shipbuilders contracted to build a tanker for the claimant shipping company. During the course of the work the US dollar, in which currency the contract price was fixed, was devalued. Although the contract had no provision for a variation in the price in step with movements in the dollar, the shipbuilders claimed an increase of 10 per cent in the contract price, threatening termination of the contract unless it was paid. Reluctantly, the shipping company agreed to pay. Some time after the ship had been delivered, the shipping company claimed the return of the extra 10 per cent arguing *inter alia* that the money was recoverable on the grounds of economic duress. Mocatta J., far from rejecting the idea of economic duress, held that, in principle, agreements might be voidable on just such grounds. Moreover, he held that, on the facts, the shipyard had applied economic duress by threatening to break the original contract, and that the agreement to pay the extra money was voidable. In the final analysis, however, he ruled that the shipping company had delayed too long in protesting and seeking the return of the money and, thus, had lost the right to avoid the contract, by effectively affirming it.

Although Mocatta J. ruled against the shipping company, his acceptance of the general principle of economic duress was clearly important and, indeed, *The Atlantic Baron* is now seen as a seminal development in the modern law. Initially, cautious use of the principle was advised, the Privy Council in *Pao On v Lau Yiu Long* (1980) emphasising that economic duress was not to be equated with inequality of bargaining power or ordinary commercial pressure. Subsequently, however, a number of pleas of economic duress have succeeded. For example, in *Atlas Express Ltd. v Kafco (Importers and Distributors) Ltd.* (1989), the plaintiff carriers, having underpriced a contract to transport the defendants' basketware goods to various retail outlets, demanded that the price should be adjusted upwards. In fact, the plaintiffs drew up a new agreement and gave their lorry driver instructions to drive away empty, without the defendants' goods, unless the defendants signed. Presented with this ultimatum, and given that this was happening in the run-up to Christmas, when the defendants could not afford to let down their retail outlets and when alternative transport was unavailable, the defendants felt that they had no reasonable alternative but to sign. Although economic duress must be distinguished from legitimate commercial pressure, and as Tucker J. put it the "borderline between the two may in some cases be indistinct" (at p.645), this was a case that clearly fell on the economic duress side of the line.

The developing case-law in this area, particularly the decisions of the House of Lords in *Universe Tankships of Monrovia Inc. v ITWF* (1983) and *The Evia Luck* (1992), indicate that a claim for economic duress cannot get to first base unless the pressure applied is *illegitimate*. The paradigm of illegitimate pressure is the situation where one party simply seizes on the vulnerability of the other to take what effectively is a monopoly profit. For example, suppose that the carriers in *Atlas Express* had not underpriced the contract but, realising that the customer was in no position to bargain, demanded an upward adjustment of the contract price (*cf. D & C Builders v Rees* (1966), p.83). Puzzles arise, however, once we move beyond this paradigm. For example, whilst one might have little sympathy for the carriers in *Atlas Express* (although *cf.* Burrows, 1993), it is perhaps arguable that the shipyard in *The Atlantic Baron*, facing a real financial loss through no fault of its own, was acting within the bounds of legitimate commercial pressure. Moreover, in *Pao On*, the Privy Council took the view that a refusal to complete a purchase of shares was no more than legitimate commercial pressure in a situation where the purchaser realised that a subsidiary buyback agreement left it vulnerable to stock market fluctuations. What, one wonders, might

the courts have made of *The Atlantic Baron* if the shipyard, prior
to the devaluation of the dollar, had applied pressure to renegotiate the contract in order to protect itself against the risk of
currency fluctuations?

It is tempting to say that the outcome of the economic duress
cases will simply track the judges' market-individualist or
consumer-welfarist predilections. However, this is one doctrinal
area where the ideological lines are not easily drawn. For market-
individualists, it is axiomatic that contractors should be held to
their bargains (for better or for worse). Certainly, sanctity of contract dictates that one-sided economic opportunism within contractual relationships should not be encouraged—for example,
there should be no encouragement to "underbid" or "under-
price" and then hold the client to ransom, which seems to imply
that the doctrine of economic duress was correctly applied in
cases like *The Atlantic Baron* and *Atlas Express* (*i.e.* to protect contractors against pressure to renegotiate bad bargains). On the other
hand, modern market thinking rejects the idea that it is always
commercially sensible comprehensively to agree the terms of dealing and to set them in classical contractual concrete—there must
be room for adjustment and the law must go some way towards
accommodating renegotiation (*cf. Williams v Roffey* (1990) p.78).
For consumer-welfarists, the development of economic duress is
a welcome doctrinal recognition of the need to encourage fair and
reasonable dealing between contractors. Conspicuous cases of
bad faith can be regulated and the emerging question of whether
the pressure was legitimate poses the issue in the right kind
of terms. Nevertheless, it is not at all clear where consumer-
welfarists will hang their hats in relation to pleas of economic
duress, because the jurisprudence of fairness and reasonableness
is far from developed in this area.

In sum, for both market-individualists and consumer-
welfarists, the doctrine of economic duress rightly shields contractors against unacceptable pressure for renegotiation, but
beyond the paradigm of illegitimate pressure (rank economic
opportunism) it is unclear how adherents of either approach will
apply this central idea in particular cases.

4. OVERVIEW

The schematic offer and acceptance model of agreement invites a
formalist approach, with judges employing it as though it were a

self-contained logical system leading mechanically to "the right answer". Resistance to formalism is weakened in various ways. First, because the general rules of the scheme and their standard application have been set largely with commercial convenience in mind, they rarely antagonise market-individualists. Secondly, judges with realist predilections may sometimes be unable to identify any better alternative than the unsatisfactory mechanical application of the rules (see, *e.g.* the *Butler Machine Tool* case). And, thirdly, even judges with realist tendencies may find the formalist approach appropriate where the case has a strong "rule of the road" element, *i.e.* it does not matter which side of the road you drive on, so long as everyone is consistent in the matter (see, *e.g.* Entores Ltd v Miles Far Eastern Corporation*, 1955, and *Brinkibon Ltd v Stahag Stahl*, 1983, both of which cases involved questions of jurisdiction (see p.60 for an illustration of the significance of this.)). This does not mean, however, that formalists have it all their own way. Consumer-welfarists, in particular, by their rejection of the conventional approach and the "logical" method (see, *e.g. Storer, Gibson, Errington* and *Holwell*), and by their protective concern for consumers (see, *e.g. Carlill*), present a standing challenge to the routine or mechanical application of the offer and acceptance model.

Where the law is less schematic (*e.g.* where the reality of agreement is at issue), the principal contest lies between the market-individualist and the consumer-welfarist approaches. Although market-individualism is concerned that the bargaining process should be consistent with the idea of free and genuine agreement, it is equally concerned that a clear line should be drawn between the *process* of bargaining and the *outcome* of the bargaining process. It is imperative, according to market-individualism, that pleas based on alleged defects in the bargaining process should not become the thin end of the wedge, opening up to judicial review the reasonableness of the outcome. It follows that the market-individualist approach favours a restrictive attitude towards such pleas as ignorance, mistake, and duress (confining economic duress, for example, to renegotiation situations). By contrast, the reasonableness of bargained outcomes is central to the consumer-welfarist approach. Consumer-welfarism, therefore, is not troubled if such pleas are the thin end of the wedge. On the contrary, if such pleas afford a toehold for reviewing the reasonableness of contractual outcomes, so much the better. It is characteristic of the consumer-welfarist approach, therefore, to take a more generous view of such pleas (see, *e.g. Thornton*).

5

THE CONDITIONS OF ENFORCEABILITY

Agreement between parties is a necessary condition for contractual enforceability, but it is not a sufficient condition. Barriers to the enforcement of an agreement may be erected by both statute and the common law. Statute, for instance, may take certain agreements outside the realm of contract altogether (*cf.* pp.217–224 where we discuss agreements involving public sector bodies), or may hold particular agreements to be void (*e.g.* gaming or wagering agreements), or may hold otherwise valid agreements unenforceable (*i.e.* no legal action can be brought on them) because of limitation periods, and so on. The common law, too, is no less obstructive, the courts having developed a catalogue of enforcement conditions, particularly in requiring that the agreement should be supported by consideration (unless the promise is made in a deed), that it should be backed by an intention to create legal relations, that its terms should be certain and complete, and that its terms should not be unconscionable or in some other way offensive to public policy (*e.g.* by being illegal, or in restraint of trade). In this chapter we will focus selectively on consideration (including the doctrine of privity of contract), intention to create legal relations, certainty and completeness, and good faith and unconscionability.

1. CONSIDERATION

When lawyers say that a simple contract must be supported by consideration, they mean that the promise must be bargained for (not in the sense of an agreement resulting from negotiation, but simply in the sense of the promise forming part of a transaction involving the exchange of economic assets). Traditionally, this is translated into a model of mutual benefit and detriment. For example, if Jack gratuitously promises to give his cow to the butcher, Jack's promise (assuming it not to have been made in a deed) would be unenforceable as lacking consideration: the promisor (Jack) incurs detriment and confers benefit, but the promisee incurs no detriment and confers no benefit. However, in the case of unilateral and bilateral contracts, consideration is returned by the promisee, either in the form of an act (as where the butcher has to climb the beanstalk and return with the giant's gold) or in the form of a promise (as where the butcher has to promise to deliver the magic beans).

(i) Adequacy and sufficiency of consideration

It is sometimes said, albeit cryptically, that the courts are not concerned with the adequacy, only with the sufficiency of consideration. The "adequacy" side of this maxim means that the courts will not review an exchange to see if it represents good value for money. If Jack made a bad bargain when he exchanged the cow for the magic beans, that was his problem. Similarly, in *Mountford v Scott* (1975), where for a mere £1 the owner of a house granted a property developer an option to purchase his house for £10,000 within the next six months, the fact that the option was purchased for a nominal consideration did not prevent it from being enforced.

Thus, a promise to pay £1 will be treated as adequate consideration irrespective of whether it buys a pig-in-a-poke, a Rolls-Royce, or a speculative opportunity in the property market. It will be appreciated that the principle of adequacy of consideration, that the parties must be left to set their own value on an exchange, is absolutely central to the market-individualist approach. As we have said already, market-individualists do not want to be drawn into reviewing the reasonableness of contractual outcomes.

Whilst the courts (at least when guided by market-individualism) will not enquire into the adequacy of consideration, the requirement of "sufficiency" traditionally means that they will not enforce an agreement unless they find mutual benefit and detriment, and are satisfied that the benefit and detriment so found are legitimate.

On occasion, the courts are easily persuaded that an agreement is supported by consideration. In *Carlill*, for instance, the court thought that the inconvenience and unpleasantness associated with the use of the smoke ball constituted consideration on Mrs Carlill's side. Alternatively, it was held that the use of the smoke ball, by promoting sales, was an indirect benefit to the manufacturers. In modern times, a court could have ruled that Mrs Carlill had a collateral contract with the manufacturers, her consideration consisting in her entering into the primary contract with the chemist from whom she purchased the smoke ball.

As *Carlill* suggests, it is important never to underrate the courts' ingenuity in finding consideration. An instructive case in this respect is *Charnock v Liverpool Corporation* (1968). Charnock's car was involved in a collision with a corporation bus, the corporation admitting liability in negligence. The garage at which the car was repaired was particularly busy, and the repair work, which normally would have taken five weeks, actually took eight weeks. While the car was undergoing repairs, Charnock hired a car. The corporation having paid five weeks' hire charges, the question arose whether Charnock could recover the outstanding three weeks' hire from the garage in respect of the latter's alleged breach of contract (*i.e.* their failure to repair the car within a reasonable time). The garage's main line of defence was that they had no contract with Charnock because it was his insurance company, and not him, which had authorised and paid for the work. Nevertheless, Charnock's claim succeeded. It was held that he had put business the way of the garage (which was to the garage's benefit) and had forgone the opportunity to entrust the repair work to another garage (which was Charnock's detriment). Of course, there had not been a conversation between Charnock and the garage at which the contract had been struck in these terms, but the law does not jib at inferring a contract from conduct.

Carlill and *Charnock* suggest that the line between promises supported by consideration and promises not so supported is not altogether clear-cut. Suppose, for instance, that the butcher says to Jack, "Here, lad, if you hold out your hand, I will give you some magic beans." Is this a gratuitous promise by the butcher, or a unilateral contract in which Jack's consideration is the act of holding out his hand as requested? Ordinarily, we might say that this is no more than a gratuitous promise. If, however, the particular circumstances warranted it, we surely could find detriment to Jack in the inconvenience of having to hold out his hand and some corresponding benefit to the butcher in seeing Jack hold out his hand as requested. Consideration, it seems, is in the eye of the beholder. If we look from one point of view we may see no consideration, while from a different viewpoint, we see consideration. As Holmes said, "The same thing may or may not be consideration as it is dealt with by the parties" (1881, pp.293–4).

Although the courts are astute in finding consideration on occasion, it does not follow that they are readily satisfied by every return promise or act which may be suggested to constitute consideration. There are standing question marks over a number of return promises or acts, particularly promises to perform (or actual performance of) existing legal (statutory, common law, contractual) duties, and past acts. In handling such questions, the courts evince two rather different approaches.

For example, in *Ward v Byham* (1956), the Court of Appeal held that the father of an illegitimate child was bound by his promise to pay the mother £1 a week as an allowance for the child, even though the mother alone was under a statutory obligation to maintain the child. Morris L.J. and Parker L.J. applying a traditional benefit and detriment analysis, held that the mother gave consideration by going beyond her statutory duties (*e.g.* by undertaking to make the child happy). Denning L.J. however, held that, irrespective of any detriment to the mother, her performance of a statutory duty was of benefit to the father and, thus, constituted sufficient consideration. The implications of this latter approach were made clear in *Williams v Williams* (1957), a case involving a similar point of law:

> "Now I agree that, in promising to maintain herself whilst she was in desertion, the wife was only promising to do that which she was already bound to do. Nevertheless, a promise to perform an existing duty is, I think, sufficient consideration to support a promise, so long as there is nothing in the transaction which is contrary to the public interest." (*per* Denning L.J. at p.307)

In short, according to this approach, it is the public policy grounds for and against the enforcement of a promise which matter (and see *Williams v Roffey* (1990), below).

The rival approaches in *Ward v Byham* reflect the general distinction between a formalist and a realist approach to the question of sufficiency of consideration. For formalists, the enforcement of promises must be consistent with traditional consideration theory, and this engenders some elaborate conceptual gymnastics. In the existing legal duty cases, like *Ward v Byham*, the record is kept pure by conjuring up "extra" detriment on the part of the person who already has a legal duty. Similarly, in the past consideration cases (where the problem is that a past service cannot, strictly speaking, support a future promise), the circle is squared by implying a prior promise to pay for the service (see, e.g. *Re Casey's Patents, Stewart v Casey*, 1892). For realists, however, sufficiency of consideration is to be determined less by "consideration considerations" than by "public policy considerations" whether market-individualist or consumer-welfarist (the latter, of course, in the case of Lord Denning). Accordingly, formalist gymnastics are both unnecessary and irrelevant.

Now, until the landmark decision of the Court of Appeal in *Williams v Roffey Bros. and Nicholls (Contractors) Ltd* (1990), one of the largest question marks about the sufficiency of consideration arose where one contracting party, B, promised to pay an additional sum to fellow contracting party, A, if A simply undertook to perform (or actually performed) his existing contractual obligations to B. The orthodox view was that A's return promise was not sufficient consideration. For example, in the classic English case of *Stilk v Myrick* (1809), it was held that a captain (B) was not bound by his promise to pay additional sums to his crew (A) if they would complete the voyage as contracted. Similarly, in the modern Canadian case of *Gilbert Steel Ltd v University Construction Ltd* (1976), the court held that a building contractor (B), having contracted with a steel supplier (A) for the supply of steel at a fixed price, was not bound by a promise to pay the steel supplier additional sums for the supply of the steel. In both cases, the clinching argument (in line with traditional contract theory) was that such actions should fail for want of consideration—the point being that A incurs no fresh detriment (promising to do nothing more than perform existing contractual obligations) and is set to get something for nothing. To allow such a claim would be to cloud the traditional distinction between contract (as exchange) and charity, and in the absence of a developed doctrine of economic duress it would license contractors to abuse their occasional bargaining strength by demanding an upward adjustment of the agreed price. However, *Williams v Roffey* put a very different complexion on all this.

In *Williams v Roffey*, the defendants were main contractors employed by a housing association to refurbish some flats. The defendants sub-contracted the carpentry work to the plaintiff, the agreed price being £20,000. Before the carpentry work was completed, however, the plaintiff ran into financial difficulty and the defendants promised to pay additional sums for the work to be completed. In the event, even with the benefit of the promised additional sums, the plaintiff failed to complete the carpentry work and, in due course, the question arose whether the defendants were bound by their promise to pay the extra money. On the face of it, applying traditional consideration principles, the plaintiff's action must fail. However, the Court of Appeal, without having to resort to any manipulation of the facts, ruled unanimously that the defendants were bound by their promise. Seminally, Glidewell L.J. summarised the (revised) legal position as follows:

(i)   if A has entered into a contract with B to do work for, or to supply goods or services to, B in return for payment by B;

(ii) at some stage before A has completely performed his obligations under the contract B has reason to doubt whether A will, or will be able to, complete his side of the bargain;

(iii) B thereupon promises A an additional payment in return for A's promise to perform his contractual obligations on time;

(iv) as a result of giving his promise, B obtains in practice a benefit, or obviates a disbenefit;

(v)   B's promise is not given as the result of economic duress or fraud on the part of A; then

(vi) the benefit to B is capable of being consideration for B's promise, so that the promise will be legally binding (at pp.521–22).

The crux of this statement lies in conditions (iv) and (v). If the promisor is to be bound, then the promisor must derive some practical benefit from the arrangement and there must not be any vitiating factors such as fraud or duress weighing against the enforcement of the promise. In *Williams v Roffey*, there was actually little contest about these matters. The case was argued on the basis that there was no economic duress applied by the plaintiff, and it was conceded by the defendants that they had obtained a practical benefit—for, the additional sums promised to the plaintiffs were likely to be less than the agreed damages that the defendants would have to pay to the client housing association if the main contract was delayed because of delays with the carpentry sub-contract.

Williams v Roffey leaves a number of questions tantalisingly unanswered (see Adams and Brownsword, 1990a). For instance, in *Re Selectmove Ltd* (1994), the Court of Appeal declined to set *Williams v Roffey* against the rule in *Pinnel's* case (1602) (see pp.83–84, below), according to which a promise by a creditor to accept a lesser sum in full and final settlement of a debt is not binding. Yet, the modern argument against the doctrine in *Pinnel* is that the creditor's promise should be binding precisely because the creditor derives some practical benefit from such an arrangement with the debtor. It is unclear, too, how the approach in *Williams v Roffey* relates to the modern doctrine of frustration (see Chapter 6, especially *Davis v Fareham* (1956)), which takes a tough line against commercial contractors seeking to excuse themselves from performance (or seeking to renegotiate the agreed price) on the grounds of mere financial hardship. Also, whilst the court emphasised that, if the plaintiff carpenter had applied economic duress to extract the defendants' promise, then the promise would not have been binding, we simply do not know what the outcome would have been if the case had been argued on the basis that there was such economic duress.

These puzzles notwithstanding, however, it is perfectly clear where *Williams v Roffey* is to be located in the recent history of the doctrine of consideration. Quite simply, the Court of Appeal has taken over from Lord Denning the baton of a benefit-led policy-sensitive theory of consideration. It is arguable that there is a welfarist element in the court's realist approach (the defendant main contractors being required to show concern for the financial difficulties of the plaintiff sub-contractor). However, the better interpretation is that the court's realism was inspired by a modern market-individualism, the central concern being that the doctrine of consideration should not impede the ability of commercial contractors to make ongoing (sometimes one-sided) adjustments to their contracts as performance proceeds. Of course, it remains to be seen whether *Williams v Roffey* will establish itself as the new orthodoxy with regard to the question of sufficiency of consideration. Certainly, the prospects are not entirely unfavourable: for, with the modern development of a doctrine of economic duress (albeit, as we have seen, a doctrine of somewhat uncertain scope and application), the courts now have more finely-tuned resources for dealing with the range of problems previously dealt with under the general rubric of the consideration requirement.

(ii) Is consideration always necessary?

It is generally accepted that certain commercial practices (*e.g.* bankers' confirmed irrevocable commercial credits (see p.17), requirements contracts, and the like) may not pass muster in terms of strict consideration theory. Such exceptions to the "no consideration, no contract" principle cause no concern, except perhaps to the obsessive formalist. It would be a different story, however, if it were suggested that a coach and horses could be driven through the traditional requirement of consideration. For this reason, there was considerable agitation when the principle of promissory estoppel was aired by Denning J. (as he then was) in *Central London Property Trust Ltd v High Trees House Ltd* (1947).

In *High Trees*, the plaintiffs granted the defendants a 99-year lease of a block of flats, at a ground rent of £2,500 a year. In 1940, the plaintiffs agreed to reduce the ground rent to £1,250 a year (by implication for as long as the war conditions made it difficult for the defendants to let the flats). The defendants paid the reduced ground rent until 1945, by which time the flats were fully let; whereupon the plaintiffs claimed the original ground rent of £2,500 a year. To test the legal position, the plaintiffs claimed £625, representing the difference between the original and the reduced ground rent for the last half of 1945. They were held to be entitled to this sum, but the interest of the case lies in Denning J.'s ruling that, following an equitable principle outlined by Lord Cairns L.C. in *Hughes v Metropolitan Railway Co* (1877):

> ". . . a promise intended to be binding, intended to be acted on and in fact acted on, is binding so far as its terms properly apply. Here it was binding as covering the period down to the early part of 1945 . . ." (p.136)

Apparently, the plaintiffs were bound by their promise to reduce the ground rent even though the defendants gave no consideration for the promise.

In *Combe v Combe* (1951) the relationship between the scope of promissory estoppel and consideration was clarified. Here, Byrne J. ruled that the *High Trees* decision permitted a wife to sue her husband on a promise (made at the time that the parties were getting divorced) to pay her £100 a year, even though the wife gave no consideration for this promise. This ruling truly bit the bullet, for it assumed that promissory estoppel allowed the enforcement of gratuitous informal promises. If this was right, the contract books would have to be rewritten. Byrne J.'s decision was, however, reversed by the Court of Appeal, Denning L.J. (as he then was) saying:

> "[Lord Cairns's] principle does not create new causes of action where none existed before. It only prevents a party from insisting upon his strict legal rights, when it would be unjust to allow him to enforce them, having regard to the

dealings which have taken place between the parties ...
Seeing that the principle never stands alone as giving a cause
of action in itself, it can never do away with the necessity of
consideration when that is an essential part of the cause of
action. The doctrine of consideration is too firmly fixed to be
overthrown by a side-wind." (pp.219–20)

As counsel for the husband suggested, the *High Trees* principle
was to be used as a shield and not a sword (see Birkett L.J. at
p.224). These suggestive statements attempt to articulate the slip-
pery distinction between the gratuitous promisee's claim in *High
Trees*, as contrasted with the claim made in *Combe*. In *High Trees*,
the principle of promissory estoppel entailed that the gratuitous
promisor could not simply ignore his promise to accept some
lesser performance from the promisee. In *Combe*, the gratuitous
promisee was trying to hold the promisor to a performance to be
undertaken by the promisor. Whatever the precise scope of the
promissory estoppel principle, *Combe* must be understood as a
limiting case. Denning L.J.'s views expressed there gain additional force when it is borne in mind that there was a real question on the facts as to whether or not the husband's promise had
been intended to be acted on. Byrne J. thought that it had, but
Denning L.J. rejected this finding. Thus he could have left Byrne
J.'s extension of the *High Trees* principle intact, and still found
against the promisee (*i.e.* on the grounds that the promise was not
intended to be acted on).

If we stand back from the details of the promissory estoppel
case-law, we can see that it reflects the long-standing question of
whether contractual liability should be based on exchange or reasonable reliance (*cf.* Collins, 1986, Chapter 3). Should a promisor
be held to his promise only where the promisee has bought the
promise by providing consideration (*i.e.* the exchange model), or
should the promisor be bound where the promisee has reasonably relied on the promise in the reasonable expectation that the
promisor meant what he said (*i.e.* the reasonable reliance model)?

As we have seen, the traditional market-individualist approach
equates contract with exchange—the paradigm of contractual
obligation is exchange-based obligation, the paradigm of contractual liability breach of exchange-based obligation. It follows that
where promises do not form part of an exchange they cannot
ground contractual obligation. However, as we have also
remarked (when discussing the developing doctrine of economic
duress and the important case of *Williams v Roffey*), modern

market-individualists must recognise that in long-term contracting the law should accommodate commercial practice where adjustments to a relationship are freely made by the parties, even if such adjustments do not constitute an exchange. Viewed in this light, the response in *High Trees* can be seen as an expression of modern market thinking: exchange still remains the paradigm for contract but, at least within a relationship founded originally on exchange, non-exchange adjustments are recognised as having some contractual effect. On the other hand, there is a more radical interpretation of *High Trees*. What *High Trees* foreshadows is the adoption of reasonable reliance as a rival, or perhaps supplementary, basis for contractual obligation and liability. In other words, if a promisee reasonably relies on a promise, then it is only fair and reasonable that the promise should have contractual effect. Put in this way, the protection of reasonable reliance in general, and the *High Trees* principle in particular, chime in with the welfarist strand of consumer-welfarism (see further Chapter 9, pp.213–215).

Since *High Trees*, there has been no shortage of litigation refining the principle of promissory estoppel (*e.g.* concerning the circumstances in which the promisor can legitimately give notice that the original contractual position is to be resumed, the precise sense in which the promisee must "act on" the promise, the scope of the principle outside contractual relations, and so on), but two aspects of the post-*High Trees* developments are worthy of short comment.

First, there is the question of the impact of promissory estoppel on the long-established rule in *Pinnel's* case (1602), which is authority for the proposition that where A owes B an undisputed sum of money, and B gratuitously agrees to accept a lesser sum in settlement of the debt, then B remains entitled to the balance (*i.e.* in more technical terms, the defence of accord and satisfaction is not open to the defendant). Of course, if B receives some bargained-for return benefit, perhaps early payment, that is another matter. Without any return consideration, however, the promise to accept less is not binding. In *High Trees*, Denning J. warned that the "logical consequence" of equitable estoppel was that "a promise to accept a smaller sum in discharge of a larger sum, if acted upon, is binding notwithstanding the absence of consideration" (p.135). Almost 20 years later, he had the chance to apply this logic in *D & C Builders Ltd v Rees* (1966), where some jobbing builders sued for the balance outstanding on a debt owed to them by the defendant. The plaintiffs had, in fact, accepted a cheque for £300 against a debt of some £482, and they had written out a receipt indicating that the £300 was "in completion of the account". However, the background to this "settlement" was that the plaintiffs were in severe financial difficulties, and the defendant, realising this, put it to the plaintiffs that they must accept £300 or get nothing. The defence rested on two grounds, first, that payment by cheque, rather than by cash, constituted payment in a different kind, and thus took the case outside the category of gratuitous promise, and, secondly, that the creditors were barred from suing for the balance by virtue of promissory estoppel. The Court of Appeal dismissed both lines of defence. The first was held to fail because payment by cheque can no longer be regarded as significantly different from a cash payment, and, to the extent that the principle of the second ground of defence was accepted, the debtors could not shelter behind promissory estoppel where they had applied unfair pressure to creditors in difficulties.

Even without the complication now presented by *Williams v Roffey* and *Re Selectmove Ltd*, it is difficult to say just where this leaves the law with regard to the rule in *Pinnel's* case. On the one side, there is Lord Denning's view that promissory estoppel has superseded both *Pinnel* and the House of Lords' confirmation of the principle in *Foakes v Beer* (1884). On the other side, there is the more traditional approach (reflected, for example, by Winn L.J.'s judgment in *D & C Builders*) that *Pinnel* is still good law, and that *D & C Builders* was really a straight application of *Foakes v Beer*. Given that the law already recognises that compositions with creditors are binding on the creditors, as are settlements for lesser sums struck with third parties, why not recognise settlements between a creditor and a debtor? One reason, perhaps, is that debtors might put creditors under unfair pressure to accept lesser sums; but, quite apart from the emerging safety net of economic duress, Lord Denning's judgment in *D & C Builders* takes care of just this point. Formalist judges will not lightly overturn a precedent of nearly four hundred years' standing, but judges who are prepared to ask whether *Pinnel* makes sense nowadays (and given that it was in any event arguably a technical decision on the defence of accord and satisfaction, and outside of that context never quite sat happily with the common law doctrine of waiver, which is somewhat akin in its effect to *High Trees*) may well decide that the rule should now be changed. Of course, abandoning *Pinnel* is very much easier for consumer-welfarists (who recognise the need to protect reasonable reliance and, concomitantly, reasonable expectation) than for market-individualists. For the latter, the question is whether the rectification of any commercial inconvenience flowing from *Pinnel* can justify an inroad into the exchange model.

The second aspect of the post-*High Trees* period concerns the difference in judicial attitudes towards promissory estoppel. Whereas some judges, notably Lord Denning himself, have seen *High Trees* as a doctrine of first resort, it is evident that many judges view the doctrine with suspicion, and prefer not to base themselves upon it.

In *Brikom Investments Ltd v Carr* (1979), for example, the question was whether the landlords of some blocks of flats, having offered 99–year leases on the flats with an assurance that they would not enforce the covenants in the leases' provisions which required tenants to contribute to the cost of roof repairs, could then claim a contribution. This point was tested in respect of three types of lessee as follows:

(i)   A, who had bought one of the flats on the faith of the landlords' representation about the roof repairs.

(ii) B, who was one stage removed from the landlords' assurance, having bought one of the flats from someone like A.

(iii) C, who was two stages removed from the landlords' assurance, having bought one of the flats from someone like B.

Lord Denning M.R. saw no problem in applying *High Trees* for the benefit of A; and it did not matter whether A was actually influenced by the representation, where, as in *Brikom*, the representation was clearly intended to influence the judgment of the reasonable representee. As for the property lawyers' objections to allowing promissory estoppel to operate for the benefit of assignees of a lease such as B and C, Lord Denning dismissed this in typical style:

> "It was suggested that if assignees are able to rely on an oral or written representation (not contained in the deeds) it would cause chaos and confusion among conveyancers. No one buying property would know where he stood.
>
> I am not disturbed by those forebodings. I prefer to see that justice is done: and let the conveyancers look after themselves." (p.484)

Of course, Lord Denning had a point here, since the lessees' argument in *Brikom* was precisely that if the landlords' assurance was not binding, then they did not know where they stood when they bought the flats.

To some extent, the conveyancers could have been assuaged by putting the lessees' claim on the alternative ground of a collateral contract; but this did not appeal to Lord Denning:

> "This seems to me a roundabout way of reaching the same result as the *High Trees* principle . . . It is a technical way of overcoming technical difficulties. I prefer the simple way . . ." (p.485)

For Roskill L.J. and Cumming-Bruce L.J., however, the technical way had its attractions. Lessee A could succeed on a collateral contract, supported by the consideration of entering into the lease; and lessees B and C could rely on Lord Cairns's principle in *Hughes*. Accordingly, as Roskill L.J. put it, it was possible, and therefore desirable, to find for the lessees without having "to resort to the somewhat uncertain doctrine of promissory estoppel" (p.490).

Thus, there are two schools of thought about *High Trees*. For realists, particularly those of a consumer-welfarist persuasion *Hughes* and *High Trees* are but illustrations of a master equitable principle. There is a coalescence of the ideas of fair dealing, and of not "blowing hot and cold", and the niceties of conceptual divisions and the requirement of consideration are quite simply irrelevant. By contrast, the traditional formalist approach treats *High Trees* with care. The ground rules here give preference to a traditional consideration explanation of a ruling (*e.g.* by finding a collateral contract, as in *Brikom*). Failing this, Lord Cairns's principle, narrowly interpreted, is the next resort, and when all else fails maybe *High Trees*. Above all, no hostages to fortune are to be offered to anyone looking to remove the necessity for consideration.

(iii) The doctrine of privity of contract

In the leading case of *Dunlop Pneumatic Tyre Co Ltd v Selfridge and Co Ltd* (1915), Viscount Haldane L.C. proclaimed:

> "[In] the law of England certain principles are fundamental. One is that only a person who is a party to a contract can sue on it. Our law knows nothing of a *jus quaesitum tertio* arising by way of contract." (p.853)

In practice the doctrine of privity of contract (that only a person who is a party to a contract can sue on it) is one of the most important obstacles to the enforcement of an agreement (though a limited relaxation of certain aspects of the doctrine has been effected by the Contracts (Rights of Third Parties) Act 1999, which we deal with at the end of this section). Thus, in *Dunlop v Selfridge*, Dunlop were prevented by want of privity from enforcing a contract between a motor accessory factor, Dew and Co (to whom Dunlop had supplied tyres), and Selfridge, whereby the latter undertook to observe Dunlop's list prices. This, it should be emphasised, was despite the fact that Selfridge were clearly in breach of contract and that their undertaking was intended (by Dew at least) to be for the benefit of Dunlop. Although resale price maintenance of the sort attempted by Dunlop is regulated nowadays (see, *e.g.* the Competition Act, 1998), the application of the privity doctrine on facts such as those in *Dunlop* prompts two thoughts. First, privity looks capable of producing unfair outcomes (a troubling thought for consumer-welfarists); and, secondly, where the dealings of contractors generate chains or networks of contracts, privity might be a commercially inconvenient doctrine (a troubling thought for market-individualists).

Before we take up these troubling thoughts, however, it needs to be said that third-party problems arise in various guises. In fact, there are four distinct privity questions (see Adams and Brownsword, 1990b: Law Commission, 1991):

(1) Can P sue on a contract to which he is not a party ("P1") (see, *e.g. Dunlop v Selfridge*, above)?
(2) Can D rely on defences based on a contract to which he is not a party ("P2") (see, *e.g. The Eurymedon* pp.89–91)?
(3) Can D rely on defences based on his own contract to which P is not a party ("P3") (see, *e.g. Morris v C.W. Martin and Sons Ltd* (1966), a case which involved both this, P3, and the previous, P2, questions)?
(4) Can P enforce his own contract against a third party ("P4") (see, *e.g. Barker v Stickney*, below).

A strict privity doctrine gives negative answers, not just to question P1, but to each of these four privity questions. For example, in *Barker v Stickney* (1919) (a P4 case), Barker assigned the copyright in his book to a publisher in return for a lump sum and a royalty. The publisher having gone into receivership, and the copyright in Barker's book having been assigned to Stickney without any stipulation as to the payment of royalties, the Court of Appeal refused to order Stickney to pay Barker's royalties even though the former had knowledge of the latter's agreement with the publisher.

Readers may feel that the result in *Barker v Stickney* is manifestly unfair and, as we have indicated, this is one line of objection to the strict application of the privity doctrine. In the simplest form of P1 situation, for example, where A and B have made a contract under which B is to confer a benefit on a third-party, C, it seems unfair that C should be left without a remedy against B if B defaults on the contract. Yet in *Tweddle v Atkinson* (1861), a third-party beneficiary was held unable to enforce a contract made for his benefit even though the contracting parties had expressly declared that the contract should be enforceable at the suit of the beneficiary. And, as we have seen, in *Dunlop v Selfridge*, the third-party beneficiary (Dunlop) was again thwarted by the privity doctrine.

Not surprisingly, in modern times, such "hard cases" have invited a consumer-welfarist response. One of the best examples of this is *Beswick v Beswick* (1968). Under the contract in *Beswick*, Peter Beswick agreed to sell his coal business to his nephew John in consideration that John should pay him £6.10s per week for the remainder of his (*i.e.* Peter's) life, and, in the event of his predeceasing his wife, £5 a week thereafter to his widow for the remainder of her life. The nephew proved to be the villain of the piece for, after Peter's death, he made only one payment to Peter's widow. The widow sued on the contract which, quite clearly, had been made, in part, for her benefit. Although the trial judge ruled against her, the Court of Appeal and the House of Lords found in her favour. In so ruling, the House overcame two lines of defence pleaded by the nephew: first, that privity blocked the claim, and secondly, failing that, that the claim must be restricted to nominal damages. With respect to the first of these defences, the House held that while privity barred Mrs Beswick's claim in her personal capacity she was, nevertheless, eligible to claim as administratrix of her deceased husband's estate. As for the second line of defence, the House had no sympathy for the proposition that, since the £5 a week should have been paid to Mrs Beswick and not to the estate, then strictly speaking the estate had lost nothing and, therefore, could recover no more than nominal damages. If ever the law wanted to look an ass, here was the perfect opportunity. In Lord Pearce's apt words:

> "Why should the estate be barred from exercising its full contractual rights merely because in doing so it secures justice

for the widow who, by a mechanical defect of our law, is unable to assert her own rights? Such a principle would be repugnant to justice and fulfil no other object than that of aiding the wrongdoer." (p.89)

To prevent young John from cocking a snook at the law, Mrs Beswick had to be granted an order for specific performance of the agreement.

Beswick seems to be the model situation for a third party to enjoy direct enforcement rights of a contract. The contract was made for the benefit of the third party, and the principal parties had not released one another from their contractual obligations. It is also, of course, a model situation for bringing formalists (defending the technical doctrine of privity) into conflict with consumer-welfarists (determined to secure justice for the third party).

As *Dunlop* hints, however, privity can equally well produce commercial inconvenience as injustice. To some extent, potential commercial inconvenience has been neutralised by special exceptions (*e.g.* concerning third-party beneficiaries under certain common types of insurance contracts, and holders of bills of exchange, and bills of lading—see pp.17–19). Nevertheless, privity may still impede commercial objectives. For example, in *The Eurymedon* (1975), the question was whether a firm of stevedores could avoid liability for negligently damaging a drilling machine during unloading, by taking advantage of the time-limit provisions of a contract made between the shipper of the cargo and the carrier (the carrier being a wholly owned subsidiary of the stevedores). The majority of the Privy Council ruled in favour of the stevedores.

The gist of the majority judgment, delivered by Lord Wilberforce, was that documents comprising the undoubted contract between the shippers and the carriers also constituted the basis for a unilateral contract between the shippers and the stevedores. The stevedores gave consideration for this unilateral contract by unloading the cargo. This interpretation required both a certain amount of technical manipulation of the documents, and confirmation that cases such as *Scotson v Pegg* (1861) had correctly decided that A's (the stevedores') performance of a contractual obligation (unloading the cargo) owed to B (the carriers) could stand as good consideration for a second contract with C (the shippers). The overriding principle, as Lord Wilberforce made abundantly clear, was that privity must not be allowed to obstruct commercial convenience:

"If the choice, and the antithesis, is between a gratuitous promise, and a promise for consideration, as it must be in the absence of a *tertium quid*, there can be little doubt which, in commercial reality, this is. The whole contract is of a commercial character, involving service on one side, rates of payment on the other, and qualifying stipulations as to both. The relations of all parties to each other are commercial relations entered into for business reasons of ultimate profit. To describe one set of promises in this context as gratuitous, or *nudum pactum*, seems paradoxical and is *prima facie* implausible. It is only the precise analysis of this complex of relations into the classical offer and acceptance, with identifiable consideration, that seems to present difficulty, but this same difficulty exists in many situations of daily life, *e.g.* sales at auction; supermarket purchases; boarding an omnibus; purchasing a train ticket; tenders for the supply of goods; offers of rewards; acceptance by post; warranties of authority by agents; manufacturers' guarantees; gratuitous bailments; bankers' commercial credits. These are all examples which show that English law, having committed itself to a rather technical and schematic doctrine of contract, in application takes a practical approach, often at the cost of forcing the facts to fit uneasily into the marked slots of offer, acceptance and consideration." (p.167)

Moreover, Lord Wilberforce thought that if this brought Commonwealth law into line with American law so much the better, for "Commercial considerations should have the same force on both sides of the Pacific" (p.169). There really could not be a clearer example than this of technical doctrine (*i.e.* that governing formation) yielding to commercial reality (*i.e.* market-individualism).

Against the majority view. Viscount Dilhorne and Lord Simon were not prepared to make the same leaps with the technical imagination. (Indeed, the majority's somewhat strained unilateral contract solution in *The Eurymedon* was eschewed by the Supreme Court of Canada in *London Drugs Ltd v Kuehne and Nagel Ltd* (1993), the court preferring a frontal assault on the privity doctrine—see Adams and Brownsword, 1993). In part, no doubt, this reflected a formalist unwillingness to do more than a limited amount of violence to the words of a contractual document (the fact that the exemption in question in this case was in conformity with an international convention designed to cut carriage costs by minimising double insurance highlights the formalist nature of this approach in its concentration on the rules at the expense of a detailed consideration of the actual factual context). However, there was more to it than that. What impressed Viscount Dilhorne, in particular, was the fact that the stevedores had been careless. Thus (at p.173) he cited with approval Fullagar J.'s observations in the Australian case of *Wilson v Darling Island Stevedoring and Lighterage Co Ltd* (1956) 95 C.L.R. 43, p.70:

> "And yet we seem to discern in . . . recent cases, a curious, and seemingly irresistible, anxiety to save grossly negligent people from the normal consequences of their negligence— an anxiety which refuses to be balked even by so well established a general doctrine as that of [privity]."

Commercial convenience might favour protecting the stevedores, but should the courts put such convenience ahead of protecting customers against fault? Viscount Dilhorne thought not, and, as we shall see, he is not the only judge to have taken such a protective view in recent times.

It will be apparent that the case-law dealing with the privity questions presents a particularly neat illustration of our ideological contest. While formalists defend the technical doctrine, market-individualists attack it as commercially inconvenient, consumer-welfarists as unjust. Outside the courts, various proposals for reform were made. Even before the Second World War, relaxation of the doctrine was proposed by the Law Revision Committee (1937) and, through the second half of the twentieth century, the balance of academic opinion moved steadily in favour of reform (see, too, the comments by Lord Goff in *The Pioneer Container* (1994) and by Steyn L.J. in *Darlington Borough Council v Wiltshier Northern Ltd.* (1995)). Eventually, this led to recommendations from the Law Commission (1996) (on which see Adams, Beyleveld, and Brownsword, 1997) which, in turn, led to a modest reform to the doctrine being effected by the Contracts (Rights of Third Parties) Act 1999.

The centrepiece of the new Act is the so-called test of enforceability. By s.1(1) of the Act, a third party is given the right to enforce a contract term if:

(a) the contract expressly provides that he may, or
(b) subject to subs.1(2), the term purports to confer a benefit on the third party.

These two limbs ((a) and (b)), it should be emphasised, are alternatives. The first limb is a relatively straightforward test. However, the second limb invites some tricky case-law on the interpretation of "purports to confer a benefit" (this being more restrictive than, say, "is of benefit") and it is subject to the important reservation in subs.1(2), namely that the presumptive right to enforce does not apply if, on a proper construction of the contract, it appears that the contracting parties did not intend the contract to be enforceable by the third party. To take advantage of either limb of the test of enforceability, the third party (as subs.1(3) stipulates):

"... must be expressly identified in the contract by name, as a member of a class or as answering a particular description but need not be in existence when the contract is entered into."

Where the test of enforceability is satisfied, the rights and remedies of the third party are effectively those that would have been available to him had he been a contracting party (see subss.1(4) and 1(5)). Whilst these provisions are fairly clearly targeted at improving the position of the third party in a case such as *Beswick v Beswick*, it is left to subs.1(6) to provide that the test of enforceability also applies, in principle, to cases (such as *The Eurymedon*) where the third party seeks to take the benefit of a contractual exclusion or limitation of liability. The Act also sets out, in s.2, some limits on the contractors' right to vary or rescind the contract. The intention underlying the somewhat complex provisions in s.2 is to preserve the rights of third parties whose expectations would be unreasonably defeated if the contractors were able to change their mind at will; and, in fact, the thinking underlying s.2 is a particularly interesting example of legislation seeking a pragmatic accommodation of the ideologies of contract (see further Brownsword and Hutchison, 2000).

Relating the new legislation to the four types of privity question that we identified earlier in this section, we can say that the intention is to relax the privity principle in relation to questions P1, P2, and P3, but to leave the position in relation to P4 basically unaltered. By doing this, the legislation largely tracks judicial practice, which had become increasingly adept at finding ways of avoiding negative answers to questions P1, P2, and P3, while remaining content to hold the strict privity line in relation to question P4 (see, *e.g. Law Debenture Corp. v Ural Caspian Ltd* (1993)).

2. INTENTION TO CREATE LEGAL RELATIONS

Although the question of whether the parties to an agreement intended to enter into a legal relationship may always have been a background factor for the purposes of identifying benefits and detriments as sufficient consideration, and indeed for identifying statements as "offers", it did not emerge *in name* as an independent requirement until the earlier part of the twentieth century. In the leading case of *Balfour v Balfour* (1919) the Court of Appeal had to decide whether a husband was contractually bound by his informal promise to pay his wife £30 maintenance until she was able to return from England to rejoin him in Ceylon. On the face of it, this was an easy case: the husband surely could not be liable on an informal gratuitous promise. However, the significance of the case is that the court (at least in the judgments of Warrington L.J. and Atkin L.J.) went beyond the consideration question, saying that the wife's claim must fail anyway because the husband's promise was not intended to create legal relations.

Following on from *Balfour*, it is now a commonplace that agreements, fit for enforcement in every other respect, will not be enforced unless the parties intended to create legal relations. Of course, this is no simple question of fact, such as whether the plaintiff has red hair. In the case of intention to create legal relations, we are dealing with one of those open-ended law-application questions so typical of contract, where the concept of the parties' intentions is pivotal. To operationalise the requirement of intention to create legal relations there is a rebuttable presumption that domestic and social agreements (as in *Balfour*) are not intended to create legal relations, whereas business agreements are so intended.

In many ways, the pattern of the law on intention to create legal relations is akin to that surrounding the distinction between offers and invitations to treat. Policy considerations dictate that certain general situations are marked out with rebuttable presumptions (displays of goods are invitations to treat, domestic agreements are not intended to create legal relations, etc.), but realist judges (particularly consumer-welfarists) respond to the merits of particular disputes in an ad hoc way.

Thus, in *Balfour*, Atkin L.J. identified two general policy considerations which militated against treating domestic agreements as legally binding. First, there was the floodgates argument. If, Atkin L.J. contended, agreements such as that in *Balfour* were to be legally enforceable "the small Courts of this country would have to be multiplied one hundredfold" (see further at p.579). To be blunt, this beggars the imagination, but that is beside the point. Secondly, it was suggested that the "sanctioning" presence of the courts might inhibit social relationships which proceed in a context of love, affection, trust, and the like (*cf.* the reasoning behind the courts' unwillingness to enforce collective agreements made between employers and unions, see *Ford Motor Co Ltd v Amalgamated Union of Engineering and Foundry Workers*, 1969).

Whatever the thinking behind the setting of the general presumptions, realist judges are not thereby prevented from manipulating the basic framework. Thus, cases like *Simpkins v Pays* (1955) (where a social agreement to share any winnings resulting from a Sunday newspaper competition was held to be legally binding) and *Horrocks v Forray* (1976) (where, in order to protect a man's wife, it was held that an agreement between the man and his mistress, that she could remain in occupation of a house after his death, was not intended to create legal relations) bear all the hallmarks of an ad hoc consumer-welfarist response to the merits.

3. CERTAINTY AND COMPLETENESS

If an agreement is to be enforceable, its terms must be sufficiently certain and complete for the courts to be able to identify the meaning of the agreement on the point at issue.

(i) Ambiguity, vagueness, incompleteness

Occasionally, the terms of an agreement are so ambiguous that it simply is not possible to choose between the rival interpretations. For instance, in *Peter Lind & Co Ltd v Mersey Docks and Harbour Board* (1972), Lind in effect submitted two tenders (offers) to build a container freight terminal. One tender was to do the work for a fixed price, the other to do it for a price subject to variation in the light of the cost of labour and materials. The Board purported to accept "your tender", but with no way of resolving this ambiguous acceptance there was no contract on the terms of either tender.

Vagueness is a subtly different defect, a vague provision being so imprecise that it could be read in any number of ways, without any one meaning having sufficient foundation to warrant short-listing it as plausible. In *Scammell (G) & Nephew Ltd v Ouston* (1941), for instance, the offending provision simply stipulated that the price for a new lorry should be paid "on hire-purchase terms" over two years. Without any means of establishing what sort of hire-purchase terms were in contemplation, the House of Lords ruled that the agreement was too vague to be enforceable.

Predictably, uncertainty is often argued by parties looking for an escape route from an agreement. For example, in *Carlill*, one of the Carbolic Smoke Ball Company's many unsuccessful arguments was that the terms of the agreement were too vague to be enforced, for it was not clear to which group of smoke-ball users the offer applied, and it was uncertain to which period the offer referred in promising protection against influenza. There is an important lesson here: no court can be expected to be particularly sympathetic to a plea of uncertainty, where the party making the plea is arguing that his own terms are uncertain. As Denning L.J. said in *Nicolene Ltd v Simmonds* (1953):

> "It would be strange indeed if a party could escape from every one of his obligations by inserting a meaningless exception from some of them." (p.551)

Parties are not to be allowed to escape from their obligations by resorting to uncertain provisions planted in their contracts.

Apart from ambiguity or vagueness, agreements may also fail for incompleteness. This may be because no provision whatsoever is made for the matter, or because the parties indicate in their agreement that the matter remains to be settled between them. In this latter context, two cases regularly drive students to despair: *May & Butcher v The King* (1934) (although actually decided in 1929) and *Foley v Classique Coaches Ltd* (1934). In the former case, an agreement to purchase some tentage at prices to be agreed upon from time to time between the vendors and the purchasers was held to be too uncertain to be enforced. Yet, in the latter case, it was held that an agreement to purchase petrol at prices to be agreed from time to time between the parties was enforceable. A number of dubious grounds are usually offered to distinguish the two cases, *e.g.* that the agreement in *Foley* was contained in a stamped document, and that the arbitration clause in *Foley*, unlike that in *May & Butcher*, covered failure to agree on price. The truth is, however, that the cases evince two contrasting approaches to the requirement of certainty.

The approach of the House of Lords in *May & Butcher* is stringently formalist. As Viscount Dunedin explained:

"To be a good contract there must be a concluded bargain, and a concluded contract is one which settles everything that is necessary to be settled and leaves nothing to be settled by agreement between the parties."(p.21)

Thus, in *May & Butcher*, the House did not jib at the fact that they were holding to be uncertain an agreement which, had there been no mention of price at all, could have been salvaged under s.8 of the Sale of Goods Act 1893 (as then applicable), by implying that the buyer should pay a reasonable price for the tentage. This, for the House, was irrelevant: the fact of the matter was that the parties had indicated their intention with regard to price (namely that it was still to be agreed), and so the legal position, had the parties remained silent, was beside the point.

The approach in *Foley*, by contrast, draws its inspiration from the far more flexible market-individualist principle employed by the House of Lords in a case of the same period, *Hillas & Co Ltd v Arcos Ltd* (1932):

"Businessmen often record the most important agreements in crude and summary fashion; modes of expression sufficient and clear to them in the course of their business may appear to those unfamiliar with the business far from complete or precise. It is, accordingly, the duty of the court to construe such documents fairly and broadly, without being too astute or subtle in finding defects; but, on the contrary, the court should seek to apply the old maxim of English law, *verba ita sunt intelligenda ut res magis valeat quam pereat*. That maxim, however, does not mean that the court is to make a contract for the parties . . ." (*per* Lord Wright, p.503)

Applying this principle, the House in *Hillas* upheld an option to buy some timber despite the particulars relating to the kind or size of timber, or the manner of shipment, being undefined. And, in *Foley*, the Court of Appeal (led by Scrutton L.J.) ruled that it could legitimately imply a term that the petrol should be supplied at a reasonable price, with any failure to agree on a reasonable price being referrable to arbitration under the express terms of the agreement. Quite apart from any predisposition to follow the *Hillas* rather than the *May & Butcher* approach, the court in *Foley* was faced, it must be said, with facts which strongly invited a rejection of the uncertainty argument. The background to the case was that Classique Coaches entered into an agreement to purchase petrol for their business from Foley as a condition of Foley selling them a plot of land. For three years the petrol was purchased without dispute, but then Classique, thinking they could make a better deal for the petrol elsewhere, tried to back out of the agreement. Understandably, the court was not inclined to assist Classique's attempt to use uncertainty as an escape clause, when the agreement, which had worked perfectly well for three years, no longer suited their commercial interests.

The market-individualist driving force behind *Hillas* and *Foley* and the reaction against the traditional formalist approach is vividly demonstrated by Scrutton L.J.'s reflections (in *Hillas*) upon his earlier lone dissenting judgment in *May & Butcher*:

> "I am afraid I remain quite impenitent. I think I was right and that nine out of ten businessmen would agree with me. But of course I recognize that I am bound as a judge to follow the principles laid down by the House of Lords. But I regret that in many commercial matters the English law and practice of commercial men are getting wider apart . . ." (See (1932) 147 L.T. 503, p.506—see our comments at pp.31–32.).

The parallel between this and Lord Wilberforce's views in *The Eurymedon* is striking, though it should be noted that Scrutton L.J. felt bound to follow the House's decision in *May & Butcher* and hold that there was no contract (a result overturned on appeal).

In this section, we have been considering a degree of uncertainty that is so serious that it threatens the very formation of a contract. However, uncertainty concerning the meaning of a provision in a written contract is by no means uncommon, particularly when teams of lawyers are employed to tease out ambiguities or gaps in the terms of a contract. If the commercial courts routinely resolved disputes concerning the interpretation of contracts by declaring that the contract fails for uncertainty, this would soon put them out of business. Needless to say, the courts do not do this. Uncertainty, as a formation defect, is exceptional; by contrast, contested interpretation of contractual terms is almost the rule in litigation. We will discuss the way in which the courts address this important part of their work in section (iv), below.

(ii) Agreements to negotiate

Commercial contractors sometimes enter into a so-called "negotiation contract", an agreement to negotiate. Does the law regard such an agreement as contractually binding? Or, is such an agreement doomed to fail for lack of certainty? In the light of what we have just said about judicial approaches to the question of certainty of terms in general, we might anticipate that, in relation to this specific issue, there will again be a tension between formalist and market-individualist approaches—and, indeed, that is precisely what we find.

For many years, English law on this particular question has been unsettled. On the one hand, in *Hillas v Arcos*, Lord Wright tentatively indicated that, in principle at least, an agreement to negotiate might be contractually binding. However, when the point was argued before the Court of Appeal in *Courtney and Fairbairn Ltd v Tolaini Brothers (Hotels) Ltd* (1975) Lord Wright's view was rejected as unsound. Ironically, on this occasion, it fell to Lord Denning to deliver the leading formalist homily:

> "If the law does not recognize a contract to enter into a contract (when there is a fundamental term yet to be agreed) it seems to me it cannot recognize a contract to negotiate. The reason is because it is too uncertain to have binding force. No court could estimate the damages because no one could tell whether the negotiations would be successful or would fall through: or if successful what the result would be. It seems to me that a contract to negotiate, like a contract to enter into a contract, is not a contract known to the law." (p.720)

In *Walford v Miles* (1992), the legal standing of negotiation contracts came up for authoritative resolution in the House of Lords. There, the Walford brothers, who were negotiating to buy a photographic processing business from Mr and Mrs Miles, entered into a "lock-out" agreement with the Miles, according to which the Miles agreed to terminate negotiations with any third-parties and not to consider any alternative offers. In due course, the Miles having sold to a third-party, the Walfords argued that the Miles were in breach of the lock-out agreement. One of the problems with the lock-out agreement, however, was that it was uncertain for how long the Miles were bound to eschew dealing with any party other than the Walfords. In the Court of Appeal, Bingham L.J. suggested that the validity of the lock-out agreement might be saved by reading it as enduring "for such time as is reasonable". But, of course, this begged the question of what would constitute a reasonable time. In a last ditch attempt to salvage the validity of the lock-out agreement, it was argued before the House that the lock-out agreement implied a duty on the Miles' part to negotiate in good faith with the Walfords and that, effectively, a reasonable time was such time as was necessary to permit good faith negotiations either to come to fruition or to fail. However, the House, following the *Courtney v Tolaini* line that an agreement to negotiate is not enforceable, was not persuaded that the argument for the Walfords was improved by glossing a bare agreement to negotiate with a duty to negotiate in good faith. Indeed, in Lord Ackner's view, the Walfords' argument was fundamentally at odds with the adversarial ethic of contract law:

> "However, the concept of a duty to carry on negotiations in good faith is inherently repugnant to the adversarial position of the parties when involved in negotiations. Each party to the negotiations is entitled to pursue his (or her) own inter-est, so long as he avoids making misrepresentations ... A duty to negotiate in good faith is as unworkable in practice as it is inherently inconsistent with the position of a negoti-ating party." (pp.460–1)

Clearly, the Walfords' argument was up against a potent ideolog-ical combination—a formalist concern for certainty of terms in conjunction with a robust market-*individualism*.

Although *Walford v Miles* has settled the matter for the time being, the evidence of other jurisdictions (see, *e.g.* Farnsworth, 1987) is that *Walford* is unlikely to be the last word. The point is that market-individualists who emphasise the *market* side of the approach will be concerned to offer some protection to contrac-tors who rely on preliminary agreements, such as agreements to negotiate. This sentiment is perfectly expressed by Kirby P. in the Australian case of *Coal Cliff Collieries Property Ltd v Sijehama Property Ltd* (1991):

> "Courts and lawyers may expect the agreements of business people to be clear and complete. Unfortunately, in the mar-ketplace, agreements often fall short of these lawyerly desires. Yet the law of contracts serves the marketplace. It does not exist to satisfy lawyers' desires for neat rules. In the market-place, this has been described as 'an era of "deals".'" (p.21)

Some business deals, like that in *Walford v Miles*, are very much of a one-off kind; others, like the deals litigated in *Hillas v Arcos*, *Courtney v Tolaini*, and *Coal Cliff Collieries*, are more in the nature of a joint venture (more "relational" as Ian Macneil has famously put it, see p.28). To this extent, the occasion for relaxation of the certainty requirement in respect of agreements to negotiate was *Courtney v Tolaini* rather than *Walford v Miles*. However, the opportunity will surely come round again, and the *market-individualists* will have their day (*cf. Pitt v PHH Asset Management Ltd* (1993)).

(iii) Implied terms

Although the courts are not, so it is commonly said, in the business of writing agreements for contracting parties, this does not mean that they have no power to supplement an agreement (*i.e.* complete an incomplete agreement); rather, it means that any supplementation of the agreement *via* implied terms must not be inconsistent with the parties' intentions. Terms may be implied on the basis of statute, or custom or trade usage, or case law (where precedent establishes that there are standard implied terms in a certain type of contact), or on an ad hoc basis in the particular situation. Subject to contrary statutory provision, however, the golden rule throughout is that implied terms cannot be read in where this would be inconsistent with the tenor of the express terms of the agreement.

In the modern law there has been a division of opinion about the basis on which the courts can read in implied terms of an ad hoc nature. One view, canvassed most openly by Lord Denning, permits the courts to imply terms where it is reasonable to do so. The opposed traditional view holds that the courts are authorised to imply terms only where it is necessary to do so in order to effectuate the parties' intentions. This conflict of opinion came to a head in *Liverpool City Council v Irwin* (1977), where the focus of attention was a tower block of council flats which, in view of its vandalised condition, was known locally as "The Piggeries". In protest against the state of the flats, some tenants withheld rent and the council sought an order for possession. The tenants counterclaimed *inter alia* on the ground that the council was in breach of its implied contractual obligations relating to the maintenance of the common parts of the building, *i.e.* the lifts, lighting of the stairs, etc. The tenancy agreements used by the council imposed various obligations on the tenants, but were silent as to the council's own obligations. On appeal from the trial judge's ruling in favour of the tenants' counterclaim, the counterclaim was held to fail on three different grounds as follows:

(i)   The majority of the Court of Appeal, applying a test of necessity for implied terms, held that no term should be implied putting the council under an obligation to maintain the common parts of the building.

(ii) Lord Denning M.R. in the Court of Appeal, applying a test of reasonableness for implied terms, held that the council was under an implied obligation to take reasonable steps to maintain the common parts, but that, on the facts, there was no breach.

(iii) The House of Lords, applying a test of necessity for implied terms, held that the council was under an implied obligation to take reasonable steps to maintain the common parts, but that, on the facts, there was no breach.

On the question of principle (*i.e.* the appropriate test for reading in implied terms), therefore, whilst Lord Denning favoured the apparently broader reasonableness approach, both the majority of the Court of Appeal and the House of Lords reasserted the supposedly narrower traditional approach. Nevertheless, their Lordships allowed that it was proper to take account of reasonableness in laying down a scheme of implied terms for contracts of common occurrence (*e.g.* contracts for building work, contracts of sale, hire, carriage, etc.); and on the *Irwin* facts, the House actually implied precisely the same term as that implied by Lord Denning. What are we to make of this?

The cynical view of *Irwin*, given that the supposedly rival approaches led to identical interpretations of the contract, is that the House basically agreed with Lord Denning that reasonable terms should be implied but preferred not to shout this from the rooftops. On this view, the coded message in *Irwin* is that it is perfectly proper to imply terms as reasonable provided that this is presented as a matter of necessary implication. In fact, though, *Irwin* went some way beyond this.

As we have seen, the House in *Irwin* conceded that in contracts of common occurrence it is legitimate to employ the reasonableness approach. It follows that, provided one can present a contract as representative of a particular category of contracts, the reasonableness test for implied terms is legitimately in play. The significance of this concession was underlined by the case of *Scally v Southern Health and Social Services Board* (1991). There, the House held that the defendant employers had an implied contractual obligation to bring to the attention of their plaintiff doctor employees the existence of an opportunity to enhance their pension entitlements. Considerable emphasis was laid by the House on the special features of the case, in particular that the rules concerning the doctors' pension entitlements were not directly negotiated between employer and employee but were set by Regulations issued by the Department of Health. According to Lord Bridge, these special features signified that the House was dealing with a particular category of contract, namely one where: (i) the terms of a contract of employment have not been individually negotiated with individual employees but result from negotiation with a representative body or are otherwise incorporated by reference; (ii) a particular term makes available to employees a valuable right contingent upon appropriate action being taken by employees; and (iii) employees cannot reasonably be expected to be aware of this term unless it is drawn to their attention. What *Scally* highlights is that post-*Irwin* it is possible to use the reasonableness approach quite openly not just in relation to a recognised general category of contracts (such as contracts of employment in general), but also in relation to a narrowly drawn sub-class of contract within the general category. Obviously, the more narrowly drawn these sub-classes become the more contracts of common occurrence and the reasonableness approach will openly take over the field of implied terms.

Although the cynical reading of *Irwin* has some plausibility, it should not be thought that the tension between the traditional and the reasonableness approach to implied terms is merely an empty war of words. It is true that in some cases the two approaches will lead to identical results. However, this will not always be the case. The point is that the traditional approach picks up the individualist ethic of market-individualism by disallowing any implication which a self-interested contractor would not clearly have agreed to. At the same time, it seeks to distance itself from any view that licenses judges to impose their own ideas of reasonableness in the teeth of the contractors' apparent intentions. From this perspective, a greater sensitivity to the (reasonable) expectations of contractors in particular business settings and even to the fact that some parties do operate on a cooperative basis perhaps might be acceptable (*cf.* Collins, 1992). However, if the reasonableness approach is a blank cheque for judges to tap into consumer-welfarist principles as and when they see fit (and the opposed self-interest of contractors notwithstanding), this simply will not do. Moreover, the general strategic importance of implied terms must not be forgotten. If consumer-welfarists can capture implied terms they not only have a base from which they can operate their philosophy of reasonableness, they can also feed reasonableness into other contract doctrines (*e.g.* common mistake and frustration—see Chapter 6) traditionally linked to implied terms. Therefore, when the cry goes up against the reasonableness approach to implied terms, this is not simply cosmetic—market-individualists are genuinely anxious to avoid offering their consumer-welfarist rivals any hostages to fortune.

(iv) Interpretation

In many ways the interpretation (or construction) of contracts is akin to the interpretation of legislation. In both cases, the traditional default position is a literal approach. Hence, the language employed by contractors is normally to be given its plain and ordinary meaning—the courts should no more make the parties' bargain by interpretation than by implication. Such literalism, however, is heavily qualified by a battery of presumptions and canons of construction which permit courts to give the language a wider or narrower meaning as is appropriate in the particular context. For example, in relation to legislation, it is often said that penal statutes should be construed restrictively (so that, for instance, the scope of criminal offences is to be confined narrowly to the express terms of their enactment) and, conversely, that legislation should be read broadly in the light of the UK's international obligations (a particularly important presumption as pressure built up for the domestic incorporation of the UK's human rights obligations). In the same way, we will note in the next chapter (at p.142) that the courts were able to exert some control over unfair exclusionary clauses in contracts, particularly in consumer contracts and in standard form contracts, by appealing to various background interpretive presumptions. To some extent, the need to resort to such interpretive strategies has been lessened by the enactment of legislation that expressly authorises the courts to disallow reliance on unfair contract terms (see below at p.143). However, just as traditional literalism in the interpretation of legislation has been overtaken by a new purposive approach (see Adams and Brownsword, 2003, pp.105 *et seq.*), so we find in the interpretation of commercial contracts the displacement of literalism by a new contextualism (see Brownsword, 2003a).

The principal source of the new contextual approach to the interpretation of contracts lies in the judgments handed down by

Lords Hoffmann and Steyn in *Mannai Investments Co Ltd v Eagle Star Life Assurance Co Ltd* (1997) and then, in particular, by Lord Hoffmann in *Investors Compensation Scheme Ltd v West Bromwich Building Society* (1998). The impact of the latter has been such that it is now one of the most frequently cited precedents, with one commentator being moved to describe his Lordship's speech as "rapidly becoming the bible for the Courts in contract interpretation disputes" (McLauchlan, 2000), at 147).

In *Mannai Investments*, Lord Hoffmann prefigured the key aspects of his approach in *Investors* in the following way:

> "The meaning of words, as they would appear in a dictionary, and the effect of their syntactical arrangement, as it would appear in a grammar, is part of the material which we use to understand a speaker's utterance. But it is only a part; another part is our knowledge of the background against which the utterance was made. It is that background which enables us, not only to choose the intended meaning when a word has more than one dictionary meaning but also ... to understand a speaker's meaning, often without ambiguity, when he has used the wrong words." (at p.376)

Context (or background), thus, can assist our understanding of the contractors' intentions, particularly by correcting for simple slips of the tongue or pen. As Lord Hoffmann says, when Mrs Malaprop talks about "an allegory on the banks of the Nile" a contextualist will realise that she is actually intending to say "an alligator on the banks of the Nile" (or, even more correctly perhaps, a crocodile on the banks of the Nile). Applying this approach to the dispute in *Mannai Investments*, Lord Hoffmann and his fellow majority Law Lords held that, even though a tenant had slipped up by specifying the wrong date (by one day) for the termination of a lease, the notice to terminate was nevertheless effective—for, in the particular context, the landlord clearly understood that the tenant intended to serve notice to terminate. And so we come to the landmark case of *Investors Compensation*.

The background to the litigation in *Investors* is quite complex. Briefly, in the late 1980s, many elderly homeowners were encouraged to invest in so-called "home income plans". Unfortunately, these plans proved to be disastrous investments. In consequence, investors sought to recoup their losses by pursuing claims against various parties, particularly their financial advisers, but also building societies and solicitors who had dealt with the mortgages. Where investors had unsatisfied claims against financial advisers belonging to the Financial Intermediaries, Managers and Brokers Regulatory Association (FIMBRA), they could seek compensation under a scheme set up by the Financial Services Act, 1986. This scheme was administered by a management company, the Investors Compensation Scheme Ltd (the ICS).

The particular context for the litigation in *Investors* was that a number of home income plan investors had claimed compensation under the statutory compensation scheme which generally covered between half and three-quarters of their losses. Under the terms of the compensation scheme, the ICS treated the investors' claims as having been assigned to the company and it commenced action against the relevant building society, the West Bromwich Building Society. However, the investors, too, proceeded against the building society. Faced with competing claims for damages, by the ICS and by the investors, the building society raised the question of whether (and, if so, to what extent) the investors' claims had been assigned to the ICS.

For the most part, the provisions of the standard form claims agreement made between the investors and the ICS were drafted in the best legalese. However, an accompanying explanatory note tried to put matters more straightforwardly. Paragraph 4 of this note stated that it was to be agreed that "ICS should be able to use any rights which you now have against anyone else in relation to the claim." This seemingly general assignment of third party claims was mirrored in the claims agreement under which the investors agreed to "assign absolutely to ICS each and every Third Party Claim and the benefit thereof . . ." Section 3(b) of the same claims agreement, however, provided for an *exception* to the assignment of third party claims. According to s.3(b), the investors did *not* assign:

> "Any claim (whether sounding in rescission for undue influence or otherwise) that you [*i.e.* the investor] have or may have against the West Bromwich Building Society in which you claim an abatement of sums which you would otherwise have to repay to that Society in respect of sums borrowed by you from that Society in connection with the transaction and dealings giving rise to the claim (including interest on any such sums)."

The interpretation of these provisions was crucial. Had the investors reserved "any claim" against the building society in which they sought a reduction of the amounts due under the mortgage loans (as the investors submitted), or had they reserved a narrower range of claims sounding in rescission (as the ICS contended)? The majority of the House, led by Lord Hoffmann, ruled that s.3(b) should be understood as reserving only the narrower band of claims. Instead of reading s.3(b) literally, it should be read contextually as follows: "Any claim sounding in rescission (whether for undue influence or otherwise). . . "

We shall say more in a minute about the split opinions in both *Mannai Investments* and *Investors Compensation*. First, however, we must draw in a third case of contextualism, again in the House of Lords, and again leading to division at the highest level. This case is *Bank of Credit and Commerce International SA v Ali* (2001). There, in 1990, following reorganisation by the bank, Mr Naeem was made redundant. His basic redundancy package purported to settle in full all known claims arising from the termination of his employment. However, the bank offered Mr Naeem the option of receiving a further payment, equivalent to one month's salary, if he would sign a general release (on ACAS form COT 3). Having talked this through with an officer from ACAS, Mr Naeem duly signed a general release which provided:

> "The Applicant [Mr Naeem] agrees to accept the terms set out in the documents attached in full and final settlement of all or any claims whether under statute, Common Law or in Equity of whatsoever nature that exist or may exist and, in particular, all or any claims rights or applications of whatsoever nature that the Applicant has or may have or has made or could make in or to the Industrial Tribunal, except the Applicant's rights under the Respondent's [the bank's] pension scheme."

Subsequently, of course, there was a huge scandal about corruption at BCCI; the bank collapsed; and the courts inherited a legacy of litigation. One question to arise was whether the bank's ex-employees might be entitled to so-called stigma damages; but it was not until *Mahmud v Bank of Credit and Commerce International SA* (1998) that it was authoritatively ruled that such claims were sustainable in principle. In the light of this ruling, would it now be open to Mr Naeem to seek stigma damages; or would such a claim be barred by the general release that he had signed eight years earlier? The House applied a contextual approach, the majority holding that the release properly interpreted did not bar such an unknown claim.

These are not easy cases. The fact that each case generates a division of opinion in the House indicates that contextualism does not guarantee consensus. If we add in the fact that, whereas, in *Mannai Investments* and *Investors Compensation*, Lord Hoffmann is in the majority, he hands down the minority opinion in *BCCI v Ali*, we might well wonder what to make of these cases. Is our ideological framework able to throw any light on how we should "interpret" the interpretation of contracts?

First, traditional literalism invites a rather formalistic approach. It is an approach that has some appeal to market-individualists (because contractors are able to rely on the language of the contract taken at face value; see, *e.g.* Staughton, 1999). However, unqualified literalism can produce absurdity that makes a mockery of the market. For example, in *Segovia Compania Naviera S.A. v R. Pagnan & Fratelli* (1977), a charterparty provided that the charterers could order the vessel to any port in the United States of America that was to the east of the Panama Canal. The vessel was ordered to New Orleans, a port (surprisingly perhaps) that is actually to the west (*sic*) of the Panama Canal. To stand on the literal terms of the charterparty would be to defeat the intentions and reasonable expectations of the parties.

Secondly, contextualism is predicated on an implicit principle of fair and reasonable dealing. If A realises that, although fellow contractor B has said or written one thing, B actually means something else, it is neither fair nor reasonable for A to stand on the language used by B. In a sense, this is an application of the reasonable reliance principle that we saw underpinning the doctrine of equitable estoppel. A is precluded from asserting the literal meaning against B because, in the particular context, it is not reasonable for A to rely on what B has seemed to say when A has understood perfectly well what B intends to say. The majority's approach in *Mannai Investments* is a fairly straightforward application of this line of thinking.

Thirdly, where it is not perfectly clear that A has detected the slip by B, the application of contextualism becomes much less straightforward. To say that it would be unreasonable for A to rely on the apparent meaning of the contract is no longer convincing without further argument. Such is the position in *Investors Compensation*. Given the documentary legalese in that case, to hold that the investors must have understood that the ICS would be taking over pretty much all their claims is far from compelling. For the majority (including Lord Hoffmann), this reading nevertheless makes best (or most reasonable) sense of the compensatory arrangements. However, Lord Lloyd, who dissents, has a good point. The investors, it will be recalled, had *not* been *fully* compensated by the ICS and so they had a perfectly good reason for advancing claims against the Building Society. Thus:

> "It is common ground that the investors have retained rights of some kind against WBSS. That being so it would seem to me as likely as not, commercially, that the agreement would provide for the investors to retain the whole of their rights against WBSS, including the right to claim damages in reduction of their loans. Such a consequence cannot be regarded as 'ridiculous' or 'extraordinary' or 'very unreasonable'." (p.107)

Clearly, the key to *Investors Compensation* is not that the investors realised, when they read s.3(b), that the bracket was in the wrong place and that the words needed to be re-ordered. Instead, the differing opinions evince a degree of realism driven by various background judgments as to what is the more reasonable resolution, all things considered, in the circumstances.

Fourthly, in *BCCI v Ali*, we have much the same pattern. It is inconceivable that, when Mr Naeem signed the release, he thought: "Of course, I am signing away not only the claims that we know about but also those that we do not know about, including claims of a kind that presently are not even recognised in principle in English law." Nor is it plausible to suppose that those who drafted the release intended it to have such a comprehensive application but had slipped up in their drafting. Yet, if the context was to be decisive, it had to settle whether a reasonable person in Mr Naeem's position would have understood that he was signing away the possibility of pursuing a claim against the bank for compensation: (a) in relation to facts which were not then generally known; and/or (b) where the claim pleaded was of a kind which would only be recognised in English law some years later. For Lord Hoffmann (dissenting), the business sense of the release in *BCCI v Ali*—very much as his Lordship sees the business sense of the arrangement in *Investors Compensation*—was that "unknown claims" must have been swept up. Against this reading, the majority's view is put most explicitly by Lord Nicholls:

> "I consider these parties are to be taken to have contracted on the basis of the law as it then stood. To my mind there is something inherently unattractive in treating these parties as

having intended to include within the release a claim which, *as a matter of law*, did not then exist and whose existence could not then have been foreseen. This employee signed an informal release when he lost his job, in return for an additional month's pay. The ambit of the release should be kept within reasonable bounds." (p.974)

Rather like Lord Lloyd's view in *Investors Compensation*, the majority's approach in *BCCI v Ali* speaks to a conception of reasonableness that puts the burden on the party who drafts the documentation and protects the interests of the non-professional contractor against the professional party.

To take stock, where contextualism precludes manifestly unreasonable reliance, functioning as a corrective to literalism, it is tolerably calculable. Seen in this light, *Mannai Investments* is a relatively easy case. However, both *Investors Compensation* and *BCCI v Ali* are deeply problematic because there is no clear contextual understanding on which to ground the reasonableness of the preferred interpretation. In these cases, contextualism invites a realist approach, the result being measured either by a reasonable business perspective (a rendition of market-individualism of the kind favoured by Lord Hoffmann in both *Investors Compensation* and *BCCI v Ali*) or by the consumer-welfarism of Lord Lloyd in *Investors Compensation* and the majority in *BCCI v Ali*. This involves something of an irony: for the contextualism launched by Lord Hoffmann as a modest corrective to literalism, opens the door to a consumer-welfarist approach that he would be the first to discourage (see further, his Lordship's views in *Union Eagle Ltd v Golden Achievement Ltd* (1997) below at p.119).

4. THE GENERAL CONDITIONS: GOOD FAITH AND UNCONSCIONABILITY

In many legal systems, the enforceability of an agreement is subject to two general conditions—that the parties have acted in good faith and that the terms of the agreement are not unconscionable. Although these general conditions have not been explicitly adopted as such in the English law of contract, any attempt to regulate transactions must grapple with these ideas in one form or another.

(i) Good faith

According to Art. 1134(3) of the French *Code civil*, agreements are "to be performed in good faith"; similarly, s.242 of the German Bürgerliches Gesetzbuch (BGB) imposes a good faith requirement on contractors. It should not be thought, however, that the adoption of good faith clauses is peculiar to civilian legal systems—for example, Art. 1–203 of the American Uniform Commercial Code (in force in all but one jurisdiction) provides for a requirement of good faith in the performance and enforcement of contracts. Although these good faith clauses (particularly s.242 of the BGB) have been widely used in their respective legal systems, and although the jurisprudence of good faith is quite well-developed (see Summers, 1968), English lawyers tend to be suspicious of the idea that a party must act in good faith. For, what precisely does "good faith" mean? Does it simply mean that a party must act with a clear conscience or are there some external standards of good faith dealing? If the latter, are these external standards set by a particular commercial community, or is there a critical moral benchmark for good faith (*cf.* Powell, 1956)? Moreover, where are the boundaries of a good faith requirement to be drawn—does good faith relate only to performance and enforcement of contracts (as many of the good faith clauses explicitly provide) or does it also cover negotiation? Given all this, was it really so surprising that the House of Lords in *Walford v Miles* should reject the idea of an enforceable agreement to negotiate in good faith?

If the notion of good faith is not to be dismissed out of hand, the Court of Appeal's decision in *Interfoto Picture Library Ltd v Stiletto Visual Programmes Ltd* (1989) is a helpful starting point. In *Interfoto*, the defendants contracted to have the use of some photographs from the plaintiffs who ran a library. The photographs were sent to the defendants, along with a delivery note which specified the date for the return of the photographs to the plaintiff. The delivery note also set out nine printed conditions, condition 2 of which specified the holding charges for late return of the photographs. The defendants, having forgotten about the photographs, returned them some two weeks late and, under the terms of condition 2, incurred a holding charge of £3,783.50. The defendants refused to pay but the trial judge ruled in favour of the plaintiffs.

On appeal, it was argued by the defendants that the plaintiffs had failed to take proper steps to draw their attention to the level of the holding charges set by condition 2, these charges being well above comparable rates elsewhere. Effectively, as Bingham L.J. observed, the defendants alleged that the plaintiffs had failed to act in good faith:

> "In many civil law systems, and perhaps in most legal systems outside the common law world, the law of obligations recognizes and enforces an overriding principle that in making and carrying out contracts parties should act in good faith. This does not simply mean that they should not deceive each other . . .; its effect is perhaps most aptly conveyed by such metaphorical colloquialisms as 'playing fair,' 'coming clean' or 'putting one's cards face upwards on the table.' It is in essence a principle of fair and open dealing. In such a forum it might, I think, be held on the facts of this case that the plaintiffs were under a duty in all fairness to draw the defendants' attention specifically to the high price payable if the transparencies were not returned in time and, [after the date set for return], to point out to the defendants the high cost of continued failure to return them." (p.439)

However, Bingham L.J. continued, English law's preference for pragmatic solutions has meant that no such overriding principle has been adopted. Instead, English law responds to perceived cases of unfairness by developing piecemeal solutions. And, indeed, to deal with the perceived unfairness in *Interfoto*, such a solution was readily at hand. As we saw in the previous chapter, the Court of Appeal in *Thornton v Shoe Lane Parking*, developed the classical "reasonable notice" requirement in such a way that unusually onerous terms would only be incorporated if exceptional steps were taken to draw such terms to the attention of the contracting party. Given that the holding charges specified by condition 2 in *Interfoto* were unusually onerous, and given that the plaintiffs took no exceptional steps to draw the defendants' attention to these charges, the clause failed for lack of reasonable notice.

Whilst *Interfoto* is a fairly straightforward application of the *Thornton* principle, the *Interfoto* context is not quite identical to that in *Thornton*. In *Thornton*, the plaintiff suffered personal injury; and, although he was a professional musician on his way to work, it would be distorting the facts to characterize his contract with the car-park as anything other than a consumer contract. By contrast, in *Interfoto*, the defendants' loss was purely economic and, as an advertising agency contracting for the use of the photographs for a particular promotion, the defendants clearly made the contract in a commercial capacity. Accordingly, whilst the approach of the court in *Thornton* represents textbook consumer-welfarism, the court in *Interfoto* carries a protective concern—to disallow condition 2, which Bingham L.J. described as an "unreasonable and extortionate clause" (p.445)—into commercial contracting. It is tempting to interpret this as a welfarist intervention in the commercial sector; however, it might be read, instead, as a "hard look" version of market-individualism in which even unreasonable and extortionate clauses will be enforced provided that the contracting party subject to such clauses has had proper notice of, and has freely agreed to, the terms.

If English law does not yet *explicitly* recognise an overriding requirement of good faith in contracts, but does on occasion implicitly draw on such an approach (see, *e.g. Timeload Ltd v British Telecommunications plc* (1995)), two questions arise. First, how far are the courts prepared to take this implicit approach; and, secondly, is it simply a matter of time before the doctrine is explicitly recognised? Certainly, if we take our lead from *Walford v Miles*, the answers are: (i) not very far; and (ii) not unless the adversarial ethic of English contract law is abandoned.

In relation to the first of these questions, the willingness of the courts to allow explicit doctrine to be stretched by implicit good faith ideas was tested in the important case of *Baird Textile Holdings Limited v Marks and Spencer plc.* (2001). In that case, there was a long-running co-operative relationship between the parties, Baird having been a principal supplier to Marks and Spencer for 30 years. Even Marks and Spencer's director for procurement attested that the relationship with suppliers, such as Baird, was close to that of a partnership. Given this background, Baird were understandably aggrieved when, without warning, Marks and Spencer notified them that, as from the end of the then current production season, all supply arrangements were to be determined. In response, Baird appealed implicitly to the ideal of good faith to argue that they were entitled to a reasonable period of notice (some three years) during which time they could make the necessary adjustments to their business. If there had been an express framework contract governing the relationship between the parties and including a termination clause, Baird might have argued that the notice period should be extended to reflect the duration of the dealings between the parties. However, in the absence of such an express contract, Baird relied on the co-operative nature of their relationship with Marks and Spencer to argue that their entitlement to long notice arose either under an implied contract or by way of an estoppel. The Court of Appeal, taking their bearings from classical individualistic thinking, rejected this argument. As Mance L.J. put it:

> "It is evident that Baird felt, quite rightly, that it had achieved a long and very close relationship, an informal business 'partnership', with M & S, and that it could, as a practical matter, rely on this and M&S's management's general good-will and good intentions. But managements, economic conditions and intentions may all change, and businessmen must be taken to be aware that, without specific contractual protection, their business may suffer in consequence. I do not think that the law should be ready to seek to fetter business relationships, even—and perhaps especially—those as long and as close as the present, with its own view of what might represent appropriate business conduct, when the parties have not chosen, or have not been willing or able, to do so in any identifiable legal fashion or terms themselves." (para. 76)

So, even in a co-operative context, where, if anywhere, good faith might flourish, we find individualistic doctrinal thinking continuing to assert itself.

Nevertheless, such hesitation to adopt good faith by stealth might be overcome eventually by the pressures building up for explicit adoption of the principle. The sources of this pressure are various. In both the common law and civilian law worlds, it is now almost axiomatic that good faith dealing is a cornerstone of any regime of contract law (see, *e.g.* Priestley J.A. in *Renard Constructions (ME) Property Ltd v Minister for Public Works* (1992); and Brownsword, Hird, and Howells, 1999). Moreover, national legal systems are no longer self-contained communities. With the development of harmonised law for larger regional markets and model contracts for international trade, it becomes ever more difficult for local contract law to maintain a parochial attitude or idiosyncratic doctrinal positions (see, *e.g.* Beatson and Friedmann, 1995; and Forte, 1999). In this setting, perhaps the most acute pressure on English contract law is exerted by EC law. Already, two Directives—one, Directive 86/653 on Commercial Agents (implemented by SI 1993/3053), the other, Directive 93/13 on Unfair Terms in Consumer Contracts (implemented initially by SI 1994/3159, now replaced by SI 1999/2083)—have introduced explicit pockets of good faith into English law. Whereas the former provides for reciprocal duties on principals and agents to "act dutifully and in good faith" in relation to one another's interests, Art. 3 of the latter famously provides that a term is unfair if "contrary to the requirement of good faith, it causes a significant imbalance in the parties' rights and obligations arising under the contract, to the detriment of the consumer." The Recitals to the Directive attempt to capture the spirit of good faith by saying that the requirement "may be satisfied by the seller or supplier where he deals fairly and equitably with the other party whose legitimate interests he has to take into account."

Notwithstanding the fears of those market-individualists who believe that good faith is simply too vague to be doctrinally healthy, there is now a substantial body of jurisprudence associated with the application of Art. 3 of the Directive. Much of this is out-of-court jurisprudence in the sense that it is to be gleaned from the Bulletins published by the Unfair Contract Terms Unit within the Office of Fair Trading, whose responsibility it is to enforce the implementing regulations (see further p.223, below). These Bulletins show that the OFT is acting against both procedural and substantive unfairness (for an overview, see Bright, 2000). As for the in-court jurisprudence of good faith, we now have the views of the House of Lords in *Director General of Fair Trading v First National Bank* (2001).

The complaint in the *First National Bank* case concerned a standard form provision to the effect that, where borrowers fell into arrears, interest at the contractual rate would continue to accrue on the outstanding sum even where the bank obtained judgment for repayment (that is, the court order would not serve to roll up the entire debt and preclude the independent contractual accumulation of interest on the debt). In order to bring this home to defaulting borrowers, the bank sent a standard letter saying that, whilst borrowers need only pay the amounts ordered by the court, interest continued to accrue and, thus, it was in the borrower's interest to increase their repayments "otherwise a much greater balance then the judgment debt may quickly build up." The Director General of Fair Trading formed the view that a significant number of borrowers had been unfairly caught out by this term and that the Bank could not in good faith rely on this provision. However, the Bank disagreed, leaving the Director General to fall back on his reserve powers by seeking an injunction to restrain further use of the term.

Although it was the 1994 version of the regulations that governed this particular dispute, the guidance given by their Lordships as to the meaning of good faith, and the span of potential unfairness, is equally applicable to the current 1999 version. Giving the leading judgment, Lord Bingham largely echoes the procedural emphasis (on fair and open dealing) that we have already seen in his remarks in the *Interfoto* case; and the same is true of Lord Steyn's judgment. However, both their Lordships are clear that good faith also has a dimension of substantive fairness. According to Lord Bingham:

> "The requirement of good faith in this context is one of fair and open dealing. Openness requires that the terms should be expressed fully, clearly and legibly, containing no concealed pitfalls or traps. . . . Fair dealing requires that a supplier should not, whether deliberately or unconsciously, take advantage of the customer's necessity, indigence, lack of experience, unfamiliarity with the subject matter of the contract, weak bargaining position or the like. Good faith in this context . . . looks to good standards of commercial morality and practice. [The implementing regulations lay] down a composite test, covering both the making and the substance of the contract, and must be applied bearing clearly in mind the objective which the regulations are designed to promote [*i.e.* improving the functioning of the single market and protecting consumers in that market]." (at para. 17)

Similarly, Lord Steyn (at para. 36) cautions that "[a]ny purely procedural or even predominantly procedural interpretation of the requirement of good faith must be rejected." Despite taking this broad view of good faith, the House held that the term was not unfair. In so ruling, the House was guided by the jurisprudence of the European Court of Justice, where it is settled that the average consumer is to be assumed to be "reasonably well-informed and reasonably observant and circumspect" (see *Gut Springheide GmbH v Oberkreisdirektor des Kreises Steinfurt* (1998), para. 37). Whilst this is the settled view of the ECJ, not all Member States accept this benchmark. In particular, in both Belgium and Germany, there are decisions that take a more protective line towards consumers. And, whilst consumer-welfarists will surely welcome the expansive approach towards good faith reflected in *First National Bank*, they might feel that the actual decision is not altogether in line with Lord Bingham's avowal that good faith precludes taking advantage of the customer's necessity, indigence, lack of experience, and so on. With good faith now firmly embedded in the consumer law of contract and with English contract law under pressure to harmonise with contract regimes that operate with a good faith doctrine, this is a space to be watched. So long as good faith is perceived to be a blank cheque for judicial discretion, market-individualists will resist its adoption. However, once the reasonable expectations that good faith seeks to protect are seen as being rooted in the practice of identifiable business communities, even market-individualists might accept that what works for consumer contracting might also have a place in commercial contracting.

(ii) Unconscionability

Article 2–302 of the Uniform Commercial Code provides:

> "If the court as a matter of law finds the contract or any clause of the contract to have been unconscionable at the time it was made the court may refuse to enforce the contract, or it may enforce the remainder of the contract without the unconscionable clause, or it may so limit the application of any unconscionable clause as to avoid any unconscionable result."

Although English law lacks any equivalent general principle, it does recognise, albeit in a piecemeal fashion, the idea of unconscionability. Indeed, one commentator has observed:

> "Despite lip service to the notion of absolute freedom of contract, relief is every day given against agreements that are unfair, inequitable, unreasonable or oppressive. Unconscionability, as a word to describe such control, might not be the lexicographer's first choice, but I think it is the most acceptable general word." (Waddams, 1976: 390)

According to this view, it is the idea of unconscionability which explains the courts' refusal to enforce manifestly unfair salvage agreements (see, *e.g. The Port Caledonia and The Anna*, 1903); and oppressive agreements with expectant heirs (who sell their inheritances for a song, see, *e.g. Evans v Llewellin*, 1787; *Fry v Lane*, 1888) and with poor and ignorant persons (see, *e.g.* the two previous cases, and more recently *Cresswell v Potter*, 1978).

Similarly, the notion of unconscionability is seen to underlie the courts' willingness to grant contractors relief against penalties and forfeitures, and the like.

This academic commentary is not without judicial support. For example, in *Schroeder (A) Music Publishing Co Ltd v Macaulay* (1974), Lord Diplock said (with some poetic licence as to historical accuracy):

> "Under the influence of Bentham and of laissez-faire the courts in the 19th century abandoned the practice of applying the public policy against unconscionable bargains to contracts generally, as they had formerly done to any contract considered to be usurious; but the policy survived in its application to penalty clauses and to relief against forfeiture and also to the special category of contracts in restraint of trade. If one looks at the reasoning of the 19th century judges in cases about restraint of trade one finds lip service paid to current economic theories, but if one looks at what they said in the light of what they did, one finds that they struck down a bargain if they thought it was unconscionable as between the parties to it, and upheld it if they thought it was not." (p.623)

In line with these sentiments, the courts have tended to uphold restraint of trade provisions (*e.g.* "no competition" clauses) in contracts for the sale of a business, but to take a much tougher line on restraints which occur in contracts of employment (where employees are judged to be in need of protection) (*cf. e.g. Nordenfelt v Maxim Nordenfelt Guns and Ammunition Co*, 1894, and *Mason v Provident Clothing and Supply Co Ltd*, 1913). Quite consistently with this paternalistic approach, the House in *Schroeder* struck down a covenant between a music publisher and a young songwriter as unreasonably in restraint of trade (and, see further, Brownsword, 1998).

Not surprisingly, Lord Denning was in the vanguard of those judges who attempted to foster the idea of unconscionability, most notably in *Lloyds Bank Ltd v Bundy* (1975). Mr Bundy, an elderly farmer, stood as guarantor, with his farmhouse charged as security, to his own bank in respect of loans made by the bank to his son's ailing plant-hire company. Eventually, the guarantee and charge were increased to the point where they exceeded the value of the farmhouse. In due course, the company collapsed and the bank took steps to enforce the guarantee and charge (which effectively meant taking possession of the farmhouse).

The Court of Appeal set aside the guarantee and charge. There was no suggestion that the bank had been guilty of sharp practice, but there was clearly a conflict of interest (on the one side the bank's interest in securing its loans to the company, and on the other side its interest in protecting its client Mr Bundy); and the bank erred in not insisting that Mr Bundy should take independent advice. Although Sir Eric Sachs and Cairns L.J. put their reasoning on a traditional understanding of the principle of undue influence (*cf. Allcard v Skinner*, 1887), Lord Denning M.R. saw a broader principle at stake:

> "Gathering all together [*viz.* duress of goods, unconscionability and the expectant heirs, undue influence, undue pressure—foreshadowing economic duress—and the salvage cases], I would suggest that through all these instances there runs a single thread. They rest on 'inequality of bargaining power'. By virtue of it, English law gives relief to one who, without independent advice, enters into a contract upon terms which are very unfair or transfers property for a consideration which is grossly inadequate, when his bargaining power is grievously impaired by reason of his own needs or desires, or by his own ignorance or infirmity, coupled with undue influences or pressures brought to bear on him by or for the benefit of the other." (p.339)

Apart from the fact that it is presented as "inequality of bargaining power", this might be read as a charter for the principle of unconscionability.

Since Bundy, the courts have, in general, shied away from developing the idea of inequality of bargaining power *simpliciter* as a relieving ground against enforcement. Hence, in *National Westminster Bank plc v Morgan* (1985), a case of a superficially similar kind to *Bundy* but which was eventually decided the other way, Lord Scarman gave notice that the starting point for contract law is, in effect, the market-individualist one: that one makes one's bargains and sticks to them folly notwithstanding. Similarly, the courts have been cautious about appealing to a general doctrine of unconscionability (rather than using established doctrines such as undue influence). Interestingly, though, in *Credit Lyonnais Bank Nederland v Burch* (1997), the Court of Appeal emphasised that the jurisdiction to relieve against unconscionable bargains, "although more rarely exercised in modern times, is at least as venerable as its jurisdiction to relieve against those pro-

cured by undue influence" (at p.151). Moreover, the court emphasised that "the jurisdiction is in good heart and capable of adap-
tation to different transactions entered into in changing
circumstances" (*ibid*.). These dicta, however, should be treated
with some caution.

First, the actual basis of the decision in *Burch* was undue
influence; so the comments about the possible availability of
unconscionability as a ground for relief must be seen as mere dicta.
Secondly, the situation in *Burch*—where a vulnerable party gives a
guarantee (involving a charge over the property in which that
party lives) for the benefit of a close third party (a member of the
family; or, in *Burch*, a trusted employer)—is one of the paradigms
for protective relief. On its facts, *Burch* is in the same family as
Bundy; and, it was a similar story that led the House of Lords to
review the law on undue influence and notice in *Barclays Bank plc
v O'Brien* (1994) as well as encouraging the Australian High Court
to develop its well-known doctrine of unconscionability in the
Amadio case (1983). Thirdly, alongside *Burch*, we should take heed
of the significant decision of the Privy Council in *Union Eagle Ltd v
Golden Achievement Ltd* (1997). There, it was an express term in a
contract for the purchase of a flat on Hong Kong Island that,
should the purchaser fail to complete by the specified time, the
vendor had the right to keep the 10 per cent deposit and withdraw
the property. In the event, the purchaser sought to complete a few
minutes after the deadline had passed, whereupon the vendor
purported to exercise his contractual right (*i.e.* to withdraw and
keep the deposit). The purchaser argued that the court should
exercise its discretion to relieve him against the allegedly
"unconscionable" application of the express terms of the contract.
However, Lord Hoffmann explained why, contrary to the
purchaser's plea, the strict terms of the contract should be adhered
to:

> "The principle that equity will restrain the enforcement of
> legal rights when it would be unconscionable to insist upon
> them has an attractive breadth. But the reasons why the
> courts have rejected such generalisations are founded not
> merely upon authority . . . but also upon practical considera-
> tions of business. These are, in summary, that in many forms
> of transaction it is of great importance that if something hap-
> pens for which the contract has made express provision, the
> parties should know with certainty that the terms of the con-
> tract will be enforced. The existence of an undefined discretion

to refuse to enforce the contract on the ground that this would be 'unconscionable' is sufficient to create uncertainty. Even if it is most unlikely that a discretion to grant relief will be exercised, its mere existence enables litigation to be employed as a negotiating tactic. The realities of commercial life are that this may cause injustice which cannot be fully compensated by the ultimate decision in the case." (218–219)

Having expressed these general considerations, Lord Hoffmann then qualified his remarks by conceding that "the same need for certainty is not present in all transactions and the difficult cases have involved attempts to define the jurisdiction in a way which will enable justice to be done in appropriate cases without destabilising normal commercial relationships" (219).

Lord Hoffmann's qualifying comment neatly captures the dilemma: while consumer-welfarists need lose no sleep over the prospect of a general doctrine of unconscionability, for market-individualists such a prospect threatens to undermine the security of transactions and to devalue the currency of the law of contract. (For the "economic analysis" argument against the employment of such relieving doctrines, see Posner, 1992: 113–117).

(iii) Human rights

In some legal systems, general (or blanket) clauses of the kind that we have been discussing operate as conduits carrying background constitutional values (particularly the values set out in human rights instruments) into the private law of contract (see, *e.g.* Heldrich and Rehm, 2001). With the enactment of the Human Rights Act, 1998, (the HRA) the background values of English public law have been sharpened; and we need to consider whether these values might impact on the private law of contract and, if so, how.

There is one, relatively uncontroversial sense, in which the HRA's domestic incorporation of the rights set out in the European Convention on Human Rights (ECHR) will supplement the private law of contract. Quite simply, no contract will be enforced if it is contrary to public policy; and, after the HRA, it surely cannot be doubted that respect for human rights is an aspect of public policy. To illustrate, in the case of *Horwood v Millar's Timber and Trading Company Limited* (1917), decided long before the HRA, the Court of Appeal unanimously held that an oppressive loan agreement was unenforceable as contrary to public policy. The effect of the agreement, Scrutton L.J. remarked, was tantamount to making the debtor "the slave of the money-lender" (at 317). If this decision seemed to be correct at the time, then bearing in mind that Art. 4(1) of the ECHR prohibits "slavery or servitude", this must seem all the more so now. So much, as we have said, is relatively uncontroversial. However, the potential significance of the HRA with regard to the private law of contract is a major debating point. This is so for the following principal reasons.

First, the original driver of the Convention rights, as the Lord Chancellor pointed out during the passage of the Bill, was "a desire to protect people from a misuse of power by the state, rather than from actions of private individuals" (Hansard HL Vol. 582, col. 1232 (November 3, 1997)). In line with this appreciation of the primary purpose of the legislation, s.6(1) of the HRA places the obligation to respect the Convention rights on "public authorities". Taking this at face value, one might conclude that the HRA applies only to contracts made by public authorities (by no means an insignificant volume of contracting, see Chapter 9) and not at all to the heartland of private contracting. Following the decisions of the Appeal Courts in *Wilson v Secretary of State for Trade and Industry* (2001, CA; 2003, HL), however, it seems that such a conclusion would be wrong. (We discuss *Wilson*, below).

Secondly, if the HRA has some application to contracts made between private parties, how does this work? Prior to *Wilson*, speculation about this question focused on the so-called "horizontal" application of the HRA to disputes where neither party contracts as a "public authority". In the absence of any express guidance in the HRA, while some commentators (notably Wade, 2000) argued for a robust horizontal application, the balance of opinion tended to favour some version of *indirect* horizontality (see, *e.g.* Phillipson, 1999). According to this view, which is in line with much of the jurisprudence elsewhere in the common law world, background human rights do not operate as free-standing pegs on which to hang (novel) private law causes of action; but, once a claim is grounded in settled private law doctrine, then it must be handled by the courts in a way that is compatible with Convention rights (see, *e.g.* Clapham, 1993). So, for example, if there was a dispute about the interpretation of a term in a contract, then the HRA might apply indirectly to disallow a reading of the contract that was judged to be incompatible with one of the Convention rights. Such an indirect application, it will be appreciated, involves no fundamental change to the framework of the private law of contract. By contrast, if the HRA had a *direct* horizontal application, it would be possible, in principle, for an action to be based directly on the alleged violation of a Convention right. For instance, if a restaurant owner refused to serve a would-be customer on the basis of the latter's religious or political convictions, or because of the latter's (old) age, or his sexual orientation or sporting allegiances, the claimant might contend that such a discriminatory refusal violates Convention rights. In the absence of a general clause requiring good faith in negotiation, such a direct application of the Convention rights would be particularly significant in English law, cutting deeper into classical freedom of contract (see Brownsword, 2003).

Thirdly, even if we assume that the HRA has horizontal effect, there is the question of whether the substance of the Convention rights (which are essentially "first generation" political and civil rights) is such as will engage with the kind of questions that typically arise in disputes between contracting parties. We have referred already to Convention provisions that relate to slavery, freedom of conscience, and discrimination; and, as the _Wilson_ case (below) reveals, Convention rights might engage more commonly with contract than we might suppose.

In _Wilson v Secretary of State for Trade and Industry_, the courts were able to place some of this speculative jurisprudence in a concrete context. On the face of it, _Wilson_ was a most unlikely looking case for HRA purposes. The parties were private contractors; their dispute concerned a loan agreement; the court was a "public authority" for the purposes of the HRA (because it is so included by the definition thereof in s.6(3)(a)); but, otherwise, _Wilson_ was a dispute between private contractors, a creditor and a debtor, coming into the courts in the usual way. Briefly, the parties had entered into a loan agreement that was regulated by the Consumer Credit Act 1974. However, the agreement was improperly executed (the amount of the credit being mis-stated). Generally, such agreements, despite being improperly executed, are enforceable against the debtor but only on the order of a court. In exercising its discretion as to enforcement, the court is to consider various factors as to the justice of doing so including any prejudice occasioned by the contravention as well as its power to reduce or discharge the debt. By way of exception to this general regime, however, s.127(3) of the Act provides that a court has no discretion as to enforcement where the debtor has not signed a document containing all the prescribed terms of the agreement: in such a case, the agreement is not enforceable against the debtor. The particular contravention in _Wilson_ brought it within this exceptional category. Moreover, in such a case, the creditor is not permitted to enforce any security provided. Again, *Wilson* was in this category, with the result that the creditors were unable to enforce the security by way of pledge that Mrs Wilson had given them over her BMW car.

In these somewhat improbable circumstances, and with reference to the HRA, the question arose whether the relevant provisions of the Consumer Credit Act are consistent with Convention rights, in particular the *creditor's* right to a fair trial under Art. 6(1) of the ECHR and the *creditor's* right to peaceful enjoyment of one's possessions as provided for by Art. 1 of the First Protocol to the Convention. Four issues arose for consideration: (i) whether the HRA applies retroactively to an agreement, such as that in *Wilson*, which was actually made before the HRA came into force; (ii) whether, if so, s.127(3) of the Consumer Credit Act is compatible with Convention rights; (iii) whether, if the provisions of s.127(3) are incompatible with the Convention rights, it is possible (following s.3(1) of the HRA) to "read down" the former provisions to render them compatible with the latter rights; and (iv) whether, if this is not possible, the court should make a declaration of incompatibility under s.4(2) of the HRA. The Court of Appeal, taking the view that as a public authority, the court has a statutory obligation to make orders that are compatible with the Convention rights, ruled that the law regulating the loan agreement made by the parties in *Wilson* must be tested for HRA compliance. Having found the relevant provisions of the Consumer Credit Act wanting in relation to the Convention rights, and having found no plausible way of "reading down" the Act to secure compatibility, the court issued a declaration of incompatibility. The practical effect of such a declaration is to leave the offending law intact but to excuse and explain the court's application of such law and to put pressure on the government to introduce appropriate legislative changes. So far as the impingement of the HRA on contract law is concerned, the signals sent out by *Wilson* are pretty startling: the HRA applies retrospectively to contracts; and, even if the disputants are parties to a private contract, the court (as a public authority) must adjudicate their dispute in a way that achieves an HRA-compliant outcome—or, at any rate, where legislation governs their dispute, every effort must be made to read it down in a way that is compatible with Convention rights.

Wilson went on appeal to the House of Lords. It took a couple of years before their Lordships' judgments were ready to be handed down, during which time the Appeal Courts had shown themselves to be reluctant to give the Convention rights anything other than a prospective application and, even then, in a less than full-blooded fashion. It seemed unlikely that the robust approach in *Wilson* could survive—and so it proved. On pretty much every point, the House judged that the Court of Appeal had got it wrong. First, the HRA should not be applied retroactively. No matter how it was argued, the House judged that it simply could not have been Parliament's intention to permit the Act to be applied so as to impinge on rights of the kind already vested in the debtor in *Wilson*. In chorus, the House protested that to permit such an application would be unfair, productive of uncertainty, and arbitrary. Secondly, the House held that, even if the HRA had applied to the agreement in *Wilson* (as it would have done if the agreement had been made after the commencement of the Act), the right to a fair trial was plainly not engaged and the property right under Art. 1 of the First Protocol was either not engaged or, if engaged, it was legitimately restricted. In short, the court had no jurisdiction to consider making a declaration of incompatibility; and, even if there had been jurisdiction, no such declaration was warranted.

Both market-individualists and consumer-welfarists will find reasons to be cheerful about the outcome in *Wilson*. For the former, the House's concern to close off any possibility of retrospective application coupled with its antipathy towards uncertainty will sound the right note; and, for the latter, the House's concern for the consumer's interests (not least its vindication of the extremely protective terms of s.127(3) of the Consumer Credit Act) will seem well-directed. However, defenders of neither faith can be entirely confident about the prospective application of the HRA to disputes between *private* contractors? For market-individualists, it might be worrying that, with the exception of Lord Rodger (who merely mentions it in passing at para. 174), the Law Lords make no reference to this being a case with an arguably "horizontal" application. What seems to most trouble their Lordships is the retrospective effect of the Court of Appeal's decision, not its application to a dispute between private contractors. Indeed, all the indications are that, if the agreement in *Wilson* had been made after the HRA was in force, the Court of Appeal would have been right to try to read down the relevant provisions of the Consumer Credit Act and, if necessary, issue a declaration of incompatibility (see, *e.g.* Lord Scott at para. 158). On the other hand, for consumer-welfarists, it must be unsettling that the first serious attempt to invoke the HRA in the field of contracts is made on behalf of a bank.

Finally, it should be said that, while we can plot *Wilson* by reference to the general adjudicative ideologies (*viz.* formalism and realism) and the specific ideologies of contract (*viz.* market-individualism and consumer-welfarism), this is a case where the ideologies of human rights more generally are inevitably implicated. In the longer run, what might prove to be more significant than the House's concern to confine the application of the HRA is its restrictive interpretation of the Convention rights that the Court of Appeal took to be at issue. The point is that, in the coming century, there is a new agenda of human rights concerns—particularly to do with the possibility of genetic discrimination by contractors, access to reproductive technologies, and the commercialisation of the human body and body parts. Accordingly, even if the House leaves open the door to the HRA having some horizontal impingement on private contracting, *Wilson* reminds us that it can soon close it by conservative or restrictive application of the Convention rights and the values that underlie them (see Brownsword, 2001a).

5. OVERVIEW

Disputes centred on the conditions of enforceability clearly bear the imprint of the triangular ideological contest. English law's schematic approach to contract formation is a breeding ground for formalism, and this expresses itself in the traditional benefit and detriment analysis of consideration (see, *e.g.* the majority approach in *Ward v Byham*), the defence of the traditional scheme (see the majority line in *Brikom*), the technical approach to privity, and the hard line on certainty (see, *e.g. May & Butcher* and *Walford v Miles*). Market-individualists deviate from such a formalist approach where it is out of line with commercial practice and expectation and where it impairs commercial convenience (see, *e.g. The Eurymedon, Hillas,* and *Foley*); and consumer-welfarists depart from it where ad hoc fairness so requires (see, *e.g.* Denning L.J.'s approach in *Ward, Charnock, Simpkins* and *Horrocks*). The tensions between market-individualist and consumer-welfarist thinking centre on the concept of reasonableness, in particular with regard to whether reasonableness should be explicitly crafted into doctrine and, if so, as to whose standards of reasonableness should govern. The nervousness of market-individualism in relation to giving reasonableness a doctrinal foothold is evident in individual decisions such as *Irwin, Bundy,* and *Marks and Spencer,* in opposing the adoption of a general principle of good faith, and in seeking to maintain the exchange-based paradigm of contractual obligation as against models based on reasonable reliance or reasonable expectation. Once the idea of reasonableness has insinuated itself into doctrine, the question of whose standpoint governs becomes critical. While modern market-individualists will argue for the standards and expectations of reasonable business people (compare the thinking in *High Trees* and *Williams v Roffey*), consumer-welfarists tend to favour the views of reasonable consumers or more vulnerable contractors. Where there is no settled reference point, or no clear expectation or standard, the application of doctrines driven by reasonableness becomes much less predictable—and market-individualists might sense that the seemingly progressive "contextualism" of *Investors Compensation* threatens to take the interpretation of commercial contracts away from familiar and calculable bearings.

To these cross-cutting ideological tensions, the HRA has added a further layer of complexity. If the private law of contract is to be constitutionalised, this will inevitably mean that some of the ideological differences of public law will spill over into contract disputes.

6

THE CONCEPT OF RISK

A recurrent theme in modern discussions of contract is the idea that a contract is a device for allocating risk. The most direct way of isolating the risk element of contract is by posing in relation to any particular contract the question, "What if X?" (where "X" stands for some past, present, or future circumstance). For example, suppose that Jack agrees to exchange his cow for the butcher's magic beans. We can ask, "What if the cow, unbeknown to the parties, is tubercular? Whose risk is it?" or, "What if the government, shortly after the parties have struck their agreement and before delivery of the beans, requisitions all magic beans? Whose risk is this?" If the parties have planned for the particular risk, the agreement will provide an answer to our question (*e.g.* Jack might have disclaimed any responsibility for the health of the cow, indicating that the butcher has agreed to buy it at his own risk). In such circumstances, the question for the courts is whether they will enforce the agreement. However, if the parties have made no provision for the risk (*e.g.* if Jack and the butcher did not consider the possibility of the government requisitioning magic beans), then the courts must decide where the risk lies.

In this chapter we will consider, first, the problem of unplanned-for risk, particularly with reference to the doctrines of common mistake and frustration; and, secondly, we will consider planned-for risk, focusing on the special problems arising out of exemption clauses.

1. UNPLANNED-FOR RISKS: TALES OF THE UNEXPECTED

Contracts are made in an uncertain world. The more precisely the parties specify their mutual obligations, the fewer the risks left at large. Where the parties plan their relationship, it does not follow that they will make provision for all anticipated risks (see Macneil, 1974) and, a *fortiori*, for those risks which are not anticipated. Where risks are unsuspected or unexpected, and thus unplanned for, we move into the area of common mistake and frustration.

Risk analysis of common mistake and frustration is illuminating for at least two reasons. First, it aids the interpretation of judicial decisions. For instance, in the classic case of *Couturier v Hastie* (1856), the House of Lords ruled that a buyer did not have to pay for a cargo of corn which, unbeknown to either buyer or seller, had been sold prior to the contract in order to prevent deterioration. *Couturier* is regularly cited as authority for the proposition that a fundamental common mistake between the parties (concerning the existence of the cargo of corn) released them from their contractual obligations (though the application of s.28 of the Sale of Goods Act 1979 would lead to the same result that the seller could not recover the price). However, if we put the question, "Whose risk would it be if the subject-matter of the contract of sale had already been sold to prevent deterioration?" we might come up with any one of the following answers:

(i)   the seller took the risk (*i.e.* failure to deliver the cargo would be a breach);

(ii) the buyer took the risk (*i.e.* the buyer must still pay the agreed price); or

(iii) neither party took the risk (*i.e.* both seller and buyer would be released from their obligations).

The standard interpretation of *Couturier* implies answer (iii), and this may be correct. Nevertheless, in principle, the House could have defeated the seller's claim for the price by following answer (i). The only copper-bottomed interpretation of *Couturier* is that the House rejected answer (ii).

A second attraction of risk analysis is that it brings into relief the relationship between common mistake and frustration. Students may be puzzled why textbook discussions of these doctrines often take place many chapters away from one another, when the facts grounding the cases may be virtually identical. For example, in both *Griffith v Brymer* (1903) and *Krell v Henry* (1903), the dispute centred on whether contracts for the hire of rooms overlooking the route of the coronation procession of Edward VII continued to bind the hirers when the processions were cancelled (owing to the King's sudden illness). *Griffith* appears in the chapter on common mistake, because the decision to cancel the procession had already been taken prior to the formation of the contract; whereas *Krell*, where the contract was formed prior to the cancellation, appears as a leading case on frustration. In both cases, however, the material question was, "Whose risk is it if the coronation procession has already been, or is, cancelled?" For our purposes, the fact that common mistake and frustration deal with a similar problem is of more than passing interest. The occurrence of some unsuspected or unexpected risk, like the cancellation of the procession, often turns a satisfactory arrangement into an extremely bad bargain. Consequently, the doctrines of common mistake and frustration are potential avenues of escape from contracts and, as we shall see, this makes them important arenas for the conflict between market-individualism and consumer-welfarism (*cf.* Brownsword, 1985).

(i) Common mistake: the "hawks" and the "doves"

In a famous American case, *Sherwood v Walker* (1887), the plaintiff purchased a cow, known as "Rose 2d of Aberlone", from the defendants. If the cow had been a breeder, she would have been worth at least $750; whereas if the cow had been barren, her value would have been only $80 as beef. The parties agreed upon a value for beef price, and the plaintiff duly tendered $80. However, by this time the defendants had discovered that Rose was not barren, but was with calf, and they argued that the contract should be set aside on the grounds of common mistake. The majority of the Supreme Court of Michigan found in favour of the defendants holding that the difference between a beef cow (worth $80) and a breeding cow (worth at least $750) went beyond a question of mere quality and affected the substance of the whole consideration.

It is not altogether easy to contrast the dissent in *Sherwood* with the majority view, for the dissent was predicated on the assumption that the buyer purchased the cow on the basis of a speculative hunch that the cow might not be barren, and both views are couched in a terminology deriving from Roman law (Dig. 18.1.9). Nevertheless, both sides of the court started with the market-individualist premise that contracts are not lightly to be discharged, and with the concomitant principle that common mistakes as to quality are no ground for relief.

In England, there are two contrasting approaches to common mistake. First, there is the so-called "common law" approach, which tackles the problem along the market-individualist lines of *Sherwood*. Accordingly, relief for common mistake is regarded as exceptional. This is the mews of the "hawks". Secondly, there is the so-called "equitable" approach, which applies the very different ideas associated with consumer-welfarism. Relief for common mistake is judged here in the light of principles of fairness: this is the "dovecote".

In the leading case on the common law approach, *Bell v Lever Brothers Ltd* (1932), Levers bought out the service agreements of two of their employees, Bell and Snelling, for £30,000 and £20,000 respectively. Shortly afterwards, Levers discovered that Bell and Snelling had committed serious breaches of contract during their employment (by taking advantage of their special position to deal in cocoa). Had Levers realised this, they could have terminated both contracts without compensation, and the question was whether the £50,000 could be recovered. At the trial, the jury found that there had been no fraud on the part of the defendant employees. This meant that Levers' claim for the return of the money rested on common mistake and/or the employees' (non-fraudulent) failure to disclose their illicit cocoa dealings. Levers won at the trial and before the Court of Appeal, but the House of Lords ruled three to two against them, with Lord Atkin's majority speech dominating.

Lord Atkin approached both the common mistake and non-disclosure questions in a textbook market-individualist manner, though presented in a *form* which derives from Roman law (see Dig. 18.1.9). On the common mistake issue, having noted exceptional cases such as *Couturier v Hastie*, he tackled the thorny area of common mistakes as to quality:

> "Mistake as to quality of the thing contracted for raises more difficult questions. In such a case a mistake will not affect assent unless it is the mistake of both parties, and is as to the existence of some quality which makes the thing without the quality essentially different from the thing as it was believed to be." (*Bell* at p.218)

Applying this principle, Lord Atkin indicated that he would regard a common mistake as inoperative where, for instance, a purchaser bought a horse which, although unsound, was assumed by the parties to be sound, the purchaser paying the price of a sound horse. In the same way, according to Lord Atkin, there would be no operative mistake where a fake painting, assumed by the parties to be an old master, was sold for an old master's price. Such contracts work a hardship on the purchaser, but, in the absence of representation or warranty, common mistake must not be used to undermine sanctity of contract. Thus, whilst conceding the weight of Levers' contention, Lord Atkin did not judge the mistake to be anything more than an expensive inoperative mistake of quality—Levers got what they bargained for, they simply made a bad bargain. Moreover, Levers could not get round this principle by arguing that there was an implied condition in the golden handshake agreements, to the effect that those agreements were predicated on the assumption that the employees' service contracts could not be terminated without compensation:

> "Nothing is more dangerous than to allow oneself liberty to construct for the parties contracts which they have not in terms made by importing implications which would appear to make the contract more businesslike or more just. The implications to be made are to be no more than are 'necessary' for giving business efficacy to the transaction, and . . . a condition should not be implied unless the new state of facts makes the contract something different in kind from the contract in the original state of facts." (see further at p.226)

Lord Atkin was no less tough on the question of non-disclosure: there was no special duty on the employees to disclose their breaches of contract, and so Levers could fare no better here either (notice how closely this follows the restrictive market-individualist line on mutual and unilateral "collateral" mistakes—*cf.* Chapter 4).

For the dissenting Law Lords in *Bell*, however, the case was relatively straightforward. Following the same sort of legal principle as the majority, the minority held that the mistake was "as fundamental to the bargain as any error one can imagine" (*per* Lord Warrington, *ibid.* at p.208). So, according to the minority, this was no hard case, where the law would have to be shoe-horned to fit the merits—this was a perfectly clear case, the law plainly favouring Levers.

If we assume that the thinking of all judges concerned in *Sherwood* and *Bell* was market-individualist, then there is evidently some scope for disagreement within the market-individualist camp. Given that relief for common mistake must not jeopardise the security of market transactions, the question is how the minority in *Bell* (in the House of Lords) and the majority in *Sherwood* could defend their softer approach. An attractive argument is that while market-individualists should not allow common mistake to be used to renegotiate the terms of a transaction, it is safe to release a party from a contract which, had the true facts been known, he would not have been prepared to make *on any terms* (an alternative way of putting it is to say that the mistake went beyond the risks exchanged by formation). Applying this argument, the majority in *Sherwood* seem to have stretched common mistake to the limit, for this looks like a renegotiation case. With regard to *Bell*, however, the dissenting Law Lords seem to have good grounds for saying that, had the facts been known, Levers would not have entered into the golden handshake agreements *at all*. Hence, the uncompromising view of the majority was inappropriate. This prompts the mischievous thought that the market-individualists (judged by their own standards) got it wrong in both *Sherwood* and *Bell*.

Alongside the common law approach to common mistake runs the equitable approach, which is usually traced to the majority decision of the Court of Appeal in *Solle v Butcher* (1950). Here, the parties purported to enter into the lease of a flat at £250 per annum. Under the Rent Acts, the maximum rent was only £140 per annum; but the defendant lessor could have taken steps to increase the rent to £250 prior to the execution of the lease. However, acting on the mistaken advice of the plaintiff (his business partner) that the rent was not controlled at £140, the defendant had, in fact, taken no such steps and the rent could not now be raised. Effectively, this meant that the flat had been let at £140 when, had the mistake not occurred, it could have been let lawfully (after the service of proper notices) at £250. The tenant sought to recover the rent he had overpaid. On the face of it, such a mistake, calling merely for an adjustment of rent, could not possibly qualify under the restrictive approach adopted in *Bell v Lever Bros*. In *Solle*, however, Denning L.J. by-passed *Bell* by saying that the question there had been whether the agreement was void for mistake, not whether it was voidable for mistake under broader equitable principles. Thus:

> "A contract is also liable in equity to be set aside if the parties were under a common misapprehension either as to the facts or as to their relative and respective rights, provided that the misapprehension was fundamental and that the party seeking to set it aside was not himself at fault." (*Solle*, at p.693)

Accordingly, the lease was set aside on the grounds of a common misapprehension as to the application of the Rent Acts, with the plaintiff being given the option of taking a new lease at a reasonable rent (not exceeding £250 per annum).

The *Solle* approach does not start with market-individualist thinking. Rather, it turns on consumer-welfarist ideas of reasonableness and fair play between the parties. In *Solle* itself, Lord Denning was struck by the unreasonableness of the plaintiff first advising the defendant that the rent could lawfully be set at £250 and then turning round "quite unashamedly" (*per* Denning L.J. at p.695) and trying to take advantage of the parties' common misapprehension. No court of conscience could stand by and let this happen.

Following the lead given in *Solle*, support for the equitable approach can be found in a number of subsequent cases (*e.g. Grist v Bailey*, 1967, *Laurence v Lexcourt Holdings Ltd*, 1978, and *Magee v Pennine Insurance Co Ltd*, 1969). *Magee* makes instructive comparison with *Bell*. In *Magee*, the question was whether an insurance company could have a contract settling a claim made on a car insurance policy set aside in the light of the parties' mistaken assumption that the company could not avoid liability under the insurance policy. By a majority the Court of Appeal ruled that the contract could be set aside for mistake. Lord Denning M.R., applying the *Solle* principle, said that it would not be "fair to hold the insurance company to an agreement which they would not have dreamt of making if they had not been under a mistake" (*Magee* at p.515). Fenton Atkinson L.J. agreed with Lord Denning that the "right and equitable result" (at p.518) demanded that the insurers be allowed to set aside the agreement. But Winn L.J. (dissenting), applying *Bell*, ruled that this was not a mistake which was fundamental. The insurance company assumed (wrongly) that the insured had rights under the policy; the contract settled whatever rights the insured had; there was no mistake as to the essential subject-matter of the contract.

Is there any way of reconciling the market-individualism that underpins the common law doctrine of mistake with the consumer-welfarism that underpins the equitable approach? In *Associated Japanese Bank v Crédit du Nord SA* (1988), Steyn J. (as he then was) observed that "respect for sanctity of contract and the need to give effect to the reasonable expectations of honest men" (at 903) are recurrent themes in contract law (see, too, Steyn, 1997). Generally, these principles pull in the same direction; to hold contractors to what seem to be the terms of their bargain is to act in the way that reasonable parties normally expect; and the common law approach to mistake is in line with this thinking. However, according to his Lordship's bringing together of the two approaches, equity supplements the common law by providing a degree of flexibility to respond to reasonable expectations in special cases—hence, applying the equitable approach, contracts are treated as merely voidable for mistake, rather than void. On the facts of the *Associated Japanese Bank* case, where Crédit du Nord agreed to act as a guarantor in relation to what it understood to be a sale and lease-back agreement for some machines, Steyn J. held that the existence of the machines was a condition precedent to the guarantor's liability. However, he also indicated that, where the machines did not exist, the mistaken impression under which the guarantor contracted would suffice to bring into play either the common law or the equitable doctrine of mistake.

More recently, in *Great Peace Shipping Limited v Tsavliris Salvage (International) Ltd* (2002), the Court of Appeal was in a less accommodating mood. There, the defendant salvage company were seeking to salvage a stricken vessel. Being concerned about the safety of the crew, the defendants contracted for the hire of the claimants' vessel (*Great Peace*) which (relying on information supplied by a third party, Ocean Routes) they understood was a mere 35 miles away from the stricken vessel. In fact, the claimants' vessel was actually some 410 miles away; and, once the defendants appreciated this, they contracted for a vessel that was closer and cancelled the contract for the hire of the *Great Peace*. The question was whether the defendants' mistaken impression as to the position of the *Great Peace* sufficed to relieve them from liability to pay the agreed hire. It is not altogether clear where the merits of this case lie. On the one hand, there is no denying that the defendants acted with good intentions. On the other hand, would it be a reasonable expectation that the owners of the *Great Peace*, who were acting with commercial intent and who did not contribute to the defendants' misunderstanding, should forego their hire? On the face of it, if anyone should be bearing the financial risk of the mistake, it should be the owners of the stricken vessel or Ocean Routes (who gave the misleading information about the proximity of the *Great Peace*).

The court took a more formalistic approach. After an extensive review of the authorities in the area of common mistake, Lord Phillips M.R. concluded that there was really no difference between the operative criteria applied by the common law and equitable approaches (even though one results in a contract being treated as void, the other merely in a contract being avoided). If this is correct, it is a nonsense to ask whether the contract is void at common law and then, if the answer is negative, to apply precisely the same test to ask whether it is nonetheless voidable in equity—and even more of a nonsense, presumably, if the two questions produce different answers. The only conclusion, therefore, is that the equitable jurisdiction in *Solle v Butcher* simply cannot be reconciled with *Bell v Lever Bros*. Accordingly:

> "[i]f coherence is to be restored to this area of our law, it can only be by declaring that there is no jurisdiction to grant rescission of a contract on the ground of common mistake where the contract is valid and enforceable on ordinary principles of contract law."(para.157)

Eschewing the equitable jurisdiction, the court held, on the facts, that the contract for the hire of the *Great Peace* had not become impossible and nor was it essentially different from what the parties had bargained for.

In an attempt to gather together these strands, the famous American case of *Wood v Boynton* (1885) concentrates the mind. There, a girl sold a jeweller a stone for $1. The stone proved to be an uncut diamond worth $700, but the Wisconsin Supreme Court refused any relief to the girl. Obviously, this was a hard case from the girl's point of view, and a fortunate windfall from the jeweller's. The hawkish (market-individualist) approach to such a situation is that the girl had simply made a bad bargain. It would not have mattered if the stone had been worth one cent (in which case the jeweller would have made a bad bargain), $100 (in which case the girl's bargain would not have been quite so bad), or $1,000 or more (in which case the girl's bargain would have been even worse). These variations, from the hawk's standpoint, are immaterial. The point is that the market is replete with good and bad bargains, and the courts cannot (and should not) get into the business of adjusting unequal exchanges or exchanges based on collateral mistakes (notice, again, how this parallels the restrictive market-individualist approach to unilateral and mutual mistake). Against this, the (consumer-welfarist) doves operate on broad principles of fairness and reasonableness. *Wood* concerns a renegotiation type of mistake, but this would not deter the doves from granting relief. Indeed, in *Grist v Bailey* (1967), Goff J. held that a mistake as to the nature of the tenancy affecting a property was sufficient to allow the vendor to set aside the sale of the property at under-value, it having been sold for £850 as against its real value of about £2,250. Assuming that the girl in *Wood* was not at fault, and given the huge disparity between contract price and real value, one can well imagine a consumer-welfarist thinking it only reasonable that relief should be granted.

(ii) Frustration: more "hawks" and "doves"

Where, subsequent to the formation of a contract, but prior to completion of performance under the contract, performance is rendered either impossible or more onerous by some dramatic change of circumstances, it is open to a party to plead that the contract has been frustrated. If the plea succeeds, the parties will be released from their outstanding contractual obligations and the Law Reform (Frustrated Contracts) Act 1943 makes some rough and ready provision for financial adjustment of the parties' positions. The traditional account of the development of the doctrine of frustration suggests that the idea gathered ground rapidly in the nineteenth century, reaching its high point at the beginning of the twentieth century when a number of contracts were held to be frustrated by the cancellation of the coronation celebrations of Edward VII. Thereafter, a harder line set in, the courts being less willing to accede to pleas of frustration, and this culminated in the landmark decision of the House of Lords in *Davis Contractors Ltd v Fareham UDC* (1956).

Implicit in this traditional account of the development of the doctrine of frustration is the notion that, as with mistake, the courts are capable of taking either a hard or a soft line. We can see such conflicting approaches in the instructive case of *British Movietonews Ltd v London and District Cinemas Ltd* (1951, CA; 1952, HL). There, the plaintiff film distributors, by a contract made in 1941, agreed to supply newsreels to the defendant exhibitors for showing at the Pavilion Theatre, Aylesbury. Under the contract the defendants were to pay 10 guineas a week for the newsreels, the agreement being determinable by giving four weeks' notice. In 1943, the Board of Trade issued the Cinematograph Film (Control) Order, which controlled the supply of film to distributors. Whereupon, the parties entered into a supplemental agreement, to apply "during the continuance of the Cinematograph Film (Control) Order 1943". In 1948, notwithstanding the fact that the 1943 Order was still in force, the defendants gave notice to terminate the 1941 contract. The distributors maintained that the supplemental agreement of 1943 (which incorporated the obligation to pay 10 guineas a week for newsreels) remained binding so long as the 1943 Order remained in force, that the defendants could not, therefore, yet revert to their right of termination under the 1941 agreement, and, accordingly, that the defendants must continue to pay 10 guineas a week.

The essential argument put for the defendants was that, while the 1943 Order admittedly remained in force, its whole rationale had changed. In 1943, the purpose of the Order was to aid the military effort. After the war, however, the Order was retained first to secure a fair distribution of scarce resources and latterly to discourage the use of imported film. The Court of Appeal held that the parties must be released from the supplemental agreement, because they could not have contemplated that the 1943 Order would continue in force in such changed circumstances. According to Denning L.J., where a contract is thus held to be frustrated:

> ". . . the court really exercises a qualifying power—power to qualify the absolute, literal or wide terms of the contract—in order to do what is just and reasonable in the new situation." (*ibid.* at p.200)

The House of Lords, however, reversed the Court of Appeal, and ruled that the exhibitors remained bound by the supplemental agreement. Moreover, strong reservations were expressed about Lord Denning's account of frustration as a doctrine granting the courts a qualifying power to do what is just and reasonable in changed circumstances:

> "The suggestion that an 'uncontemplated turn of events' is enough to enable a court to substitute its notion of what is 'just and reasonable' for the contract as it stands . . . appears to be likely to lead to some misunderstanding. The parties to an executory contract are often faced . . . with a turn of events which they did not at all anticipate—a wholly abnormal rise or fall in prices, a sudden depreciation of currency, an unexpected obstacle to execution, or the like. Yet this does not in itself affect the bargain they have made." (*per* Viscount Simon, at p.185)

According to Viscount Simon, when a court holds that a supervening event frustrates the contract, it does not exercise a qualifying power to do what is just and reasonable; it is simply a matter of unpacking the parties' intentions.

As with the debate about the basis of implied terms, there is more to this than a verbal quibble. It is not simply a case of

Viscount Simon linking the doctrine of frustration to the rhetoric of contractual intention, whereas Lord Denning presents the doctrine as a matter of just and reasonable interpretation. Behind these familiar façades, rival substantive philosophies are in contention. For Lord Denning, frustration—like mistake—is to be approached on the basis of fairness and reasonableness, and this encourages a soft line. The parallels between the Court of Appeal's response to the frustration argument in *British Movietonews* and to the mistake argument in *Solle v Butcher* are obvious. For Viscount Simon and the other Law Lords in *British Movietonews*, however, frustration is to be used with great caution. It must not become an escape route whenever there is an unexpected turn of events. The parties must remain masters of their bargain, not only in the sense that lip service be paid to contractual intention, but also in the sense that the courts must not lightly relieve parties from their apparent contractual obligations. Such a hard line on frustration evinces all the market-individualist hallmarks which underpin *Bell v Lever Bros*.

Whilst the hawkish line on mistake, as set out in *Bell*, has to some extent been offset by the equitable approach stemming from *Solle*, the hawkish line on frustration pretty well has the field to itself. Occasionally Lord Denning subsequently nodded in the direction of his views as expressed in *British Movietonews* (see in particular *Staffordshire Area Health Authority v South Staffordshire Waterworks Co*, 1978). But modern thinking on frustration is dominated by the hard line, and particularly by Lord Radcliffe's seminal judgment in *Davis Contractors Ltd v Fareham UDC* (1956).

The facts of *Davis* were that the contractors agreed to build seventy-eight council houses for the local authority, the work to be completed within eight months. In fact, owing to the post-war shortage of skilled labour and building materials, it took the contractors 22 months to complete. The contractors, having incurred additional expense, pleaded frustration (somewhat unusually) as a way of grounding a claim for additional payment. Confirming the tough line established in *British Movietonews*, the House of Lords in *Davis* rejected the plea. In a landmark judgment Lord Radcliffe explained the principle of frustration as follows:

> "... frustration occurs whenever the law recognizes that without default of either party a contractual obligation has become incapable of being performed because the circumstances in which performance is called for would render it a thing radically different from that which was undertaken by

the contract ... The court must act upon a general impression of what its rule requires. It is for that reason that special importance is necessarily attached to the occurrence of any unexpected event that, as it were, changes the face of things. *But, even so, it is not hardship or inconvenience or material loss itself which calls the principle of frustration into play.* There must be as well such a change in the significance of the obligation that the thing undertaken would, if performed, be a different thing from that contracted for." (*ibid.* at p.729, our emphasis)

In the circumstances, Lord Radcliffe felt that the contractors' claim was "a long way from a case of frustration" (*ibid.* at p.729), and while he sympathised with the contractor undeservedly suffering loss he thought it "a misuse of legal terms to call in frustration to get him [*i.e.* the contractor] out of his unfortunate predicament" (*ibid.* at p.731). (We can safely assume, too, that if the sub-contractor carpenters in *Williams v Roffey* (pp.78–80) had been able to address a frustration argument to Lord Radcliffe, they would have enjoyed no more success than the builders in *Davis* itself).

The essential feature of Lord Radcliffe's judgment (confirmed in a number of cases arising out of the closure of the Suez Canal, see especially *Tsakiroglou and Co Ltd v Noblee Thorl GmbH*, 1962) is that contractors cannot expect to be bailed out of unprofitable or less profitable agreements simply by invoking the doctrine of frustration. The doctrine is reserved for exceptional cases, not for the routine, albeit unexpected, ups and downs of market dealing. This important limitation on the doctrine was vividly illustrated in *Amalgamated Investment and Property Co Ltd v John Walker & Sons Ltd* (1976), where the plaintiff developers agreed to pay £1,710,000 for an old whisky warehouse belonging to the defendants. Unbeknown to the parties, the building was about to be listed by the Department of the Environment and, in fact, the building was listed a couple of days after the parties had made their contract. The listing effectively killed any redevelopment potential and the market value of the property was slashed to £210,000. Naturally, the plaintiff purchasers wanted to get out of this extremely adverse contract, to which end they pleaded both mistake and frustration. It was held that both arguments failed because, at the time of the contract, there was no mistaken assumption that the building was free of listing, and the purchasers' mere economic hardship was precisely the sort of loss counted out by *Davis*.

Amalgamated Investment provides a useful focus for gathering together our thoughts on common mistake and frustration. The policy question in such a case is whether the law of contract through the doctrines of common mistake and frustration should relieve the purchaser from an unfavourable bargain. Both *Bell* (with respect to common mistake) and *Davis* (with respect to frustration) take the market-individualist line that this is a clear case in which the purchaser should derive no assistance from the courts. As it happened, the facts in *Amalgamated Investment* presented the live issue as one of frustration (because the building was listed after the contract was formed) and so *Davis* straightforwardly covered the claim. However, if the building had been listed prior to the formation of the contract, and the live issue had been presented as one of common mistake, the outcome of the case would have been less predictable. For, although *Bell* would have disposed of the purchasers' arguments as swiftly as *Davis*, there is no guarantee that the Court of Appeal hearing *Amalgamated Investment* would have applied *Bell* in preference to the equitable approach of *Solle*. If the equitable approach had been applied, it is also unclear whether consumer-welfarists would think it reasonable that the purchasers, being commercial speculators, should stand their own loss, or whether this would be treated as a case for relief, analogously to *Grist v Bailey*. None of this implies that frustration is free of the tensions so clearly evident in mistake. It is simply that the hard line of *Davis* has achieved an apparent ascendancy which the corresponding hard line in *Bell* has yet to attain. One explanation for this is that the pattern of the case-law depends to a considerable extent on the kind of disputes that happen to be litigated and then find their way into the law reports. If disputes between commercial contractors (unlike disputes involving consumers or non-business contractors) tend to elicit a tough judicial response, and if the frustration cases (unlike the mistake cases) tend to be of a commercial character, then this accounts for the apparent difference—and, sure enough, when mistake was pleaded in *Great Peace*, a textbook commercial case, the Court of Appeal seized the opportunity to underline the authority of *Bell*. Alternatively, it may be that the fact situations in the mistake cases have brought up particularly striking instances of advantage-taking (as in *Solle*); and it is this that has prompted the courts to show their welfarist colours.

2. PLANNED-FOR RISKS: TALES OF THE SMALL PRINT

Although the courts generally welcome explicit planning and risk-allocation by the parties, they are particularly sensitive about the parties stipulating their own remedies. Remedy stipulation clauses come in various guises, and the law's response has by no means been consistent (see Brownsword, 1977). For example, whereas it has long been settled that penalty clauses (which effectively over-compensate the innocent party by stipulating a fine in the event of a breach) are void, other types of remedy stipulation clauses, which might be thought equally objectionable, have been enforced. In this section, we focus on one type of remedy stipulation provision, the exemption clause.

No aspect of contract law has received greater attention in modern times than exemption (or exclusion, or exception) clauses. There is, in fact, considerable academic controversy as to the nature of such clauses, but, for our purposes, exemptions can be regarded as clauses whereby a contractor purports to narrow his general contractual obligations or to restrict his liability for breach of contract. Exemptions have dimensions of both breadth and depth. Along the dimension of breadth, the question is to what extent the obligations are shrunk, or to how many of the obligations the restriction of liability applies. Along the dimension of depth, it is a matter of how severely liability is reduced for a particular breach. An outright exemption reduces liability to zero; a so-called "limitation clause" restricts it to a stipulated maximum figure.

Whatever their niceties, in the post-war period, particularly where they were contained in standard form contracts, exemption clauses became a by-word for contractual abuse, and have been commonly regarded as a "bad thing". A well-known case indicating the problem is *L'Estrange v Graucob Ltd* (1934). Here the plaintiff, having purchased an automatic slot-machine from the defendants, sued the defendants for breach when the machine did not work satisfactorily. The contract which the plaintiff had signed contained an exemption providing that "any express or implied condition, statement, or warranty, statutory or otherwise not stated herein is hereby excluded". The exemption worked better than the machine, and the plaintiff lost her claim. The court regretted the small print in which, and the brown paper on which, the exemption was printed, but this could not avail her.

Thirty years later, Lord Reid was able to put the problem of exemption clauses in perspective:

"Exemption clauses differ greatly in many respects. Probably the most objectionable are found in the complex standard conditions which are now so common. In the ordinary way the customer has no time to read them, and if he did read them he would probably not understand them. And if he did understand or object to any of them, he would generally be told he could take it or leave it. And if he then went to another supplier the result would be the same. Freedom to contract must surely imply some choice or room for bargaining.

At the other extreme is the case where the parties are bargaining on terms of equality and a stringent exemption clause is accepted for a *quid pro quo* or other good reason." (in *Suisse Atlantique*, 1967, at p.406)

What this boiled down to was that exemptions were being used to deny *consumers* their ordinary contractual rights, and the need to afford some protection to the consumer began to be felt.

The story of the post-war campaign against exemption clauses is a long one, which we propose only to summarise. Essentially, the courts had two main strategies for controlling exemptions. First, they developed the notion of "breach of a fundamental term", or of a "fundamental breach" (whether or not the two were different was a matter of some debate), the effect of which was to deprive exclusion clauses of any protective power (see, *e.g. Karsales (Harrow) Ltd v Wallis*, 1956). Secondly, they applied a battery of restrictive rules of construction (see our discussion of interpretation, above at p.103). The central principles were that exclusion clauses should not be allowed to derogate from the "main purpose" of the contract, or to protect conduct falling outside the "four corners" of the contract. Moreover, applying the *contra proferentem* principle, ambiguities or gaps in words of exclusion were to be read against the party relying on the protective clause. In the celebrated case of *Suisse Atlantique* (1967), the House of Lords came down firmly in favour of the second strategy. This particularly satisfied formalists, who were troubled by the conceptual impurity of the fundamental breach doctrine (see Coote, 1964 for a critique of that doctrine), and it pleased market-individualists by reasserting the importance of freedom of contract. Consumer-welfarists, however, remained unperturbed. On occasion, they persisted with the discredited first approach (see, *e.g.* Lord Denning's notorious judgment in *Harbutt's 'Plasticine' Ltd v Wayne Tank and Pump Co Ltd*, 1970). More importantly, however, although the second approach paid lip service to contractual intention and freedom of contract, in practice it was easy enough for consumer-welfarists to defeat exemptions by the construction method. This intriguing chapter came to an end with the enactment of the Unfair Contract Terms Act 1977 (UCTA).

The salient features of UCTA are as follows. First, it provides a dual scheme of control over exclusion clauses. Some types of clause are, in effect, declared to be void (*e.g.* s.2(1) provides that a person cannot contract out of liability for death or personal injury resulting from negligence). Other types of clause are declared to be valid provided that they satisfy the test of reasonableness (*e.g.* s.2(2) provides that a party can contract out of liability for any other kind of loss or damage resulting from negligence, for example damage to property or economic loss, subject to the requirement of reasonableness). Secondly, the Act is particularly protective of any party who "deals as consumer" (this being, roughly speaking, someone who while himself not making the contract in the course of a business enters into a contract with someone who is contracting in the course of a business—s.12). This special concern for "consumers" manifests itself in specific provisions which give such parties the benefit of the more stringent level of control. For example, s.6(2)(a) provides that, as against a party who deals as consumer, sellers cannot contract out of their implied statutory obligations relating *inter alia* to the quality and fitness of goods. However, where the purchaser is not dealing as consumer, the parallel provisions of s.6(3) permit sellers to contract out of the equivalent obligations to the extent that the exclusion satisfies the requirement of reasonableness. Consumers also enjoy special attention in the sweeping provisions of s.3 which extend the reasonableness test to any exclusion applied against a party who deals as consumer, or where the exclusion appears in a contractor's "written standard terms of business" (see s.3(1)). In many ways, this catch-all provision is the heart of the Act. Thirdly, the reasonableness requirement gives the courts a very open-ended discretion. The relevant question under s.11(1) is whether the exclusion was "a fair and reasonable one to be included having regard to the circumstances which were, or ought reasonably to have been known to or in the contemplation of the parties when the contract was made". Schedule 2 of the Act offers some "guidelines" for the application of the test of reasonableness where the question arises under s.6 (sale of goods and hire-purchase) or s.7 (other types of contract in which goods pass, *e.g.* contracts for work and materials), but generally the courts have been left to apply the test as they see fit. The upshot of UCTA, therefore, is to license judges to police contracts for their unreasonableness in precisely the way that the consumer-welfarists wanted.

Although UCTA puts judicial intervention in contracts on a legitimate statutory basis, the tensions in the law have not been resolved. Whilst the judges pretty uniformly understand their role under UCTA as guardians of the consumer interest (see, *e.g.* *Smith v Eric S. Bush* (1989)), their future role with respect to *commercial* contracts is altogether more problematic. On the one hand, the reasonableness discretion under UCTA threatens to sweep away a large number of exclusions. On the other hand, the courts have a strong market-individualist tradition of respect for standard form commercial arrangements, exclusions included (quite rightly, for in many contexts such standard terms fulfil useful functions such as eliminating double insurance).

The cases tend to display two philosophies of reasonableness, one of a non-interventionist type (emphasising parity of bargaining strength, implied consent, and the insurance infrastructure in the commercial sector), the other of an interventionist type (emphasising fault and alleviation of loss) (see Adams and Brownsword, 1988a). In *Photo Production Ltd v Securicor Transport Ltd* (1978, CA; 1980, HL), a case not directly on UCTA but widely regarded as authoritative on its application, the House of Lords tried to maintain continuity with *Suisse Atlantique* by accentuating the non-interventionist approach in the commercial context.

In *Photo Production*, Securicor were under contract to provide a night patrol service at Photo Production's factory. One of Securicor's patrolmen, while making his patrol, deliberately started a fire at the factory, but the fire got out of control and a large part of the premises was burnt down. The agreed loss to Photo Production was £615,000, and the question was whether Securicor could take shelter behind exemption clauses in the contract. The trial judge ruled that Securicor could take advantage of their exemptions; the Court of Appeal reversed this ruling; but the House of Lords unanimously restored the trial judge's ruling in favour of Securicor. Predictably, Lord Wilberforce, delivering the leading speech, reiterated a non-interventionist line:

> "After this Act [*i.e.* UCTA], in commercial matters generally, when the parties are not of unequal bargaining power, and when risks are normally borne by insurance, not only is the case for judicial intervention undemonstrated, but there is everything to be said, and this seems to have been

Parliament's intention, for leaving the parties free to apportion the risks as they think fit and for respecting their decisions." (*ibid.* at p.843)

Here we have the classic market-individualist doctrines of freedom of contract and sanctity of contract applied to commercial exemption clauses. Commercial contractors must be left free to apportion risks as they think fit (not as the courts think fit), and, having apportioned the risks as they see fit, commercial men must expect to have the bargain enforced in those terms (not in the terms that the court now judges to be reasonable).

Such textbook market-individualist thinking can be represented in terms of reasonableness as follows. First, it is perfectly reasonable to hold parties to their agreements where both sides understand well enough what they are doing, and where there is no element of involuntary agreement. Secondly, where exemptions relate to insurance risks, such as the fire risk in *Photo Production*, it is reasonable to allow the parties to cover that sort of risk as they deem most convenient. Thus, in *Photo Production*, the House clearly thought that convenience favoured the factory owners taking the fire risk, and presumably this enabled Securicor to provide the patrol service more cheaply than would otherwise have been the case (first-party insurance is generally cheaper than insurance against uncertain liabilities to third parties—but on the insurance relevant to this particular case see the passage quoted from Lord Denning's judgment below). Thirdly, it is reasonable for commercial people to expect to be able to rely on their agreements, for this enables them to know where they stand when risks materialise.

In the more recent case of *Watford Electronics Limited v Sanderson CFL Limited* (2001), the Court of Appeal echoed this market-individualist conception of reasonableness. According to Chadwick L.J.:

"Where experienced businessmen representing substantial companies of equal bargaining power negotiate an agreement, they may be taken to have had regard to the matters known to them. They should, in my view, be taken to be the best judge of the commercial fairness of the agreement which they have made; including the fairness of each of the terms in that agreement. They should be taken to be the best judge on the question whether the terms of the agreement are reasonable. The court should not assume that either is likely to commit his company to an agreement which he thinks is unfair, or which he thinks includes unreasonable terms. Unless satisfied that one party has, in effect, taken unfair advantage of the other—or that a term is so unreasonable that it cannot properly have been understood or considered—the court should not interfere." (para. 55)

In short, if it is reasonable to assume that business contractors effectively self-regulate in their dealings with one another, it is unreasonable for the court to intervene. But, of course, there are two sides to this coin—and, in *Britvic Soft Drinks Ltd v Messer UK Ltd* (2002), the Court of Appeal thought that a very different commercial and contractual background militated against the assumption made in *Watford Electronics*. Unlike *Watford Electronics*, where financial loss was caused by software that failed, in *Messer* the stakes were potentially rather higher, traces of benzene having found their way into carbon dioxide that was supplied for the production of fizzy drinks. This was not at all the kind of risk that the drinks producers would expect; it was certainly not a risk to which consumers should be exposed; and any attempt to exclude or limit liability in relation to such a health-threatening and uncontemplated risk was unreasonable. Nevertheless, after *Photo Production*, there is clearly a significant market-individualist disinclination to become involved in reviewing the reasonableness of routine commercial dealing and the way that business contractors apportion run of the mill risks.

For the rival philosophy, however, we need only turn to Lord Denning's judgment in the Court of Appeal in *Photo Production*:

"Whilst the judge was, I think, right to apply the test of reasonableness, I do not agree with his application of it. I would point out that, whilst the owner of the premises insured against fire (save for £25,000), Securicor insured against liability for acts of their servants (save for £10,000). So to my mind the insurance factor cancels out: and we are left with the question as between the two parties. Is it fair or reasonable to allow Securicor to rely on this exemption or limitation clause when it was their own patrolman who deliberately burned down the factory? I do not think it is fair and reasonable." (*per* Lord Denning M.R. at p.154)

No doubt this will strike many readers as, at least, an equally plausible view. After all, what sort of contractual agreement was it that allowed Securicor to escape liability when their patrolman, far from securing the building, burned the factory to the ground? It surely cannot be reasonable to allow Securicor, or any other commercial contractor, to get away with such serious *prima facie* breaches of contract.

The tensions apparent in *Photo Production* surfaced again in *George Mitchell (Chesterhall) Ltd v Finney Lock Seeds Ltd* (1983). Here, the plaintiffs, who were farmers, ordered Dutch winter white cabbage seeds from seed merchants. The parties had dealt with one another over a period of years, and the contract was on the suppliers' standard terms, which included a clause purporting to limit liability for defective seeds to the price of the seeds (some £201). The question was whether the seed suppliers could rely on this clause in response to a claim for some £61,000 made by the farmers, the seeds supplied having been commercially useless. At all levels up to the House of Lords it was held that the suppliers could not shelter behind their limitation clause.

The agreement in *George Mitchell* was regulated by s.55 of the Sale of Goods Act 1979, which is substantially similar to the equivalent UCTA provisions, except that whereas UCTA ties the test of reasonableness to the circumstances as reasonably foreseen by the parties at the time of the contract, s.55(5) enjoins the court to determine whether reliance on the term would be reasonable having regard "to all circumstances of the case". This means that, under s.55, post-formation circumstances (*e.g.* surrounding the breach and post-breach) are relevant. Now, in *George Mitchell*, given the Denning Court of Appeal's track record, it is not surprising that they found against the suppliers. But why did the House of Lords, especially in the light of *Photo Production*, disallow the suppliers' defence? Apparently the key factor was that the suppliers had effectively "estopped" themselves from pleading the reasonableness of the limitation clause because they had already, in accordance with their standard practice, offered more than £201 (the ceiling set by the clause) in an attempt to settle the farmers' claim. Quite apart from any reservations that one might have about this particular reason, it would, strictly speaking, be invalid under UCTA because it involves judging the reasonableness of the provision in the light of post-formation conduct. If we ignore this reason, however, the explanation for the House's intervention remains to be identified.

One possibility is that the Law Lords in *George Mitchell* were more attracted by the interventionist philosophy of reasonableness than were their colleagues in *Photo Production*. Certainly, intervention was strongly encouraged by the unreasonableness of the suppliers' behaviour (in supplying not only defective seeds, but also seeds of the wrong type) and by the scale of the farmers' loss. Yet it is hard to believe that this was the landmark decision, when the House finally cut itself free from non-interventionism. The better explanation is that the standard non-interventionist considerations were not altogether compelling. And, indeed, this was so, for there was evidence that the suppliers could insure against the risk without materially increasing the price of the seeds. *George Mitchell*, therefore, was probably a case where all but the most hard-nosed non-interventionists would favour intervention.

Two other aspects of *George Mitchell* merit brief mention. First, the House made it clear that appeal courts will not interfere with a trial judge's ruling under the UCTA discretions unless he has asked the wrong legal question or answered the right legal question in a wholly unreasonable way. This gives us another slant on *Photo Production* and *George Mitchell*, for in both cases the House upheld the trial judge's ruling (although *c.f. Watford Electronics* above at p.145). Indeed, one of the striking aspects of *Photo Production* is the perfunctory way in which the House allowed the exemptions. This was consistent not only with the non-interventionist philosophy of reasonableness (market-individualist thinking in disguise), but equally with appeal court restraint with regard to trial court rulings.

Secondly, the House in *George Mitchell* evinced a continuing concern to purify doctrine with regard to exclusion clauses (*cf. Photo Production* where the House overruled the heretical doctrine of the Court of Appeal in *Harbutt's 'Plasticine'*, and where Lord Diplock devoted his judgment to restoring the traditional principle that express contractual provisions continue to regulate the parties' remedies notwithstanding a serious breach). Accordingly, in *George Mitchell*, Lord Bridge was quick to criticise the trial judge and Oliver L.J. below, whose judgments were thought to "come dangerously near to re-introducing by the back door the doctrine of 'fundamental breach' which this House in [*Photo Production*] had so forcibly evicted by the front" (at p.813). However, the purge goes beyond the substantive doctrine of fundamental breach: the mood of the House is to give protective clauses (particularly limitation, rather than outright exclusion, clauses) a natural, plain interpretation. Thus, while the House in *George Mitchell* could no doubt have defeated the suppliers' clause as a matter of construction, it chose rather to handle it directly under the reasonableness test.

If, in the context of commercial contracts, the tension between a non-interventionist (market-individualist) and an interventionist (consumer-welfarist) approach is evident in relation to the application of the UCTA reasonableness requirement, it is apparent, too, in relation to the prior question of the scope of UCTA (*i.e.* the question of the kinds of contractual provisions to which UCTA applies). This particular manifestation of the tension is neatly captured by a pair of Court of Appeal cases, *Phillips Products v Hyland* (1987) and *Thompson v T. Lohan (Plant Hire) Ltd* (1987). The facts of these two cases were strikingly similar. Both cases concerned contracts for the hire of plant (namely JCB excavators, the drivers of which in both cases were supplied by the plant owners). Both contracts were subject to the Contractors' Plant Association (CPA) model conditions for plant hire, cl. 8 of which provided that the hirer was to be responsible for claims arising from the negligent operation of the plant by the drivers. In *Phillips*, the driver's negligent operation of the JCB resulted in damage to the hirer's buildings; in *Thompson* the driver's negligence led to the death of Mr Thompson. In both cases, it fell to be decided whether the owners of the JCB could rely on cl. 8 to pass on to the hirers the risk of negligence by the driver. If the owners were able to do this, it would mean in *Phillips* that the hirer (actually, the hirer's insurers) would have to repair his buildings at his (his insurer's) own expense; while, in *Thompson*, it would mean that the owner would be able to indemnify himself at the hirer's expense against the cost of compensating Mr Thompson's widow. In both cases, the hirers objected to this on the grounds that cl. 8 fell within the ambit of s.2 of UCTA.

Section 2 of UCTA applies to terms which purport to "exclude or restrict" liability for negligence. According to s.2(1), where negligence leads to death or personal injury (*e.g.* the death of Mr Thompson), a clause which so excludes or restricts liability for negligence is, in effect, void; according to s.2(2), where negligence leads to some other kind of loss or damage (*e.g.* damage to buildings as in *Phillips*), a clause which so excludes or restricts liability for negligence is subject to the reasonableness test. A critical question, therefore, in both *Phillips* and *Thompson* was whether cl. 8 of the CPA conditions was to be interpreted as a clause which purports to "exclude or restrict" liability for negligence within the meaning of s.2 of UCTA.

In *Phillips*, the Court of Appeal saw little merit in the argument that cl. 8 was not to be viewed as an exclusion of the owner's liability, but rather as a clause which allocated responsibility for the driver's negligence as between owner and hirer. Thus, in a robust judgment, Slade L.J. said:

> "There is no mystique about 'exclusion' or 'restriction' clauses. To decide whether a person 'excludes' liability by reference to a contract term, you look at the effect of the term. You look at its substance. The effect here is beyond doubt. [The owner] does most certainly purport to exclude its liability for negligence by reference to Condition 8." (p.626)

By contrast, in *Thompson*, the court thought that it was perfectly appropriate to characterise cl. 8 as a term which allocated, rather than excluded, liability for negligence. Putting this in the context of the legislative policy underlying UCTA, Fox L.J. said:

> "In my opinion, s.2(1) is concerned with protecting the victim of negligence, and of course those who claim under him. It is not concerned with arrangements made by the wrong-doer with other persons as to the sharing or bearing of the burden of compensating the victim. In such a case it seems to me that there is no exclusion or restriction of liability at all. The liability has been established . . . The circumstances that the defendants have between themselves chosen to bear the liability in a particular way does not affect that liability; it does not exclude it, and it does not restrict it." (pp.638–9)

The upshot of this, therefore, was that, in *Phillips*, cl. 8 was held to fall within the range of s.2(2) of UCTA and was, as such, subject to the reasonableness test (which the Court then proceeded to find was not satisfied on the facts), while in *Thompson* the same clause was held to be outside the scope of s.2(1)—it simply was not to be characterised as a clause which purported to exclude or restrict liability.

The official reconciliation of *Phillips* and *Thompson* (see Adams and Brownsword, 1988b) runs as follows. The Court of Appeal in both cases was concerned that there should be judicial control of contractual provisions that purport to bar or limit relief for the victims of negligence. In *Phillips*, the victim was the hirer; in *Thompson* the victim was a third-party. To protect the victim in *Phillips*, it was necessary to apply UCTA to cl. 8; but, to protect the victim in *Thompson*, this was not necessary because the owner had already compensated Mr Thompson's widow (the victim). This implies a fairly discriminating consumer-welfarist approach in both cases. It is at least as plausible, however, that the non-interventionist approach in *Thompson* was driven by market-individualist thinking. For, even if UCTA did not need to be applied to protect the victim in *Thompson*, consumer-welfarists might still think it arguable that cl. 8 was unreasonable in shifting the risk to the innocent hirer—and, thus, should be brought within the regulatory range of UCTA. The fact that the court did not think it was part of its function to interfere with the private risk-allocating arrangements of the owner and the hirer smacks of market-individualism rather than consumer-welfarism.

As the judges show themselves more willing to interfere with contracts on the grounds of unreasonableness, litigants will put before the courts an increasing variety of contractual provisions which allegedly fall within the scope of UCTA. Indeed, there are clear signs that this is already beginning to happen (see, *e.g. Stewart Gill Ltd v Horatio Myer and Co Ltd* (1992); and Peel (1993)), and we can be sure that as this tendency increases the tensions between market-individualism and consumer-welfarism will become all the more apparent at all levels. The modern law, therefore, sees the judges crewing the "SS *Reasonableness*" with, on the one hand, the flotsam and jetsam of fundamental breach swilling about in its wash, but, on the other hand, with some troubled waters ahead—waters to which, it should be remembered, the Unfair Terms in Consumer Contracts Regulations have now been added (see pp.113–116).

3. OVERVIEW

Common mistake, frustration, and exemption clauses are all prime areas for the conflict between the market-individualist and consumer-welfarist approaches. The state of the game in English law is that honours are divided with respect to common mistake (market-individualists securing *Bell* and *Great Peace*, consumer-welfarists *Solle* and the equitable approach); frustration has been captured by market-individualists (*Davis*); and UCTA gives consumer-welfarists the edge with regard to exemption clauses. However, as *Photo Production*, *Watford Electronics*, and *Thompson* indicate, market-individualists are by no means beaten in respect of exemptions, for the reasonableness requirement may be colonised by a market-individualist inspired non-interventionist philosophy.

The formalist involvement in these disputes differs from one area to another. Common mistake, although in the common law approach a formalist doctrine *par excellence*, presents difficulties to formalists, because the rule-book is equivocal; frustration is a fortress which, with the assistance of market-individualists, is reasonably easy to defend; and the law on exemption clauses, although resolved in favour of consumer-welfarists, is shrouded in unclear discretions. The best that formalists can do is to hang on to the rule-book where it is clear, and purge the law of any heretical accretions.

7

REMEDIES

The important thing about an agreement being enforceable at law is that the injured party will be able to take advantage of the armoury of weapons provided by the law to secure redress for him. In this chapter, we consider the principal remedies which the law provides (remember, of course, that litigation may be avoided by employing various legitimate self-help remedies, see Chapter 1).

1. REPRESENTATIONS

Suppose that Jack represented to the butcher, prior to their agreement, that the brown cow was fit and healthy in all respects. If this proved to be the case, the butcher would have no complaint. However, if the cow proved to be other than fit and healthy, what remedy might the butcher have against Jack? In the first instance, the butcher's remedy would depend upon whether Jack's representation was contractual or non-contractual. If Jack's representation was contractual (*i.e.* if Jack had given a contractual undertaking as to the fitness and health of the brown cow), then Jack would be in breach of contract and the butcher would have available to him the remedies which arise on breach (see Section 2 of this chapter). However, if Jack's representation was non-contractual, then the butcher's remedy would basically hinge on establishing that Jack's statement was a misrepresentation. If Jack's statement was a misrepresentation, the butcher might be able to "unscramble" the contract (*i.e.* exercise the remedy of rescission) and, in some circumstances, he might also be able to recover damages. In this section, we consider first the drawing of the line between contractual and non-contractual representations, and then the remedies available for misrepresentation.

(i) Non-contractual or contractual representation?

Until the enactment of the Misrepresentation Act 1967, it was very much easier for a representee to recover damages for a contractual rather than a non-contractual representation. Although the distinction is no longer quite so important, the law concerning the classification of representations as contractual or non-contractual remains notoriously difficult.

Let us illustrate this by comparing *Hopkins v Tanqueray* (1854) and *Couchman v Hill* (1947). In *Hopkins*, the plaintiff purchased the defendant's horse at an auction at Tattersalls. On the previous day, the defendant, having found the plaintiff examining the horse's legs, had said: "You need not examine his legs: you have nothing to look for. I assure you he is perfectly sound in every respect." In *Couchman*, the defendant's heifer was put up for auction, described in the sale catalogue as a "red and white stirk, heifer, unserved." Before the bidding, when the heifer was in the ring, the plaintiff confirmed with both the defendant and the auctioneer that the heifer was indeed unserved. The plaintiff bought the heifer which, shortly afterwards, had a miscarriage and died as a result of carrying a calf at too young an age. Despite the similarities between these two cases, the seller's representation in *Hopkins* was held to be non-contractual whereas, in *Couchman*, the Court of Appeal held that the seller's representation was contractual (thus, entitling the plaintiff to recover damages for breach of contract).

The traditional view is that the classification of representations turns on an objective test of intention assisted by certain guidelines (*e.g.* concerning the proximity of the representation to the moment of contract, the importance attached to the representation by the representee, the degree of special knowledge held by the representor, and so on). However, these criteria do not provide us with much assistance in trying to reconcile *Hopkins* and *Couchman*. In order to make much sense of the thing, we have to allow for the possibility of a realist judge manipulating the criteria to produce a particular desired result. In this light, we may contrast *Oscar Chess Ltd v Williams* (1957) and *Bentley (Dick) Productions Ltd v Harold Smith (Motors) Ltd* (1965).

The defendant in *Oscar Chess* traded a Morris motor car against a new Hillman car which he acquired on hire-purchase through the plaintiff dealers. The defendant, relying in good faith upon the registration book, described the Morris as a 1948 model, whereupon the plaintiffs made him a part-exchange allowance of £290. Eight months later, the plaintiffs discovered that the Morris was in fact a 1939 model, for which the appropriate trade-in value was only £175. Therefore, they sought to recover £115 damages, pleading that it was a contractual representation that the car was a 1948 model. A number of elements pointed strongly to the defendant's representation being contractual. It was proximate to the sale, a matter of importance, and to some extent something which the dealers might have supposed to be within the defendant's special knowledge (though, as we have said, he in fact supposed it to be a 1948 model). Nevertheless, the majority of the Court of Appeal ruled in favour of the defendant, saying that he could not be taken to have warranted the year of manufacture. The most he could have said was that if the registration book was accurate, then the Morris was a 1948 model. It will be appreciated that the line taken by the Court of Appeal has some affinity to the "modified subjectivism" which we met with in relation to mistake (see pp.48–49 and 64).

With this, we can contrast *Dick Bentley*. Here, the plaintiff purchased a Bentley car from the defendant dealer, who represented that the car had done only twenty thousand miles since it had been fitted with a replacement engine and gearbox. The car proved unsatisfactory and the plaintiff sued on the representation for breach of contract. The County Court judge's ruling, that the statement as to the mileage was an untrue (albeit an honest) representation and a breach of contract, was unanimously upheld by the Court of Appeal.

The court in *Dick Bentley* distinguished Oscar Chess by employing the following line of argument:

(i) there is a rebuttable presumption that serious representations by sellers, inducing representees to enter into contracts of sale, are contractual representations;

(ii) the representor can rebut this presumption "if he can show that it really was an innocent misrepresentation, in that he was in fact innocent of fault in making it, and that it would not be reasonable in the circumstances for him to be bound by it" (*per* Lord Denning M.R. in *Dick Bentley* at p.67);

(iii) in *Oscar Chess*, the seller was innocent of fault and the presumption was, therefore, rebutted; but

(iv) in *Dick Bentley* the seller was in a position to find out the history of the car, and he ought to have known better than to make the representation without any reasonable foundation. So here the presumption was not rebutted.

This, however, is unconvincing. Why, in *Oscar Chess*, was it reasonable to rely on a log-book for the year of manufacture of a car, yet unreasonable in *Dick Bentley* to rely on the odometer for the mileage? Do we seriously believe that the decisions would have been different if the representation in *Oscar Chess* had been as to mileage, and in *Dick Bentley* as to year of manufacture?

The policy question in *Oscar Chess* was the familiar one of which of two innocent parties should bear the loss occasioned by the fraud of a third party (*i.e.* the party responsible for the fraudulent alteration of the log-book). The natural market-individualist response would be to indemnify the innocent purchaser (the garage) against the representations of the innocent seller. For consumer-welfarists, it would be a matter of putting the loss on the better loss-bearer. The majority decision in *Oscar Chess* reflects a victory for consumer-welfarists who shifted the risk to the dealer-purchaser (*cf.* the same pattern in *Ingram v Little*—see p.66). In *Dick Bentley*, the policy considerations were more straightforward. By 1965, it was received wisdom that we live in a consumer society, and that consumers need protection against dealers. It follows that consumer representees must have a reasonable come-back against dealer representors. The key to understanding the case, therefore, does not lie in the rule-book, nor in the difference between log-books and odometers, but, it can be argued, in the realist consideration, operating within a consumer-welfarist paradigm, that one representor was a dealer (in *Dick Bentley*), and the other a consumer (in *Oscar Chess*).

(ii) Misrepresentations

If a representation is non-contractual, the representee's principal line of recourse is to argue that the representation is an actionable misrepresentation. As we have said, prior to the Misrepresentation Act 1967, this was a somewhat unsatisfactory state of affairs in that misrepresentees who sought damages to cover their financial losses had to prove fraud on the part of the misrepresentor, and this often presented serious difficulties. One way of aiding such misrepresentees was to treat the representation as a collateral warranty (*i.e.* as part of a collateral contract). Basically, this meant that the representor, in return for the representee entering into the main contract (*e.g.* for the sale of the horse or the cow or whatever), warranted the truth of the representation, or at least warranted that he had good grounds for believing the representation to be reliable. Conveniently, if the representation then proved false, the representee had an action in damages for breach of the collateral contract (see Lord Denning M.R.'s candid observations in *Esso Petroleum Co Ltd. v Mardon*, 1976). Although there may be contexts (*e.g.* where there are privity problems) in which the implication of collateral contracts (with concomitant questions about whether the test is one of necessity or reasonableness, as with implied terms, see pp.100–103) remains important, the enactment of a broader statutory basis for damages probably signals less use being made of the collateral device in the context of misrepresentation.

The essential rules relating to misrepresentation are as follows: a representation is a misrepresentation if: (i) it is a statement of fact, which (ii) is untrue, and which (iii) is relied upon by the misrepresentee, specifically by entering into a contract with the misrepresentor. The misrepresentor's state of mind is not critical for the purpose of allowing the misrepresentee to have rescission of the agreement. Rescission effectively means that the parties are restored to the position they were in before the contract was made. It is an equitable remedy, though, and it is therefore subject to a number of bars. In practice, this means that the misrepresentee will lose the opportunity to secure rescission unless he acts swiftly, unless he is able to restore any benefit obtained under the contract (*e.g.* return goods), if third-party rights intervene, or if he affirms the contract. This makes rescission a fragile remedy. In *Oscar Chess*, for example, the dealers unquestionably could have sought rescission of the agreement in the light of the defendant's innocent misrepresentation as to the year of the Morris; but they did not act sufficiently promptly. The misrepresentor's state of mind is of decisive importance, however, for the purpose of recovering damages for misrepresentation. Although the Misrepresentation Act 1967 is drafted in an extraordinarily convoluted way, it is now generally thought that there are three categories of misrepresentation, namely, fraudulent (where the representor knows that the representation is false, or is reckless as to the truth or falsity of the representation—see *Derry v Peek*, 1889); negligent (where the representor believes that the representation is true, but has no reasonable grounds for this belief); and innocent (where the representor believes that the representation is true, and has reasonable grounds for this belief). The Act does nothing to change the position with respect to fraudulent misrepresentation, where the law continues to allow the misrepresentee (if he can prove fraud) to recover damages. But s.2(1) of the Act permits misrepresentees to claim damages for "negligent" misrepresentations. However, the Act reverses the burden of proof which, in cases of negligent statement, normally lies on the party who has relied on the statement (see *Hedley Byrne v Heller*, 1964). Instead, s.2(1) requires the misrepresentor to prove "that he had reasonable grounds to believe and did believe up to the time the contract was made that the facts represented were true". Accordingly, the obvious strategy for the plaintiff misrepresentee is to claim damages under s.2(1), and leave it to the misrepresentor to convince the court that the belief in the truth of the representation was based on reasonable grounds (see *Royscot Trust v Rogerson*, 1991). To complete this thumbnail sketch, we need only to note that under s.2(2) of the Act, the courts have the discretion to award the misrepresentee damages in lieu of rescission where it would be equitable to do so, although not in a case of fraud. Section 2(2) must not be thought of as the misrepresentee's charter for damages. Far from it: s.2(2) puts another obstacle in the way of rescission for the victims of innocent and negligent misrepresentations.

In this section, we will focus on two aspects of misrepresentation. First, we will look at the precondition for any action based on misrepresentation, namely that the representation is a (false) statement of fact. This is important, because the requirement of a *statement* of fact puts mere silence outside the area of misrepresentation, at least ordinarily, whilst the requirement of a statement of *fact* excludes a mere "puff" and opinion. Secondly, we will consider the idea of reasonable grounds for one's belief, which is at the heart of the Misrepresentation Act's scheme for damages.

(a) Silence is golden

Roald Dahl's version of "Jack and the Beanstalk" starts:

> "Jack's mother said, 'We're stony broke!
> Go out and find some wealthy bloke
> Who'll buy our cow. Just say she's sound
> And worth at least a hundred pound.
> But don't you dare to let him know.
> That she's as old as billy-o.' "

This was good advice because English law generally is based on the market-individualist principle that there is no duty of disclosure (market-individualists suppose that contractors should be allowed to profit from their superior knowledge). This does not, of course, protect silence with respect to representations which, whilst true originally, are falsified prior to the representee's entry into the contract (see, *e.g. With v O'Flanagan*, 1936; *Spice Girls Ltd v Aprilia World Service BV*, 2000); nor does it protect partial, suggestively misleading, representations (see *e.g. Curtis v Chemical Cleaning and Dyeing Co*, 1951). However, it does mean that there is no general duty of disclosure preventing one party from keeping silent and thereby taking advantage of another's ignorance. Thus, Jack has no duty to disclose that the cow is "as old as billy-o" (misrepresentation remedies being predicated upon a false statement); and this holds even if Jack suspects that the butcher mistakenly thinks that the cow is not old (*cf.* our discussion of unilateral collateral mistakes in Chapter 4).

Now, the law could start from a different principle. It could make full and frank disclosure the rule rather than the exception. Thus, in the American case of *Obde v Schlemeyer* (1960) it was held that justice, equity, and fair dealing placed the defendant house vendors under a duty to disclose to the plaintiff prospective purchasers that the house was infested with termites. Although consumer-welfarists would endorse such an approach, market-individualists would have to treat *Obde* with great caution. For market-individualists, the absence of a general duty to disclose is an article of faith and so the most that could be conceded would be that the decision in *Obde* was defensible as an exception to the general rule. This might rest on some special features of the case, *e.g.* the Schlemeyers had employed pest control specialists so that the termite infestation was not readily observable on reasonable inspection; or, the non-disclosure went beyond simple economic loss and gain, for it involved a dangerous commodity changing hands without the transferee realising the true nature of his acquisition.

Although, generally speaking, English law treats silence as no misrepresentation, there are certain exceptional cases where disclosure is required. In addition to various direct statutory duties, there are indirect incentives in the Sale of Goods Act 1979 (and cognate legislation), aimed at encouraging dealer-sellers to disclose defects in goods. Under the common law, too, there may exceptionally be a duty to disclose, as where a special relationship of trust and confidence exists between the parties (*cf.* the undue influence cases discussed in Chapter 5, and see, *e.g. Tate v Williamson*, 1866), or because the contract belongs to the class of contracts *uberrimae fidei*, of which the prime example is the insurance contract. In the case of insurance contracts, the disclosure principle has been given an ironic twist. First, the courts (and statute) have pitched the duty to disclose in terms of the facts which a prudent insurer would treat as material, and secondly, they have allowed insurance companies to make full disclosure the basis of the contract, so that the insurers can avoid liability where there has been a failure in respect of disclosure. The net effect of this is that a claim may be avoided on the grounds of non-disclosure, even where the insured has made a frank and honest disclosure. Hence, where non-disclosure is the order of the day, profit can be taken through indecent silence; and where disclosure is the order of the day, profit can be taken through indecent insistence upon "full disclosure". Such, one might think, is the unacceptable face of market-individualism.

The silence principle emphasises the importance of there being a statement. It is equally important, though, that the statement be one of fact. This requirement allows the representor to argue that the statement was a "mere puff", or that it was a mere statement of opinion. Mere puffs are sales talk, commendatory representations which are obviously not intended to be taken seriously. Manufacturers might be able to get away with representing that "A Mars a day helps you work, rest and play", but *Carlill* gives some indication of where the line between such statements and actionable representations will be drawn. Equally, car dealers might be able to get away with describing a vehicle as "The car of the week"; but in *Andrews v Hopkinson* (1957), a dealer's representation that a car was "a good little bus", upon which he would stake his life, was held to be the basis of a collateral contract. In a world of increasing consumer consciousness, where the persuasive force of advertising techniques is recognised, it must be expected that the courts (backed up by protective legislation such as the Trade Descriptions Act 1968) will give sales talk less and less licence.

Statements of opinion, too, are to be distinguished from statements of fact. On the face of it, this looks like an opportunity for representors to immunise themselves against potential liability simply by couching their statements in the form of an opinion. The courts, however, can block this move, either by construing the opinion as entailing an implied statement of fact (that the representor has reasonable grounds for his opinion), or by construing the opinion as being accompanied by an implied warranty (that reasonable care has been taken in formulating the opinion). Consider, for example, *Esso Petroleum Co Ltd v Mardon* (1976). Here, Mardon took a tenancy of one of Esso's petrol stations, having been told by Esso's representative that the estimated throughput of petrol for the site was 200,000 gallons in the third year of operation. Despite Mardon's best efforts the throughput was far less than the estimate, and he claimed damages pleading *inter alia* that the representative's estimate amounted to a warranty. In their defence, Esso took the point that the forecast of petrol throughput was merely a statement of opinion, neither a statement of fact nor a promise. To this, the Court of Appeal retorted that forecasters with Esso's special knowledge could not escape liability so easily—they must at least have warranted that the forecast was made with reasonable care.

Mardon, like *Oscar Chess* and *Dick Bentley*, is guided by consumer-welfarist considerations of reasonableness. It is not a case of allocating loss between two innocent parties (as in *Oscar Chess*), nor of protecting a consumer (as in *Dick Bentley*). Rather, it is a case of holding those with special informational advantage to their representations. To say, as it is commonly said, that these cases hinge on special knowledge or expertise is on the right track; but it must not be allowed to conceal the fact that subtly different principles of reasonableness are in play.

(b) Reasonable grounds and reasonable beliefs

As we have seen, the centrepiece of the Misrepresentation Act 1967, and thus of the present law on non-contractual representations, is s.2(1); and the centrepiece of this section is the proviso that the non-fraudulent misrepresentor will be liable in damages "unless he proves that he had reasonable ground to believe ... that the facts represented were true". In one of the leading cases on the Act, *Howard Marine and Dredging Co Ltd v A. Ogden & Sons (Excavations) Ltd* (1978), the defendants hired two German-built barges from the plaintiffs. Lloyd's Register incorrectly showed the deadweight capacity of the barges as 1800 tonnes; in fact, the capacity of the barges was some 1055 tonnes, and this was shown in the German shipping documents which the plaintiffs held in their London office. During the negotiations for the hire of the barges, the plaintiffs represented that the capacity of the barges was some 1600 tonnes. This was an honest statement made from memory, and recalling the Lloyd's figure. When the defendants discovered the true capacity of the barges, they responded to the plaintiffs' claim for hire by counterclaiming on the representation. By a majority, the Court of Appeal (Bridge L.J. and Shaw L.J., with Lord Denning M.R. dissenting) upheld the defendants' counterclaim under s.2(1) of the Act.

For the majority, the plaintiffs failed to show reasonable grounds for their belief, because they were aware of the figures in both the shipping documents and in Lloyd's Register, and they had no "objectively reasonable ground to disregard the figure in the ship's documents and to prefer the Lloyd's Register figure" (*per* Bridge L.J. at p.598). Lord Denning M.R., however, followed the trial judge's view that, although the representor had seen the German shipping documents, this (correct) figure had not registered in his mind. What had registered was the (incorrect) Lloyd's figure, "which was regarded in shipping circles as the Bible . . . [and which] afforded reasonable ground . . . to believe that the barges could each carry 1600 tonnes pay load . . ." (*per* Lord Denning M.R., at p.593). It is possible to explain this disagreement in formalist terms (*e.g.* by picking out ambiguities in the idea of a reasonable ground to believe), but the recent history of the courts' handling of liability for representations is hardly a purist's dream. The more likely explanation, therefore, is that the majority simply thought it reasonable to award damages to the representee, whereas Lord Denning did not. The thinking underpinning these judgments will be examined shortly.

Although the representors failed to shift the burden under s.2(1) they did have a second line of defence. Clause 1 of the charterparty purported to exclude liability for misrepresentation, by deeming acceptance of the barges as conclusive that the vessels had been examined and found satisfactory. This brought into play s.3 of the Act (now amended by s.8 of UCTA) which provided that such an exclusion would be of no effect except to the extent that a court allowed reliance on it "as being fair and reasonable in the circumstances of the case". On s.3, the court again divided as it had done with respect to s.2(1), the majority ruling that it would not be reasonable for the plaintiffs to rely on their protective clause, Lord Denning disagreeing.

The majority dealt very briefly with this point, saying that they followed the trial judge in holding that it was not fair and reasonable to rely on a clause exempting the plaintiffs from liability for negligent misrepresentation as to carrying capacity. Presumably, this indicates that negligence has a special significance not simply under s.2(1), but also under s.3, at least where the negligent misrepresentation concerns a relatively important matter (as was the case with the carrying capacity of the barges). By contrast, Lord Denning was very much more expansive on the question of reasonableness:

"It seems to me that the clause was itself fair and reasonable. The parties here were commercial concerns and were of equal bargaining power. The clause was not foisted by one on the other in a standard printed form . . . It was a clause common in charterparties of this kind ... It is specially applicable in cases where the contractor has the opportunity of checking the position for himself ...

Even if the clause were somewhat too wide ... this is ... a case where it would be fair and reasonable to allow reliance on it ... Ogdens had had full inspection and examination of the barges ... Yet they seek to say that the barges were not fit for the use for which they intended them ... And in support of this case they have no written representation to go upon. They only have two telephone conversations and one interview—as to which there is an acute conflict of evidence. It is just such conflicts which commercial men seek to avoid by such a clause as this." (*ibid.* at p.594)

The pattern of these competing conceptions of reasonableness is as follows. The majority view emphasises fault: carelessness by the representor is unreasonable conduct and raises a presumption against reliance on an exemption clause and in favour of damages for the representee. Lord Denning's view, however, emphasises the parties' parity of bargaining strength and the commercial reasonableness of the exemption: damages, therefore, are inappropriate. (Readers may wish to compare this with the approach that Lord Denning took in *Photo Production*, see p.146.)

It will be recalled that, in the last chapter, we suggested that two philosophies of reasonableness would emerge, one interventionist, the other non-interventionist. The majority view in *Howard Marine* undoubtedly falls into the interventionist camp. With Lord Denning's view, however, we must be careful. Superficially, it looks like the non-interventionist conception of reasonableness; yet it is consumer-welfarist inspired rather than market-individualist derived. The significance of this is twofold. First, consumer-welfarism appears to be capable of generating both interventionist and non-interventionist conceptions of reasonableness; and, secondly, a non-interventionist philosophy of reasonableness (at least in commercial contracts) can apparently be approached from both market-individualist and consumer-welfarist angles (see further Chapter 8). To sum up, misrepresentation and exemption clauses are now in the same boat, the "SS *Reasonableness*". This facilitates consumer protection, but, as *Howard Marine* indicates, commercial disputes raise fundamental policy questions which are still to be resolved.

2. REMEDIES FOR BREACH OF CONTRACT

Faced with a breach of contract, the innocent party may in every case claim damages (subject, of course, to any exemption clauses), and in some cases the innocent party may withdraw from the contract (or, as it is often put, he may terminate, or rescind the contract, or treat the contract as repudiated). Exceptionally (except in the context of contracts for the sale of land where the remedy is common), the innocent party may be awarded specific performance (although actions by sellers and suppliers for the agreed sum, which are commonplace, amount to much the same thing in practice). We examine, first, the right of withdrawal, and then some aspects of damages.

(i) The right of withdrawal and the concept of a condition

In principle, a contractual term must be either a condition (express or implied) or a warranty (express or implied). The right to withdraw from a contract for breach (a party may expressly reserve the right to withdraw in respect of some non-breach contingency, *e.g.* a purchaser of land who reserves the right to withdraw should an application for planning permission be refused) obtains only if the term breached is a condition.

Judicial treatment of the right of withdrawal for breach is guided by the following four principles:

(i)   The principle of proportionality: it is unfair to the contract-breaker to allow the innocent party to withdraw for a breach with trivial consequences. To permit withdrawal in such circumstances would be disproportionate to the gravity of the breach.

(ii) The bad faith principle: a party should not be permitted to use a trivial breach as an excuse for withdrawal from a contract when the real reason for withdrawal is not the breach itself.

(iii) The certainty principle: the innocent party should be left in no doubt as to the remedies he has in the event of a breach. The point here is that if A is in breach, but B's withdrawal is unjustified, B (the innocent party originally) now finds his over-retaliation treated as a breach.

(iv) The principle of sanctity of contract: a party is not to be lightly relieved from the terms of his bargain.

These principles do not necessarily pull in the same direction. For example, it will be recalled that in *Schuler v Wickman* (p.39) the Law Lords were divided on the question of whether a single (trivial) breach of the visiting obligation (stipulated by the contract to be a condition) justified withdrawal. One interpretation of this division is that the majority applied the principle of proportionality (perhaps, also, the bad faith principle), whereas Lord Wilberforce's dissent was predicated upon the principles of certainty and of sanctity of contract. The competing principles, however, go beyond such a division of opinion in a particular case. They ground two competing general approaches to the question of conditions and withdrawal.

The traditional so-called "classification" approach links the right to withdraw to conditions in a strict sense. The test for such a condition (in the absence of classification by statute, precedent, or agreement) is whether a given term is essential or fundamental, or whether a breach of the term necessarily would strike at the root of the contract. In principle, the classification approach presupposes that particular terms can be identified at the time of formation as conditions or warranties, and that having been so identified the actual consequences of a subsequent breach are irrelevant to the categorisation of such terms. By contrast, the modern approach, which derives from the Court of Appeal's judgments in *Hong Kong Fir Shipping Co Ltd. v Kawasaki Kisen Kaisha Ltd.* (1962), takes the actual consequences of the breach to be a matter of considerable importance. In this case, the question was whether the shipowners' breach of their charterparty obligation to deliver a seaworthy vessel justified the charterers in withdrawing from the contract. According to the court, a term such as the seaworthiness clause could not be classified at the outset as either a condition or a warranty. Some breaches of the seaworthiness clause might have very serious consequences but, equally, some breaches might produce quite trivial consequences. Thus, unless the seaworthiness clause was pre-classified by statute or express stipulation by the parties or the like, the only sensible approach was to treat the term as "innominate" and to classify it in the light of the actual consequences of the breach. Elaborating this consequential approach, the court then declared that a breach of an innominate term would only be treated as a breach of condition (justifying withdrawal) if the actual consequences of the breach were so serious as to deprive the innocent party of substantially the whole benefit of the bargain. This, it will be appreciated, set the threshold for the right to withdraw very high;

and, indeed, applying this approach to the facts of the *Hong Kong Fir Shipping* case, the court ruled that, although the breaches of the seaworthiness clause involved the vessel having to undergo repairs for several months, these consequences did not justify the charterers' withdrawal.

The consequential approach, as in *Hong Kong Fir Shipping*, can be read broadly or narrowly. The Court of Appeal's judgments in the case support a narrow reading whereby the consequential approach is merely a supplementary approach to be employed when the traditional classification approach gives no clear answer to whether a term is to be treated as a condition or a warranty. Moreover, this interpretation of the relationship between the classification and the consequential approaches has been endorsed by the House of Lords in *Bunge Corp. v Tradax SA* (1981). However, a broader reading of the consequential approach is available, in which it displaces rather than supplements the classification approach. And, indeed, there was a period, particularly in the 1970s, when the case-law (see, *e.g. Schuler v Wickman*, and *The Hansa Nord*, 1976, below) encouraged such a view. As we shall explain, the source of these tensions lies in competing contractual ideologies.

We have intimated already that the classification approach is not entirely free of difficulty. Sometimes, the approach can be applied fairly straightforwardly: this might be because of statutory provision (see, *e.g.* the classificatory regime in ss.12–15 of the Sale of Goods Act, 1979), or because of a settled understanding in a particular sector of commerce (possibly supported by precedent), or because the parties have expressly stipulated that a particular term is to be treated as a condition (although *cf. Schuler v Wickman*). However, where the classification approach yields no straightforward answer, its tests are vague enough to permit the courts to classify terms according to the result thought to be fair in the circumstances (see, *e.g. Bettini v Gye*, 1876, and *Poussard v Spiers*, 1876). To introduce the consequential approach interstitially at this point presents no problems to market-individualists (see, *e.g.* Lord Wilberforce's approach in *Reardon Smith Line Ltd. v Hansen-Tangen*, 1976); but, for consumer-welfarists, such a marginal recognition of reasonableness fails to address the major problem with the classification approach.

The nature of this problem is clearly illustrated by the well-known case of *Arcos Ltd. v E.A. Ronaasen and Son* (1933). There, the buyers were held to be entitled to reject a consignment of timber on the grounds that its measurements were fractionally out in relation to the contractual specification. The timber thus failed to correspond to its description and, under s.13 of the Sale of Goods Act, such a breach was a breach of a condition. Now, it is often objected that this decision was unreasonable in that the buyers could have made perfectly good use of the timber for its intended purpose and without incurring any additional expense in so doing. Hence, if the buyers had sought damages for the breach, their claim would have been for next to nothing; yet the House of Lords held that they were entitled to take the draconian step of withdrawing from the contract. Whilst this objection has some force, it misses the critical point. The buyers were not withdrawing for the sake of high principle. Their motivation was purely commercial. The fact of the matter was that prices in the timber market were falling so that, if the buyers could escape from their contract, they could meet their timber requirements more cheaply by buying at prevailing (lower) market prices. We can assume, therefore, that far from being upset at the delivery of the non-conforming timber, the buyers could not believe their luck. The critical question, therefore, is whether economic opportunism of this kind is thought to be a matter for legal regulation.

In *Arcos v Ronaasen* itself, the House of Lords, being perfectly aware of what was going on, saw no problem. As Lord Atkin (adopting again the market-individualist stance evident in his speech in *Bell v Lever Bros.* (pp.130–131)) put it in *Arcos v Ronaasen*:

> "If a condition is not performed the buyer has a right to reject. I do not myself think that there is any difference between business men and lawyers on this matter. No doubt, in business, men often find it unnecessary or inexpedient to insist on their strict legal rights. In a normal market if they get something substantially like the specified goods they may take them with or without grumbling and a claim for an allowance. But in a falling market I find the buyers are often as eager to insist on their legal rights as courts of law are to maintain them." (p.480)

Contrary to Lord Atkin's view, however, the modern courts were not to prove consistently eager to maintain the right to withdraw in cases of this kind. Indeed, whilst there are several theories about the best interpretation of the thinking behind the Court of Appeal's approach in the *Hong Kong Fir Shipping* case, a plausible view must be that the court set such a difficult threshold for withdrawal precisely in order to block opportunistic withdrawals of the kind exercised by the buyers in *Arcos v Ronaasen*.

In counterpoint to *Arcos v Ronaasen*, we have *The Hansa Nord* (1976). There, a Dutch buyer contracted to buy 12,000 tons of U.S. citrus pulp pellets to be used in cattle food; the price was some £100,000. On arrival in Rotterdam, the pellets were found to be damaged by overheating. The buyers, having rejected the pellets for alleged breach of condition, promptly repurchased them from a third party for £30,000 and used them to make cattle food as intended. Although the buyers were held entitled to reject at arbitration and before Mocatta J., the Court of Appeal employed the consequential approach to defeat the buyers' opportunism. The nub of the issue was summarized by Lord Denning M.R.:

> "It often happens that the market price falls between the making of the contract and the time for delivery. In such a situation, it is not fair that a buyer should be allowed to reject a whole consignment of goods just because a small quantity are not up to the contract quality or condition. The proper remedy is a price allowance and not complete rejection." (p.63)

In brief, consumer-welfarists will not stand by and allow bad faith withdrawals of this kind to go unchecked (*cf.* Brownsword, 1992); and, seemingly in line with this approach, s.15A of the Sale of Goods Act 1979 (inserted by s.4 of the Sale and Supply of Goods Act 1994) now provides that, in a *commercial* sales contract (such as in *Arcos* or the *Hansa Nord*), the buyer's right to withdraw for breach of one of the statutory implied terms is lost if "the breach is so slight that it would be unreasonable . . . to reject".

For market-individualists, an unrestricted use of the consequential approach is doubly problematic. First, it threatens to interfere with arrangements freely struck between commercial contractors. Granted, some withdrawal provisions in commercial contracts have gained a certain notoriety (*e.g.* charterparty clauses which entitle the owner of a vessel to withdraw it if the charterer fails to make punctual payment of the hire); but, as Lord Wilberforce emphasised in *Schuler v Wickman*, (and again in *The Laconia*, 1977, which is a punctual payment clause hard case) it is not the function of the courts to suspend such provisions where their application seems unreasonable. Secondly, the consequential approach leaves the innocent party unsure about the remedies available for a particular breach—crucially, how can an innocent party ever be confident that a court will treat the consequences as being serious enough to justify withdrawal?

This uncertainty encourages litigation, gives potential contract-breakers less incentive to take their contractual obligations seriously, and unfairly exposes innocent parties to the risk of counter-claims for wrongful withdrawal (generally, see Megaw L.J. in *The Mihalis Angelos*, 1971; and the comments of Lord Hoffmann in the *Union Eagle* case, quoted above at p.119).

To return to our starting point, for the most part, the relationships between the classification and the consequential approaches, their underlying principles, and the contractual ideologies are fairly clear. The proportionality and bad faith principles are consumer-welfarist, and are currently served by the consequential approach. The certainty principle and the principle of sanctity of contract are market-individualist, and are better served by the classification approach. Although the House, in *Bunge v Tradax*, has called for a truce between the two sides, the case-law shows that the underlying ideological differences run deep and are not easily settled.

(ii) Damages

Damages for breach are not at large. The plaintiff will only be awarded such damages as fairly compensate him for losses occasioned by the breach.

Plaintiffs seeking compensation may seek protection for three types of interest as follows (see, classically, Fuller and Perdue, 1936):

(i) the restitution interest (the interest a person has in the restoration to him of benefits which the defaulting party has acquired at his expense);

(ii) the reliance interest (the interest a person has in compensation in respect of his justifiable reliance on the defaulting party's promise—the object of reliance damages is to restore the innocent party to the position he would have been in had the promise not been made); and

(iii) the expectation interest (the interest a person has in compensation for loss of the expectancy which the defaulting party's promise created—the object of expectation damages is to put the innocent party in the position he would have been in had the promise been properly performed).

To illustrate: suppose that Jack agreed to sell his prize dairy cow to the butcher for £1,000, delivery of the cow to be made within a week, payment to be made within a month. Now, if Jack delivered the cow as agreed, but the butcher failed to pay, Jack would plead his restitution interest in attempting to recover the cow together with any value obtained by the butcher from having the use of the cow (*e.g.* the value of the cow's milk); he would plead his reliance interest in seeking to recover any expenses incurred directly (*e.g.* the cost of delivering the cow) or indirectly (*e.g.* any losses incurred in expectation of having one cow less); and he would plead his expectation interest by seeking the agreed price or any profit lost by having to re-sell the cow. Where restitution damages are awarded, the defaulting party has to restore the value of any goods and incidental benefits to the innocent party. This may or may not return the innocent party to the position he was in (*vis-à-vis* the defaulting party) immediately prior to the formation of the contract. The object of reliance damages is, however, precisely to restore the innocent party to his pre-contractual position. Accordingly, the combined effect of restitution and reliance damages is to return the innocent party to his original position; the effect of the breach will have been neutralised. Expectation damages are less neutral: as we have said, the object of such damages is to put the innocent party in the position he would have been in had the contract been performed. Thus, if the innocent party has made a good bargain, expectation damages are calculated to enable him to reap his profit and not simply to indemnify him against any loss.

For the most part, damages for breach of contract are measured by reference to the innocent party's expectation interest, restitutionary awards being more at home in the context of property law and claims for unjust enrichment, and reliance awards (in the sense of returning the claimant to the *status quo ante*) being characteristic of compensation for torts. However, before we discuss expectation awards, we need to speak briefly to matters of restitution and reliance.

Suppose that Jack, having agreed to sell his cow to the butcher for £1,000, instead sells it to a neighbour who offers a better price (let us say £1,500). Suppose further that the butcher has made a generous offer for the cow and that, despite Jack's breach of contract, the butcher will have no difficulty in buying another equivalent cow for £1,000. On these suppositions, the butcher suffers no loss as measured by his expectation interest (he gets a cow for £1,000) but Jack, by breaking his contract with the butcher, is able to take advantage of the neighbour's more attractive offer; Jack, thus, ends up with £500 over and above the £1,000 value of his expectation interest. If our reaction is "Good luck to the boy—his enterprise is rightly rewarded", we will leave well alone. However, if we think that it is unreasonable that contractors in breach should profit from their wrong, then some adjustment seems to be called for and restitution seems to be the way to achieve it. In most cases of this kind, the English law of contract will not interfere. Provided that the innocent party's expectation interest is fully compensated, the remedial work of contract law is complete. However, there are exceptional cases, particularly so where the defendant profits by doing the very thing that he has contracted not to do. Inevitably, the difficulty is to know quite where the general rule ends and the exception begins.

In *Surrey CC v Bredero Homes Ltd* (1993), the Court of Appeal applied the general rule. There, the defendants increased the profitability of a housing development by building more houses than they had agreed with the vendors of the site. This breach did not cause any direct financial loss to the vendors (but see below for an arguable indirect loss); and, even if the breach resulted in a profit for the contract-breaker, there was no expectation loss to be compensated. This is to be contrasted with *Attorney-General v Blake* (1998, CA; 2001, HL), where the Court of Appeal's hints as to the appropriateness of a restitutionary award were picked up and acted on by the majority of the House of Lords. The relevant wrongdoing in this case was by George Blake, the notorious spy, whose autobiography, *No Other Choice*, contained information that was covered by the Official Secrets Act and disclosure of which was in breach of the terms of his one-time contract of employment with the Crown. The Attorney-General sought to prevent royalties, being held to Blake's account by his British publishers, from being paid to him. If ever there was a case designed to raise the heckles, this was it. Blake, having been convicted of espionage, had escaped from prison where he was serving a 42-year custodial sentence; and, years later, from the safe distance of his flat in Moscow, he claimed to be entitled to realise the profit of a publication the content of which was a testimony to his various wrongs. Outraged by this prospect, the majority of the House allowed that this was an exceptional case where, even if the Crown had suffered no loss to its expectation interest, justice required that an order be made to disgorge Blake's profits.

Looking back at *Bredero*, we might reflect that it is one thing for a house-builder to profit from a contractual wrong, quite another for a spymaster to do so. We might also think, as Lord Hobhouse argued in his dissent in *Blake*, that there is a dimension of the expectation interest (albeit indirect) that calls for compensation in cases of this kind. The argument is that, where a contractor specifically covenants not to do x (build more than so many houses, disclose classified information, or whatever), then the covenantee's contractual expectation is that x will not be done or, at any rate, that x will not be done unless it is agreed by the parties that x may be done—that is, unless the covenantee releases the covenantor from the undertaking. This proviso for possible release is critical. Had the house-builders in *Bredero* sought release, to enable them to build the number of houses that they now wanted to build, the covenantors might well have agreed *at a price*. On this analysis, the covenantee's breach deprives the covenantor of the opportunity to set a price for release and, thus, impinges on the latter's expectation interest.

Whichever way we tackle such contractual wrongdoing, in an attempt to avoid extremely unreasonable results, we generate uncertainty (*cf.* Furmston, 2000). If we follow the majority of the House in *Blake*, we have an exception (for what are, in effect, restitutionary awards) of uncertain scope; if we follow Lord Hobhouse, we have a more flexible interpretation of the expectation interest but how is a compensatory figure to be put on the lost opportunity to negotiate a release, and what if it is quite clear that the covenantee would simply not have entertained a release?

From this conundrum, we turn to the question of whether reliance or expectation should be adopted as the standard measure of damages for breach of contract. The nature of the choice can be illustrated quite simply. Suppose that the butcher leaps out into Jack's path waving a deed in which he promises to pay Jack £1,000 the following day (*i.e.* the butcher makes a binding enforceable unilateral promise). If, in reliance on the promise, Jack immediately gives £500 to the Society of Giant Slayers, should the butcher, in the event of his defaulting on his promise, be required to compensate Jack to the tune of £500 (Jack's reliance interest) or £1,000 (Jack's expectation interest)? One argument in favour of the expectation measure is that if damages are awarded in lieu of specific performance then they should, as far as possible, be a full substitute for performance. Another argument is that innocent parties should not be deprived of their deserved contractual gains. After all, why should a wrongdoer be able to neutralise an innocent party's good bargain? Against this it is argued that it is unfair to hold the defaulting butcher to more than a simple indemnity covering Jack's actual loss. Even with this limited cover, Jack has no cause for complaint, getting £500 without lifting a finger. This line of argument can be pursued from two standpoints. One may emphasise that the expectation measure gives the innocent party the benefit of the bargain without his actually having to earn it; in ordinary bilateral contracts at least (if not in Jack's case), it involves unjust enrichment for the innocent party. Alternatively, one may attack expectation from the standpoint of the defaulting party. The argument here is that while defaulters cannot complain about having to compensate innocent parties for their actual reliance losses, to put defaulters at risk with regard to expectation is to override their intentions.

Wherever the merits finally lie in this debate, the English courts have long since settled that expectation sets the standard measure of damages for breach:

> "The rule of the common law is, that where a party sustains a loss by reason of a breach of contract, he is, so far as money can do it, to be placed in the same situation, with respect to damages, as if the contract had been performed." (*per* Parke B in *Robinson v Harman*, 1848, at p.855)

This, of course, reflects market-individualist thinking, for, in the market, the expectancy is regarded as present value; the profit on a contract is as good as earned when the contract is made. Similarly, it will not do to have the rewards of the market disrupted by breach.

Given expectation as the usual measure, three refinements concerning the valuation of expectation, the innocent party's duty to mitigate his loss, and the extent to which consequential losses may be recovered must now be considered.

(a) The valuation of expectation

Expectation damages are geared to compensating for pecuniary losses as measured by the market. Generally, putting the innocent party in the same position as if the contract had been performed involves covering that party's financial losses relative to the applicable market rates. If Jack defaulted on a contract to sell his prize cow Daisy to the butcher for £1,000, and if the market price for an equivalent cow were £1,500, the butcher would need £500 (the difference between the contract price and the market price for a substitute cow) to cover his expectation loss. What more could the butcher reasonably ask for?

From a consumer-welfarist perspective, the market measure of the lost expectation will sometimes under-compensate the innocent party. Sometimes, the consumer's subjective valuation of the bargained-for performance will be such that the consumer would not be prepared to accept a buy-out in return for the going market rate. In such cases, there is a consumer surplus to which compensatory awards need to be sensitive. Accordingly, in a line of cases going back to *Jarvis v Swans Tours Ltd* (1973), the courts have awarded so-called disappointment damages over and above the ordinary expectation measure. In *Jarvis*, the claimant was a disappointed holiday-maker who found the alpine atmosphere less heady than the brochure promised. The damages, which were roughly twice the amount of the holiday, represented a refund of the holiday price plus the same again for disappointment. Since *Watts v Morrow* (1991), which was a claim arising from a negligent survey, it has become the received wisdom that non-pecuniary loss of this kind is limited to the breach of a contract whose object is to provide pleasure, relaxation, or peace of mind (see, too, *Branchett v Beaney* (1992)); and, it is clear that such compensation is not aimed at easing the frustration of commercial contractors (see *Hayes v James & Charles Dodd* (1990)). This, however, leaves considerable scope for modest awards to cover consumer disappointment. Thus, as Lord Steyn remarked in *Farley v Skinner* (2002):

> "[I] am satisfied that in the real life of our lower courts non-pecuniary damages are regularly awarded on the basis that the defendant's breach of contract deprived the plaintiff of the very object of the contract, *viz.* pleasure, relaxation, and peace of mind. The cases arise in diverse contractual contexts, *e.g.* the supply of a wedding dress or double glazing, hire purchase transactions, landlord and tenant, building contracts, and engagements of estate agents and solicitors."
> (at p.748)

In *Farley* itself, the claimant, who was on the point of retiring, was contemplating purchasing an apparently idyllic residential property in the heart of the Sussex countryside. However, the property was some 15 miles from Gatwick airport and it occurred to the claimant that there might be problems with aircraft noise. He engaged the defendant surveyor to check over the property, in particular to report back on any disturbance from aircraft en route to or from Gatwick. The surveyor reported back in reassuring terms and, in reliance on this report, the claimant went ahead with the purchase. It soon transpired, however, that the property was close to a navigation beacon where aircraft stacked up. At the trial, it was held that the survey had been carried out negligently (in breach of contract) but that the price actually paid for the property was its fair market value—in other words, the claimant could sell up without loss; his only loss was non-pecuniary (for not being able to enjoy breakfast or an evening meal outside in his garden without the interference of aircraft overhead). The simple question, therefore, was whether the claimant was entitled to disappointment damages. The trial judge awarded £10,000 for non-pecuniary loss; a two-member Court of Appeal could not agree; the majority of a fresh three member court ruled against the claimant; but the House of Lords unanimously restored the trial judge's award in favour of the claimant. Although the House expressed some anxiety that awards for disappointment damages should not encourage litigiousness (in which light, the sum of £10,000 was on the generous side), they had no desire to take a technical or restrictive approach to the availability, in principle, of awards of this kind. It was enough, Lord Steyn said, if peace of mind was an important object of the contract (as it clearly was in Mr Farley's case); it did not need to be the exclusive object.

The question of whether it is fair and reasonable to compensate for subjective valuation of performance presents another puzzle that is similar to that of disappointment damages. Suppose, for example, Mr Farley employed a contractor to divert the stream that ran through the middle of his property and to re-position his croquet lawn, but that, in breach of contract, the builder failed to carry out the work as specified. However, let us suppose that while the breach by the builder reduced the value of the property by only a small amount, it would nevertheless cost a great deal of money to rectify. If the impersonal valuation of the market rules, then Mr Farley's compensation will be no more than the diminution of the value of the property. However, if Mr Farley's subjective valuation rules, then damages to cover the far higher cost of repair will be awarded. A likely story? As the American case of *Peevyhouse v Garland Coal and Mining Co* (1962) illustrates, fact is sometimes stranger than fiction.

Here, the plaintiffs agreed to let the defendants strip-mine coal on their land for a period of five years. It was a term of the contract that, at the end of the period, the defendants should perform certain restorative and remedial work. The defendants failed to carry out the remedial work (which would have cost $29,000), thereby causing a diminution in the value of the plaintiffs' property of about $300. Were the plaintiffs' expectation damages to be measured in line with the diminution in market value, or in line with the very much greater cost of substitute performance? The court was split. The majority, working along consumer-welfarist lines, favoured the lower diminution measure, arguing that it was unreasonable (disproportionate) to expect the defendants to commit such a colossal amount of money to effect such a minute gain in market value. There was also a risk of unjust enrichment; for, if the plaintiffs were awarded $29,000 damages, but did not then use the money to reinstate the land, they would be very much better off than they would have been had the contract been performed. Against this, the dissenting minority took the market-individualist objection that the majority approach effectively rewrote the agreement (interfering with freedom and sanctity of contract), and allowed the defendants to take the benefit of the contract without shouldering its burdens.

In England, the response to the problem has been somewhat pragmatic. Cases such as *Radford v De Froberville* (1978) suggest that, if the claimant has had, or will have, the work carried out then cost of cure (or performance) damages will be awarded; but, alongside this, cases such as *Tito v Waddell (No.2)* (1977) indicate a concern that unjust enrichment should be avoided. On this basis, we might say that English law tends towards a fairly straightforward market-individualist approach (which can also protect the interests of good faith, if eccentric, consumers) but without allowing this to be a licence for unreasonable exploitation or opportunism. Such pragmatism and such an inclination towards the market-individualist response must now be read in the light of the much-debated case of *Ruxley Electronics and Construction Ltd v Forsyth* (1994 CA; 1995 HL).

In *Ruxley Electronics*, the company, having contracted to carry out various items of building work at Mr Forsyth's house, were in breach by building a swimming pool to a depth that did not conform to the agreed specification—although, as the trial judge ruled, the pool was safe, it was in fact nine inches shallower than it should have been at the deep end (and, likewise, at the point where Mr Forsyth might dive into the pool). Without doubt, Mr Forsyth was entitled to damages. However, the question was whether he should be awarded the cost of cure (some £21,560, a figure in excess of the original contract value of the pool) or the diminution in market value (nothing in this case, because it was agreed that the shortfall in the depth of the pool did not decrease the value of Mr Forsyth's property), or perhaps some other measure. Taking the view that neither cost of cure nor diminution in value seemed entirely right (the one arguably over-compensating, the other under-compensating, Mr Forsyth), the trial judge took a third course by allowing Mr Forsyth a £2,500 reduction against his bill (ostensibly for loss of amenity). By a majority, the Court of Appeal awarded the full cost of cure— controversially, this being awarded without requiring any under- taking from Mr Forsyth that the damages would be spent on re-instatement of the pool. However, the House of Lords unani- mously restored the trial judge's ruling (leaving Mr Forsyth with a modest award to set against the bill from the building contrac- tors but with, one assumes, a much larger account to be settled with regard to the legal expenses incurred in the case).

One of the striking features of *Ruxley Electronics* is that, whether we look at the opinions that prevailed in the Court of Appeal or at those that prevailed in the House of Lords, the reasonableness (or unreasonableness) of Mr Forsyth pocketing cost of cure dam- ages is a dominant consideration. In defence of a cost of cure award, Staughton L.J. said:

> "It is unreasonable of a plaintiff to claim an expensive rem- edy if there is some cheaper alternative which would make good his loss. Thus he cannot claim the cost of reinstate- ment if the difference in value would make good his loss by enabling him to purchase the building or chattel that he requires elsewhere. But if there is no alternative course which will provide what he requires, or none which will cost less, he is entitled to the cost of repair or reinstatement even if that is very expensive." (CA at p.810)

Since there was no alternative way by which Mr Forsyth could make good his loss, the majority view in the Court of Appeal was that it was not unreasonable for the cost of cure to be awarded. By contrast, in the House of Lords, the authorities were read as emphasising:

> "the central importance of reasonableness in selecting the appropriate measure of damages. If reinstatement is not the reasonable way of dealing with the situation, then diminution in value, if any, is the true measure of the plaintiff's loss . . .
>
> If the court takes the view that it would be unreasonable for the plaintiff to insist on reinstatement, as where, for example, the expense of the work involved would be out of all proportion to the benefit to be obtained, then the plaintiff

will be confined to the difference in value." (*per* Lord Lloyd at pp.284–285)

As the House of Lords saw it, the cost of reinstatement award was wholly unreasonable; difference in value might have been reasonable in some cases but, here, it would undercompensate Mr Forsyth; and, even if the trial judge's award of £2,500 was a touch generous, Mr Forsyth being "lucky to have obtained so large an award for his disappointed expectations" (289), this was a reasonable resolution of the matter.

Relative to the ideologies of contract, how should we interpret the reasoning of the judges in this difficult case? In favour of a cost of cure award, the majority judgments in the Court of Appeal have echoes of classic market-individualism in holding firmly to the idea that the innocent party is entitled to have his loss made good, expensive though reinstatement might be. Moreover, this thinking is supported by a simple form of consumerism, according to which the interests of Mr Forsyth (who, after all, contracted here as a consumer) merit protection against the builders. Hence, even if the builders saved no money by deviating from the contract specification for the pool, their incompetent performance should be corrected by a cost of cure award. Against a cost of cure measure, however, the emphasis, in the House of Lords, on the unreasonableness of committing such a large sum of money in order to rectify a perfectly usable pool picks up the idea of proportionality that, as we have seen already, is a strand in welfarist thinking. We might also find that the thinking of the House of Lords is in line with a more dynamic form of market-individualist thinking under which the reasonableness of the award is judged by reference to generally accepted standards of fair dealing (if any) in the building trade. These considerations, therefore, might be thought to cancel out the case for cost of cure and point to diminution in value. If we assume, however, that neither measure feels right in this case, then we might arrive at the actual award of £2,500 in one of two ways. Taking a consumer welfarist approach, we might judge: (i) that cost of cure was unreasonable as out of all proportion to the benefit achieved, (ii) that diminution in value was more appropriate, and (iii) that, because Mr Forsyth was contracting as a consumer, he was at least entitled to compensation for his disappointment (*i.e.* nothing for diminution plus £2,500 for disappointment). Alternatively, taking a classic market-individualist approach, we might judge: (i) that, given a presumption in favour of cost of cure, but given

too the risk of unfair enrichment, the award should be for cost
of cure with a condition that the sum be used to reinstate the
pool, (ii) that Mr Forsyth would prefer an award free of such a
condition, and (iii) that, if the parties had bargained around the
award so that Mr Forsyth was released from the condition, he
might well have settled for about £2,500 (see Poole, 1996).

(b) Mitigation and the *"White & Carter"* question

Faced with a breach of contract, the innocent party has a duty to
mitigate, *i.e.* to take reasonable steps to minimize his losses. For
example, in *Lazenby Garages Ltd. v Wright* (1976), the defendant,
having agreed one day to buy a second-hand BMW car for £1,670
from the plaintiff motor dealers, notified the dealers on the following day that he had changed his mind. In line with their duty
to mitigate, the plaintiffs took reasonable steps to resell the car.
Had they resold the car for less than £1,670, the plaintiffs could
have looked to the defendant to make up thedifference. In fact,
the plaintiffs succeeded in selling the car a couple of months later
for £1770 (*i.e.* £100 more than the defendant had agreed to pay).
On the face of it, the defendant's breach had cost the plaintiffs
nothing. However, the motor dealers argued that the breach had
actually cost them a sale—because the person who eventually
bought the BMW for £1770 might well have spent that sum on
another vehicle if the defendant had performed rather than
breached his contract. Although the trial judge was prepared to
award the plaintiffs half their alleged lost profit (on the ground
that, if the defendant had not broken the contract, there was a
50:50 chance that the plaintiffs would have sold another car to the
eventual buyer of the BMW), the Court of Appeal showed strong
consumer-welfarist colours in protecting the defendant by insisting that, because second-hand cars are all different from one
another, the defaulting buyer simply would not have contemplated a claim of this kind. *Lazenby* would have raised another
nice point if the motor dealers, notwithstanding the buyer's indication that he had changed his mind, proceeded nevertheless to
prepare the car to the buyer's order. This scenario would have
raised the vexed question of how the mitigation principle relates
to the election principle (*viz.* that an innocent party, faced with a
breach of condition, may elect either to affirm, *i.e.* continue with
the contract, or to treat it as repudiated).

The tension between these principles was highlighted in the
much-debated case of *White & Carter (Councils) Ltd v McGregor*
(1961). Here, the appellants agreed to advertise the name of the

respondent's garage on litter bins over a three-year period. The respondent purported to cancel the contract almost as soon as it had been made. Although, at the time of cancellation, the appellants had taken no steps to perform the contract, they refused to accept the cancellation, went ahead with the advertisements, and duly claimed the agreed price under the contract. The respondent argued that this action must fail, the appellants being entitled only to damages for loss of profit. On the face of it, the respondent's argument was attractive, for one of the supposed virtues of the expectation measure is that it enables an innocent party to recover his lost profit without economic waste. Critics of the expectation measure complain about the innocent party taking an unearned profit, but they would hardly approve of such wasteful expenditure (*i.e.* the advertisers' resources being committed to conferring the unwanted benefit). Nevertheless, the House of Lords ruled three to two in favour of the appellants.

The majority's reasoning was straightforward. It has long been settled that where one party clearly indicates that he is refusing or will refuse to perform his side of the agreement, then the innocent party has the option to affirm the contract or to treat it as repudiated. The appellants had simply opted to continue with the contract, and the reasonableness of their decision was irrelevant. To this, two qualifications were added. First, in practice, it may sometimes be impossible for the innocent party to continue with the contract without the co-operation of the defaulting party. In *White & Carter*, it was fortuitous that the nature of the contract allowed the appellants to proceed without the assistance of the respondent; but this was no reason to deny the appellants their rights. Secondly, if the appellants had had no legitimate interest in opting to continue with the contract, there may have been a case for relieving the respondent; but, on the facts, there was nothing to suggest that the appellants lacked such an interest. Since *White & Carter*, the courts have grappled with both these qualifications, the legitimate interest qualification remaining particularly controversial (see, *e.g. The Alaskan Trader* 1984). The point of this caveat seems to be to disqualify the option to continue where it is unreasonable. However, the majority's ruling in *White & Carter* indicates that there is nothing unreasonable *per se* in earning the contract profit rather than taking it without performance. Unreasonableness, for the purposes of undermining a legitimate interest, lies elsewhere, perhaps in the notion of bad faith or malice on the part of the innocent party.

In opposition to the majority view, the dissenting Law Lords in *White & Carter* emphasised the waste involved in permitting the appellants to run up the unwanted bill. This, for the minority, violated the principle that the innocent party has a duty to mitigate.

To answer this charge, the majority could contend, formalistically, that where the election principle is in play, the duty to mitigate simply does not arise, because until the innocent party has elected to accept the repudiation, the contract remains in being. This, however, seems arbitrary. The better argument would be to concede that the election principle is qualified by the mitigation principle, so that the option must be exercised in a way which does not wantonly inflict loss on the defaulting party and cause economic waste. This makes some sense of Lord Reid's playing around with the idea of a legitimate interest, and possibly can be tied in with the mitigation principle which, even at its strongest, demands only that reasonable steps be taken to mitigate. On this interpretation, the division in *White & Carter* essentially involves differing conceptions of reasonable steps.

We can discern a parallel between the majority approach in *White & Carter* and the standard market-individualist approach to cost of performance or diminution of value damages. Both approaches start at a similar point: a bargain has been made; the defaulting party now complains that it would be unreasonable (because economically wasteful) for the innocent party to continue with performance (as in *White & Carter*) or to insist upon cost of performance damages (as in cases like *Peevyhouse*). Both approaches, whilst resisting this argument of economic unreasonableness, nevertheless show themselves willing to compromise with reasonableness in another guise. Even market-individualists will not stand by and license the innocent party wantonly to inflict loss on the defaulter (hence the legitimate interest qualification in *White & Carter*) or to collect a windfall profit in bad faith (hence the observations in *Radford* and *Tito* concerning the use of the damages for the intended purpose).

(c) Consequential loss and remoteness

The expectation principle enjoins the court to put the innocent party in the same position as if the contract had been performed. Now, suppose that, if the contract had been performed, the innocent party would have made some exceptional gain; or, suppose that the breach causes the innocent party some exceptional loss. Is the defaulting party liable to compensate the innocent party for all consequential loss caused by the breach?

One might expect the party in default to be required to cover all such losses. After all, it is his breach which has caused the losses. However, the law operates with a principle of remoteness of damage, which has the effect of barring the innocent party's claim in respect of consequential losses which are "too remote". In the landmark case of *Hadley v Baxendale* (1854) Baron Alderson laid down the principle in the following terms:

> "Where two parties have made a contract which one of them has broken, the damages which the other party ought to receive in respect of such breach of contract should be such as may fairly and reasonably be considered either arising naturally, *i.e.* according to the usual course of things, from such breach of contract itself, or such as may reasonably be supposed to have been in the contemplation of both parties, at the time they made the contract, as the probable result of the breach of it." (*ibid.* at p.354)

In *Hadley*, the plaintiff millers delivered to the carriers, Pickford & Co, a broken crankshaft to be sent to engineers at Greenwich. The plaintiffs' mill could not operate until the engineers had supplied a new shaft, using the broken shaft as a pattern. The carriers, in breach of contract, delayed five days in delivery, and the millers sued for five days' loss of profits. Applying the remoteness principle, it was held that the millers' action failed. The millers' loss of profit did not arise "naturally, *i.e.* according to the usual course of things" (the so-called "first limb" of the rule in *Hadley v Baxendale*) because the carriers could reasonably expect the mill to be equipped with a spare shaft. Neither was the loss such as "may reasonably be supposed to have been in the contemplation" of the carriers (the so-called "second limb" of the rule in *Hadley v Baxendale*); in other words, the carriers were not put on special notice that this was a high-risk contract, that the mill would be at a standstill until the new shaft was fitted (on the two "limbs" in their historical context, see Adams, 1979).

While students are anxiously trying to commit Baron Alderson's time-honoured words to memory, the general significance of the principle of remoteness may be missed. It must never be forgotten that remoteness is about limiting the innocent party's *ordinary* right to recover. In more recent times, too, the House of Lords in *The Heron II* (1969) has emphasised the severity of this limitation. Their Lordships insisted that the defaulting party should only be liable for those consequential losses which, on the basis of his general or special knowledge, he must have regarded as substantially probable or quite likely, rather than merely possible or pretty unlikely. This was not the House engaging in hair-splitting; it was ensuring that there was no mis-understanding about the restricted range of consequential losses for which the defaulter will ordinarily be liable.

Consumer-welfarists can argue in favour of the remoteness principle on the grounds that it is only fair that special risks should be disclosed. Of course, this can become a recipe for unfairness if the potential defaulter promptly uses his bargaining strength to contract out of liability; and consumer-welfarists will certainly want to counteract this by subjecting the defaulter's exclusions to a test of reasonableness.

For market-individualists, the rationale of the remoteness principle lies in the facilitation of commerce. Ever since commerce began, commercial men have been risk minimisers. Good commerce assumes efficient covering of risk, particularly (in modern times) efficient insuring against risk. Thus, in carriage contracts (which have been central to the development of the remoteness principle), the apportionment of insurance risks between consignor and carrier has long been treated as a matter of first importance (see Adams, 1983). Now, if defaulting carriers (or defaulting contractors generally) are to be exposed to a bottomless pit of consequential losses, this threatens efficient risk coverage in two ways. First, the defaulter, unaware of the potential loss, may simply have no cover. If the innocent party has relied on the defaulter having cover, this is a loss that will rebound on the former. It is also bad for the defaulter who may be put out of business and, indeed, for third parties who may benefit from a low-cost service operated by the defaulter (*cf.* the thinking about the reasonableness of the exemptions in *Photo Production*, p.144). Secondly, even if the defaulter has cover, it may be inefficient for him to insure. For example, in carriage contracts, the remoteness principle gives the consignor an incentive to insure (*cf.* Posner, 1992, p.126), and this fits with the common assumption that it is cheaper for consignors to insure for themselves than for carriers to do that for them. There are, for this reason, various conventions limiting carriers' liability in international contracts of carriage by sea and air, and there are domestic equivalents both conventional and statutory. Of course, it is true that the incentive to disclose special risks implicit in the remoteness principle runs against the market-individualist axiom that there is no general duty to disclose. But this is one situation where self-interested non-disclosure has to yield to broader commercial considerations.

3. OVERVIEW

Conflicts between formalists and realists play only a relatively minor role in the fight to control remedies. The principal protagonists are market-individualists and consumer-welfarists, the former tending to occupy traditional doctrinal strongholds (*e.g.* the absence of a general duty of disclosure, the expectation measure of damages, the classification approach), with the latter on the offensive.

Without doubt, consumer-welfarists have made significant advances (see, *e.g.* the representation cases such as *Mardon, Oscar Chess* and *Dick Bentley*, the Misrepresentation Act 1967, the consequential approach, the development of damages for consumer disappointment and ad hoc protection as in *Lazenby*). Nevertheless, these encroachments on market-individualist territory do not necessarily signal the surrender of market-individualist positions. For example, the reasonableness provisions of the Misrepresentation Act (as of UCTA) can be made to mirror market-individualist thinking; the consequential approach can be accommodated and contained within the classification approach; and the expectation measure can be compromised at the margins where it produces extremely unreasonable results. The rise of consumer-welfarism does not necessarily entail the collapse of market-individualism.

8

THE IDEOLOGIES OF CONTRACT

We have presented judicial employment of the contract rule-book as a three-cornered fight between formalists, market-individualists, and consumer-welfarists (the reader will recall our *caveat* about such locutions in Chapter 3). This interpretive scheme, it will be recalled, was drawn from a general theoretical framework constituted by the ideologies of formalism, realism, market-individualism, and consumer-welfarism. In the light of our discussion we must now take stock of each of these ideologies, and then assess the pattern of their relationships.

1. THE INFLUENCE OF THE IDEOLOGIES

(i) *Formalism*

The formalist view gravitates around the rule-book. Its influence can be characterised in the following ways.

First, and foremost, the rule-book governs. Lawton L.J.'s observations on the problem of the "battle of the forms" (in *Butler Machine Tool*, p.57) reflect this attitude:

> "The problem is how should that battle be conducted? The view taken by the judge was that the battle should extend over a wide area and the court should do its best to look into the minds of the parties and make certain assumptions. In my judgement, the battle has to be conducted in accordance with set rules . . .
> The rules relating to a battle of this kind have been known for the past 130-odd years." (*ibid.* at p.969)

The new problem presented by the battle of the forms was to be resolved according to the traditional rules. The world may change, but the traditional rules of contract, like Ol' Man River, "jus' keep rollin' along".

Secondly, the rule-book is viewed as a closed logical system. Rule-book exercises are exercises in the logic of the concepts of contract. Just as one plus one must equal two, formalists view contractual concepts as having a logic of their own. The traditional schematic approach to formation, particularly, reflects this aspect of formalism.

Thirdly, the conceptual purity and integrity of the rule-book is to be maintained. Formalists are uncomfortable when they encounter ill-fitting or otherwise deviant doctrines. The attempt to clean up the doctrine of fundamental breach, from *Suisse Atlantique* (p.142) onwards, is a good example of a formalist purifying operation.

Fourthly, formalism tends towards doctrinal conservatism. Thus, formalists tend to confine innovations, such as the *High Trees* (p.81) principle and collateral contracts. If such "dangerous" ideas are to be used, they must be used with caution. In the same way, formalism encourages judges to base themselves on well-established rather than less well-established ground (see, *e.g.* the preference for the construction approach towards exemption clauses, the preference for an intention-based approach to implied terms, the reluctance to employ the concept of good faith, etc.).

Fifthly, as Geoffrey Lane L.J. said in *Gibson v Manchester City Council* (p.51) at p.591, "sympathy and politics" are not material considerations (*i.e.* for formalist judges—unless, of course, the rule-book makes such considerations material). Judges may sympathise with a litigant, but if the rule-book is against that party then that is conclusive. Hard cases make bad law (*i.e.* introduce ad hoc distinctions into the rule-book). In the same way, politics, interpreted broadly as judicial values and commitments, must not influence a formalist judge. A judge may regard a particular rule as unfair or inconvenient, but this must not act as an excuse for deviation from the rule-book.

Sixthly, formalism implies an uncritical acceptance, and a mechanical application, of the rule-book doctrines. Shibboleths such as "freedom of contract" and "sanctity of contract" are cited without critical reflection on their doctrinal purpose, or the social context in which they are to be applied. Formalism takes the idea that "Justice is blind" quite literally: the rule-book is to be applied blind to any consideration of the merits of the case, the purpose or point of the rules, or the context of the dispute.

Seventhly, because formalism favours the routine application of the rule-book, it works best with clear general rules which do not involve the exercise of judicial discretion. Of course, the facts have to be found, but once found, general rules promise more or less mechanical application. Accordingly, formalists prefer a rule which either straightforwardly allows or disallows exemption clauses to one which allows exemption clauses if they satisfy a requirement of reasonableness. It simply is not possible to apply a reasonableness requirement in a routine mechanical fashion, although formalists will no doubt strive to structure the discretion along the lines of certain general rules of thumb.

Finally, it is also possible to view as corollaries of a formalist outlook the tendency both to eschew responsibility for major law reform ("This is best left to Parliament"), and to interpret appeal court jurisdiction narrowly ("Provided that the trial court asked the right legal question, and provided that the answer acted upon was not totally unreasonable, then the ruling must stand"). The former tendency can be seen as a by-product of formalist caution coupled with the formalist belief that the function of judges is to apply, not to make, the rules. The latter tendency is assisted by the formalist detachment from the results of cases. Consequently, when a case comes up on appeal, the question for the appeal court is not whether the trial judge got the right result, but whether the right rules were applied.

(ii) Realism

Realism is the antithesis of formalism. It follows that each of the formalist tendencies is matched by a realist tendency which pushes in the opposite direction (*cf.* Steyn, 1996).

First, the rule-book is not decisive. The most important aspects of a dispute are the facts and the decision; rules are a secondary consideration, a mere means. If formalism is rule-orientated, realism is result-orientated. In many ways, Lord Devlin's observation that "The true spirit of the common law is to override theoretical distinctions when they stand in the way of doing practical justice" (*Ingram v Little*, 1961, p.68) enshrines the realist articles of faith.

Secondly, the logic of the rule-book concepts is by no means the be-all and end-all. Immediately one thinks here of Lord Denning's criticisms of traditional offer and acceptance analysis (see p.52), and of his cavalier exploits with regard to consideration (see pp.77–78). But Lord Denning was not alone in such a realist disregard for the logic of the concepts. For example, the logic of the concepts did not prevent the majority finding the required contractual connection in *The Eurymedon* (p.89), nor did it stop the House of Lords finding a remedy for Mrs Beswick (see pp.88–89).

Thirdly, realists do not regard blotting the rule-book as the ultimate sin. If practical justice demands some running repairs, then the elegance or conceptual neatness of the solution hardly matters. What matters is that the repair job works. Formalists may pour scorn on such realist patch-up jobs as the device of the collateral contract (see pp.156–157) or the doctrine of the fundamental term (see p.142), but realists can take such criticisms without flinching. Realists know a spatchcock solution when they see one, but a solution is at least a solution.

Fourthly, realism tends towards doctrinal and conceptual innovation. Judges are not to be discouraged from sowing new doctrinal seeds (*e.g.* promissory estoppel—see pp.81–86; unconscionability—see pp.116–120; economic duress—see pp.70–72; the doctrine of the innominate term—see p.165 *et seq.*) simply because it is not clear how the doctrinal plant will grow. Nor are judges to be discouraged from cultivating newly born ideas. If a recent innovation supports a particular decision, then there is no reason to eschew such support in favour of a traditional ground for the same decision.

Fifthly, for realist judges, "sympathy and politics" *do* matter. It is all very well complaining that hard cases make bad law; but if judges ignore the obvious merits of a case, practical justice goes by the board and the law is rightly accused of being an ass. Likewise, politics, broadly interpreted, *do* count. Where a judge considers a particular rule or its application unfair, or inconvenient, he should recognise the force of these considerations. On the realist view, judges must act as custodians of practical justice and convenience, not simply as the keepers of the code.

Sixthly, for realists, the mechanical and uncritical adoption and application of the rule-book will not do. Rules are laid down for a purpose, to defend some principle or to support some policy. When rules no longer serve their intended purpose, when they become detached from their point, slavish adherence to the rule-book undermines the spirit of their enactment. The drive towards consumer protection is the outstanding example of a realist recognition that the world changes and that, in a changing social context, the original intent of the rules may become perverted by their continued uncritical application. (To avoid misunderstanding, we should emphasise that realists are not tied to the purposes underpinning the rule-book. In the final analysis, the rule-book, whether read literally or purposively, is marginal to realism.)

Seventhly, realism is not necessarily inconvenienced by a rule-book which is riddled with discretions. At least, for realists of a consumer-welfarist persuasion, if the rules enjoin judges to decide according to the canons of reasonableness, fairness, conscionability, and the like, this is no problem, for it is precisely how such realist judges will want to decide anyway.

Finally, because realists have a passion for results rather than rules, they will tend to take a broad view of appeal court jurisdiction. For realists, the point of an appeal is not to test out whether the trial court applied the right rules, but primarily to assess the result handed down. Accordingly, appeal courts should feel free to overturn trial court rulings where they are judged to have arrived at the wrong result. Similarly, where the rule-book is in obvious and urgent need of reform, realists do not see the sense of simply exhorting the legislature to come to their rescue. If the legislature duly reforms the law, all well and good, but in the meantime realist judges will think that they have a responsibility to get on with the reforming work themselves:

> "[T]here is a bill now before Parliament which gives effect to the test of reasonableness [*i.e.* the bill which led to UCTA]. This is a gratifying piece of law reform: but I do not think we need wait for that bill to be passed into law. You never know what may happen to a bill. Meanwhile the common law has its own principles ready to hand." (*per* Lord Denning M.R. in *Levison v Patent Steam Carpet Cleaning Co Ltd*, 1978, at p.79)

Not only do realist judges put results before rules, they put pragmatism ahead of conceptual purity.

(iii) *Market-individualism*

Market-individualism has both market and individualist strands. The strands are mutually supportive, but it aids exposition to separate them. We can look first at the market side of this ideology and then at its individualistic aspect.

(a) The market ideology

According to market-individualism, the function of contract law is not simply to make a market (informal markets may exist outside the law); its function is to establish a regulated marketplace in which contractors are able to deal with security and confidence. The market is made for exchange, not gift or charity; and it should be designed for self-interested competitive trading without becoming a licence for highway robbery or exploitation. So conceived, the law of contract establishes the ground rules for competitive, calculable, and confident commerce—hence, subject to fraud, mistake, coercion and the like, bargains made in the market between eligible contractors are to be treated as enforceable. In many ways, the line drawn between (actionable) misrepresentation and mere non-disclosure epitomises this view. There are minimal restraints on contractors: the law of the market is not the law of the jungle, and this rules out misrepresentations. However, non-disclosure of some informational advantage is simply prudent bargaining—contractors are involved in a competitive situation and cannot be expected to disclose their hands or otherwise negotiate in good faith (see Lord Ackner's remarks in *Walford v Miles*, p.99). In line with these assumptions, market-individualists attach importance to the following considerations.

Firstly, the security of transactions is to be promoted. This means that where a party, having entered the market, reasonably assumes that he has concluded a bargain, then the courts will defend that assumption. The courts' acceptance of an objective approach to contractual intention, their caution with respect to subjective mistake, and their vigorous defence of third-party purchasers (see the mistake of identity cases, pp.65–70) reflect the concern for security of contract. Ideally, of course, security of transactions means that a party gets the performance he has bargained for, but, as the market reveals an increasing number of transactions where performance is delayed, the opportunities for non-performance increase. To protect the innocent party, contract espouses the expectation measure of damages (it is the next best thing to actual performance), and in the principle of sanctity of contract (which we will consider under the individualistic side) it takes a hard line against excuses for non-performance.

Secondly, it is important for those who enter into the market to know where they stand. This means that the ground rules of contract should be clear. Hence, the restrictions on contracting must not only be minimal (in line with the competitive nature of the market), but also must be clearly defined (in line with the market demand for predictability, calculability, etc.). The postal acceptance rule is a model for the market-individualist: clear, simple, and not hedged around with qualifications which leave contractors constantly unsure of their position. Similarly, the traditional classification approach to withdrawal encapsulates all the virtues of certainty, which are dear to the market-individualist. Conversely, the uncertainty inherent in the consequential approach (see pp.165–166) weakens its appeal to market-individualists, even though they may be unavoidably drawn to it where particular terms cannot be dealt with under the classification test.

Thirdly, since contract is concerned essentially with the facilitation of market operations, the law should accommodate commercial practice, rather than the other way round. Therefore, market-individualists sound the alarm bells as soon as the rules of contract fall out of line with and impede commercial practice. The majority judgment of the Privy Council in *The Eurymedon* (p.89) is an outstanding example of market-individualist realignment of the law; and *Williams v Roffey* (p.78) and *Hillas v Arcos* (p.96) testify to an evolving market-individualist recognition that technical formation requirements should be relaxed to facilitate agreed adjustments to commercial contracts. In the same way, deference to commercial practice accounts for the relatively smooth acceptance of incorporation of terms by reasonable notice, and stamps the pronouncements of the House of Lords in *Photo Production* (p.144) as thoroughly market-individualist.

Finally, we should notice the import of the commonplace that many of the rules concerning formation (*e.g.* the rules determining whether a display of goods is an offer or an invitation to treat) simply hinge on convenience. This may well be a statement of the obvious, but the obvious should never be neglected. Contract is concerned to avoid market inconvenience, precisely because its market-individualism commits it to a policy of facilitating market dealing.

(b) The individualistic ideology

The law of contract rightly assumes that market trading is informed by an element of self-interest. Contract does not condemn philanthropy; but it has its place, and the market is not it. Nevertheless, the market will have its own ethic, setting the standard for fair dealing. Essentially, the choice is between an ethic of self-reliance (where contractors are very much on their own) and one of co-operation (where contractors, although pursuing their own economic interests, view contracts as an exercise in mutual advantage) (see Brownsword, 2001). The individualist dimension of classical market-individualism treats self-reliance as the default ethic. It follows that judges should play a largely non-interventionist role, leaving it to the contractors to decide whether to enter the market, with whom they wish to deal, and on what terms. Once bargains have been struck, it falls to the courts to oversee their enforcement (or to make compensatory orders). From these individualistic premises, we derive the cornerstone doctrines of "freedom of contract" and "sanctity of contract".

The emphasis of freedom of contract is on the parties' freedom of choice. First, the parties should be free to choose one another as contractual partners (*i.e.* partner-freedom). Like the tango, contract takes two. And ideally the two should consensually choose one another. Secondly, the parties should be free to choose their own terms (*i.e.* term-freedom). Contract is competitive, but the exchange should be consensual. Accordingly, if Jack refuses to deal with the butcher because his mother has warned him about talking to strangers, this is his prerogative; he is exercising his right of partner-freedom. Equally, if Jack agrees to trade the family's last cow for the butcher's magic beans, this too is his prerogative; he is exercising his right of term-freedom (even though we may think he exercises it stupidly). Contract is about unforced choice.

One of the hallmarks of the modern law, of course, has been the increasing regulatory oversight of contracting and, with that (as many would see it), the erosion of freedom of contract. Anti-discrimination statutes restrict partner-freedom; and term-freedom has been restricted both by the common law (*e.g.* in its restrictions on illegal contracts as well as its controlling devices for the incorporation and interpretation of contractual terms) and by legislation (*e.g.* UCTA and the Unfair Terms in Consumer Contracts Regulations). In practice, too, notwithstanding recent attempts to introduce markets into the public sector (see below at p.217), weaker parties have difficulty in actually exercising the freedom of contract that they enjoy on paper. Thus, whilst consumers may have some choice about their utility supplier, they have less choice about the terms of supply and, in fact, their relationship with their supplier, although mimicking contract, may not be governed at all by the law of contract. In other cases, for example the railways, one's contractual partner is virtually self-selecting. As for the experience of freedom of contract in the heartland of the private sector, consumers are often confronted with non-negotiable standard form agreements; and, whilst competition on prices seems to be keen in some sectors, it is much less so in others. Nevertheless, none of this should obscure the thrust of the principle of freedom of contract, which is that one should have the freedoms, and that the law should restrict them as little as possible—indeed, it is consistent with the principle (in a widely held view) that the law should facilitate the freedoms by striking down monopolies.

Although the principle of partner-freedom still has some life in it (*e.g.* in defending the shopkeeper's choice of customer), it is the principle of term-freedom which is the more vital. Term-freedom can be seen as having two limbs:

(i) The free area within which the parties are permitted, in principle, to set their own terms should be maximised; and,
(ii) parties should be held to their bargains, *i.e.* to their agreed terms (provided that the terms fall within the free area).

Some of the fundamental issues in *Suisse Atlantique* (p.142) can be related to these two limbs as follows: the House of Lords' support for freedom of contract in *Suisse Atlantique* was primarily support for the first limb. Their Lordships were not prepared to prohibit certain sorts of exemption clauses in the way that, for example, penalty clauses are banned. The effect of exemption clauses remained a matter of the meaning of particular clauses in the light of the parties' intentions (as determined by the rules of construction). However, the preferred construction approach did not prevent later courts from violating the second limb of the principle of term-freedom. Of course, this meant that lip service only was being paid to freedom of contract. To give term-freedom a real bite, both limbs of the principle must be acted upon.

The second limb of term-freedom is none other than the principle of sanctity of contract. By providing that parties should be held to their bargains, the principle of sanctity of contract has a double emphasis. First, if parties must be held to *their* bargains, they should be treated as masters of their own bargains, and the courts should not indulge in ad hoc adjustment of terms which strike them as unreasonable or imprudent. Secondly, if parties must be *held* to their bargains, then the courts should not lightly relieve contractors from performance of their agreements. It will be appreciated that, while freedom of contract is the broader of the two principles, it is sanctity of contract which accounts for the distinctive market-individualistic stand against paternalistic intervention in particular cases.

A glance back over the chapters in this part of the book will reveal that the modern law is littered with examples of the principle of sanctity of contract in operation. We first encountered its non-interventionist philosophy in Lord Wilberforce's powerful dissent in *Schuler v Wickman* (p.40), and, not surprisingly, the same philosophy underpins his speech (and those of the other members of the House) in *Photo Production* (p.144). However, the principle goes beyond particular judgments. It is the foundation for such landmarks as the doctrine that the courts will not review the adequacy of consideration; the principle that the basis of implied terms is necessity not reasonableness (see *Liverpool City Council v Irwin*, p.100); the hard line towards unilateral collateral mistake (see, *e.g. Smith v Hughes*, p.64 and, common mistake (see *Bell v Lever Brothers Ltd*, p.130) and frustration (see *Davis v Fareham*, p.138; the cautious reception of economic duress; the anxiety to limit the doctrine of inequality of bargaining power; the resistance to the citation of relatively unimportant uncertainty as a ground for release from a contract (see, *e.g. Foley v Classique Coaches Ltd*, p.95); and the reluctance to succumb to arguments of economic waste or unreasonableness as a basis for release from a bargain (see, *e.g. White & Carter*, p.179). The principle of sanctity of contract is a thread which runs through contract from beginning to end, enjoining the courts to be ever-vigilant in ensuring that established or new doctrines do not become an easy exit from bad bargains. Of course, we are not suggesting that such bargains are necessarily products in the first place of free bargaining in the literal sense. Especially in those cases where standard forms are involved they are a product of some rather artificial rules of incorporation (see especially *L'Estrange v Graucob* p.141). But courts in the twentieth century tended to regard the contracts resulting from the application of such rules as exercises in term-freedom (see Adams (1978b) for a detailed analysis as to how this came about).

(iv) Consumer-welfarism

Recently, in *Johnson (AP) v Unisys Ltd* (2001), Lord Steyn remarked (at 808) that the historic denial of compensation for the manner of an employee's dismissal (in *Addis v Gramophone Co Ltd* (1909)) "was decided in the heyday of a judicial philosophy of market individualism" but that the modern law has seen "a fundamental change in legal culture", namely, towards a greater concern with the welfare of employees (and, of course, consumers). Whilst some might place the heyday of market-individualist thinking a bit earlier (in the nineteenth century), no one would dispute the rise of consumer-welfarist thinking in the modern law of contract (particularly from 1945 onwards). To the extent that legal culture reflects larger cultural currents, the rise of consumer-welfarism is no more than one might expect. In a consumer society, the law takes the interests of consumers more seriously; and, where government assumes significant welfare responsibilities, welfarist ideas inevitably show through in contract law. Of course, culture does not stand still and, in the early years of the twenty-first century, while consumerism continues unabated, pressure on government budgets has led to cut-backs on welfare programmes (including state-assisted legal aid)—the new rhetoric thus emphasises consumer choice and value for money coupled with self-reliance. It follows that whilst the ideology of consumer-welfarism should continue to be influential in the consumer law of contract, its prospects in straight commercial contracting are less certain.

Although the consumer-welfarist ideology clearly stands for a policy of consumer protection, and for principles of fairness and reasonableness in contract, it lacks the unity and coherence of market-individualism. It does not start with the market-individualist premise that all contracts should be minimally regulated. Rather, it presupposes that consumer contracts are to be closely regulated, and that commercial contracts, although still ordinarily to be viewed as competitive transactions, are to be subject to rather more regulation than market-individualists would allow. The difficulties with consumer-welfarism appear as soon as one attempts to identify its particular guiding principles (*i.e.* its operative principles and conceptions of fairness and reasonableness).

Without attempting to draw up an exhaustive list of the particular principles of consumer-welfarism, we suggest that the following number amongst its leading ideas:

(1) The principle of reasonable reliance: contractors should not "blow hot and cold" in their dealings with one another. A person should not encourage another to act in a particular way or to form a particular expectation (or acquiesce in another's so acting or forming an expectation) only then to act inconsistently with that encouragement (or acquiescence). This principle is relevant to the Court of Appeal's support for the council-house purchasers in the *Manchester City Council* cases (*i.e. Storer*, p.51, and Gibson, p.51), and (with rather different facts) for the unilateral contract offerees in *Errington v Errington* (p.55); and, of course, it is central to High Trees (p.81) and the equitable estoppel cases. The most important application of the principle is to offer some protection to those who reasonably rely in pre-contractual situations (in

anticipation of a contract) and in situations where contractual terms have been adjusted (as in *High Trees*). Potentially, the principle could operate beyond the shadow of exchange-based agreement to become the modern paradigm for contract.

(2) The principle of proportionality: an innocent party's remedies for breach should be proportionate to the seriousness of the consequences of the breach. This underwrites the *"Hong Kong"* consequential approach to withdrawal, and it explains the attitude of the majority of their Lordships in *Schuler v Wickman* (p.39). We can also see this principle at work in regulating contractual provisions dealing with the amount of damages. Thus, penalty clauses are to be rejected because they bear no relationship to the innocent party's real loss (they are disproportionately excessive), and exemption clauses are unreasonable because they err in the opposite direction.

(3) The principle of bad faith (and good faith): a party who cites a good legal principle in bad faith should not be allowed to rely on that principle. Hence, in *The Hansa Nord* (p.168), the buyer was not allowed to rely (in bad faith) on the breach as a legitimate ground for withdrawal; and in *Nicolene Ltd v Simmonds* (p.95), the seller was not allowed to rely (in bad faith) on the alleged uncertainty of the contract. In both cases, we can sense that the courts were aware of the danger of one party planting traps in the contract in order to facilitate release if so desired. The general principle of bad faith may also explain the rejection of the nephew's reliance on privity in *Beswick v Beswick* (p.88) and Rees's reliance on promissory estoppel in *D & C Builders v Rees* (p.83), and it fits with the regulation of economic duress in *Atlas Express v Kafco* (p.71). In all these cases it would have been an abuse of legal doctrine to allow (bad faith) reliance—and this would be inconsistent with the general requirement of good faith.

(4) The principle that no man should profit from his own wrong: this was a principle of which Lord Atkin was certainly conscious in *Bell v Lever Bros Ltd* (p.130), but of course it had to give way to his market-individualist thinking. However, the equitable mistake cases, such as *Solle v Butcher* (p.132), and *Magee v Pennine* (p.133) act on this principle; and the decisions in *Beswick* (p.88) and *D & C Builders* (p.83) derive support from it.

(5) The principle of unjust enrichment: no party, even though innocent, should be allowed unjustly to enrich himself at the expense of another. Accordingly, it is unreasonable for an innocent party to use another's breach as an opportunity for unfair enrichment: hence, again, the prohibition on penalty clauses, the anxiety about the use made of cost of performance damages, and perhaps the argument in *White & Carter* which (unsuccessfully) pleaded the unreasonableness of continued performance (p.179). Equally, frustration should not entail unfair financial advantage (see *e.g.* the Law Reform (Frustrated Contracts) Act 1943, and *Krell v Henry*, p.128).

(6) The better loss-bearer principle: where a loss has to be allocated to one of two innocent parties, it is reasonable to allocate it to the party who is better able to carry the loss. As a rule of thumb, commercial parties are deemed to be better loss-bearers than consumers. The decisions in *Ingram v Little* (p.66), and *Oscar Chess* (p.154) exemplify this principle.

(7) The principle of exploitation: a stronger party should not be allowed to exploit the weakness of another's bargaining situation; but parties of equal bargaining strength should be assumed to have a non-exploitative relationship. The first part of this principle, its positive interventionist aspect, pushes for a general principle of unconscionability (*cf. Lloyds Bank Ltd v Bundy*, p.117), and justifies the policy of consumer protection. The latter (qualifying) aspect of the principle, however, is equally important, for it invites a non-interventionist approach to commercial contracts (see, *e.g.* Lord Denning's views in *Howard Marine*, p.161, and in *British Crane Hire v Ipswich Plant Hire*, p.162).

(8) The principle of a fair deal for consumers: consumers should be afforded protection against sharp advertising practice (*cf. Carlill v Carbolic Smoke Ball Co Ltd*, p.49), against misleading statements (see, *e.g. Curtis v Chemical Cleaning and Dyeing Co*, p.159), against false representations (*cf. Dick Bentley*, p.154), and against restrictions on their ordinary rights (see, *e.g. Thornton v Shoe Lane Parking Ltd*, p.61, and *Karsales (Harrow) Ltd v Wallis*, p.142). Moreover, consumer disappointment should be properly compensated (see, *e.g. Jarvis v Swans Tours Ltd*, p.174).

(9) The principle of informational advantage: representors who have special informational advantage must stand by their representations; but representees who have equal

informational opportunity present no special case for protection. The positive aspect of the principle of informational advantage is protective (see, *e.g. Esso Petroleum Co Ltd v Mardon*, p.160), but its negative aspect offers no succour to representees who are judged able to check out statements for themselves (see, *e.g.* Lord Denning's views in *Howard Marine*, p.161).

(10) The principle of responsibility for fault: contractors who are at fault should not be able to avoid responsibility for their fault. This principle threatens both exemption clauses which deal with negligence (see, *e.g.* the decision in *George Mitchell*, p.147, the thinking of the minority in *The Eurymedon*, p.89, and of the majority in *Howard Marine*, p.161) and indemnity clauses which purport to pass on the risk of negligence liability (see, *e.g. Smith v South Wales Switchgear Ltd*, 1978, and *Phillips v Hyland*, p.149 and for the tensions exhibited in judicial treatment of indemnity clauses, see Adams and Brownsword, 1982 and 1988b).

(11) The paternalistic principle: contractors who enter into imprudent agreements may be relieved from their bargains where justice so requires. The case for paternalistic relief is at its most compelling where the party is weak or naive (see, *e.g. Cresswell v Potter*, p.116, *Lloyds Bank Ltd v Bundy*, p.117, *Schroeder v Macaulay*, p.117 *et seq.*). Although the consumer-welfarist line on common mistake and frustration suggests a general concern to cushion the effects of harsh bargains, it is an open question to what extent consumer-welfarists would push the paternalistic principle for the benefit of commercial contractors.

As we have seen, some of these ideas can generate novel doctrines such as equitable estoppel and unconscionability. However, consumer-welfarism also attempts to feed reasonableness into existing contractual categories. Thus, consumer-welfarists would like to see categories such as implied terms, mistake, and frustration grounded in reasonableness, in order to open the door to the employment of the particular principles of the ideology. Lord Denning's attempts to make such a move in respect of implied terms and frustration have failed, but the equitable doctrine of common mistake continues to enjoy some support. The most spectacular success has been with exemption clauses which are generally regulated under a regime of reasonableness by UCTA.

Now that consumer-welfarists have a secure base, the question is how they will operationalise their discretion. We have suggested that consumer-welfarists will not always agree about the application of the reasonableness requirement. We can assume that they will uniformly continue with the principle of a fair deal for consumers, but we can expect a division of opinion with regard to commercial contracts. Some consumer-welfarists will observe the limitations built into the principle of exploitation. This means that, because commercial contractors are assumed to be roughly equal in terms of bargaining strength, the courts will refrain from interfering with their arrangements. Such thinking parallels the market-individualist inspired approach in *Photo Production* (p.144). Against this, however, some consumer-welfarists will give priority to the principle of responsibility for fault. This means that, even though commercial contracts are not seen as exploitative, it is thought to be unreasonable to use contractual provisions to avoid liability for fault.

Consumer-welfarism suffers from its pluralistic scheme of principles. Where a dispute clearly falls under just one of its principles, there is no difficulty; but as soon as more than one principle is relevant, there is potentially a conflict. Without a rigid hierarchy of principles, the outcome of such conflicts will be unpredictable, as different judges will attach different weights to particular principles. It follows that consumer-welfarism is unlikely ever to attain the consistency or calculability of its market-individualist rival.

2. THE RELATIONSHIPS BETWEEN THE IDEOLOGIES

The ideologies exert their distinctive individual influences, but they do not operate in isolation from one another. We must attempt, therefore, to understand the dynamics of the ideologies viewed as a set. To structure our brief discussion, we will hypothesise, first, a market-individualist rule-book and then a rule-book (such as the contemporary one) where market-individualist doctrines have had to give considerable ground to consumer-welfarist ideas.

(i) A market-individualist rule-book

Where the rule-book encapsulates market-individualist values, formalist judges have market-individualism in tow. It is not that they are setting out to apply market-individualist values;

they simply cannot avoid doing so. By the same token, market-individualist realist judges, who do seek to promote market-individualism, will often find that the traditional application of the rule-book will do the trick. Accordingly, where the rule-book has a market-individualist content, genuine formalists will unintentionally advance market-individualism while market-individualist realists can produce desired results by posing as formalists.

A market-individualist rule-book presents difficulties for consumer-welfarist realists: traditional rules and concepts must be played down, the merits of cases emphasised, novel ideas employed, etc. This does not mean that consumer-welfarist realists only become realists when the rule-book is against them; it simply means that judges working across the grain of the rule-book will tend to show their true realist colours.

One must not, however, overstate the difficulties for consumer-welfarist realists. Whilst Lord Denning in particular often worked in a conspicuously realist fashion, consumer-welfarist judges have also worked in a less overt manner. On occasion, the rule-book applied to the letter will assist consumer-welfarism. Thus, some of the most notable consumer-protection cases have hinged on a strict application of the market-individualist rules concerning the incorporation of terms by reasonable notice or by previous dealings (see, *e.g. Olley v Marlborough Court Hotel Ltd.*, 1949, and *Thornton*, p.61). In one such case, *McCutcheon v David MacBrayne Ltd* (1964), where the House of Lords protected the appellant consumer against the respondent ferry operator's standard terms, Lord Devlin could scarcely conceal his satisfaction:

> "If the respondents had remembered to issue a risk note in this case, they would have invited your Lordships to give a curt answer to any complaint by the appellant. He might say that the terms were unfair and unreasonable . . . The respondents would expect him to be told that he had made his contract and must abide by it. Now the boot is on the other foot. It is just as legitimate, but also just as vain, for the respondents to say that it was only a slip on their part, that it is unfair and unreasonable of the appellant to take advantage of it and that he knew perfectly well that they never carried goods except on conditions. The law must give the same answer: they must abide by the contract which they made. What is sauce for the goose is sauce for the gander." (*ibid.* at pp.438–9.)

However, such occasional opportunities for turning the tables are not, in the final analysis, the main opening for covert realist consumer-welfarism. The point is that contract, in its traditional form, operates with numerous doctrines and distinctions which rest on the intention of the parties (see, *e.g.* the distinctions between offers and invitations to treat, and between non-contractual and contractual representations; the idea of an intention to create legal relations; the doctrine of implied terms; and the various principles of construction relevant to the interpretation of contracts). Such intention-based categories enable consumer-welfarists to pursue consumer-welfarist objectives under the cover of the rule-book. It is important to appreciate, therefore, that consumer-welfarist realists can appear to adhere to surprisingly large sections of a market-individualist rule-book. Of course, the attraction of imitating a formalist approach, for both market-individualist and consumer-welfarist realists, is that it avoids unnecessarily drawing formalist criticism.

(ii) A hybrid rule-book (reflecting both market-individualism and consumer-welfarism)

Where the hybrid rule-book is decisive on a particular point, formalist judges will apply the rule-book with whatever values it happens to have in tow. However, because formalists have a predilection for clear rules rather than open-ended discretions, they will endeavour to convert the discretionary principles at the heart of consumer-welfarism into a set of rules of thumb. Where the rule-book is unclear, in the sense that both market-individualist and consumer-welfarist doctrines can lay claim to authority (*cf. e.g.* the law of common mistake), the conservatism of formalists will incline them towards the traditional market-individualist rules.

For market-individualist realists, the hybrid rule-book is, of course, less helpful than the market-individualist rule-book. The traditional market-individualist doctrines of the rule-book must be defended—the formalists can be expected to assist in this respect—against consumer-welfarist encroachment (*e.g.* as with the principle of unconscionability); and where consumer-welfarism has already achieved a firm grip on the rule-book, damage must be limited by bringing consumer-welfarist doctrines, wherever possible, into alignment with market-individualist values.

Just as it is easy to overrate the constraints imposed upon consumer-welfarist realists by a market-individualist rule-book, it is a mistake to imagine that market-individualist realists will constantly be forced into the open by the consumer-welfarist doctrines of a hybrid rule-book. If consumer-welfarists can infiltrate intention-based rules, then market-individualists can certainly infiltrate reasonableness-based doctrines. Indeed, as we have seen, market-individualists have already set in motion a defensive strategy against UCTA by promoting the idea that it is unreasonable to interfere with consensual and insurance-efficient commercial arrangements.

From the standpoint of consumer-welfarist realists, the hybrid rule-book represents a definite advance. The consumer-welfarist side of the rule-book must be consolidated and the attack intensified against the remaining market-individualist doctrines. Obviously, no assistance can be expected from the market-individualists; but the formalists might at least make a small contribution to the consolidation work.

(iii) Natural affinities

The picture so far suggests nothing more than occasional alliances between the ideologies, conditioned by the contingent content of the rule-book. In particular, the extensional similarity between formalism and market-individualism appears to hinge on a market-individualist rule-book. It is possible, however, to discern certain features of the ideologies which create a natural affinity, on the one hand between formalism and market-individualism, and on the other between realism and consumer-welfarism. (For a seminal discusson of the relationship between private law *form*—general rules or equitable standards—and *substance*—individualism or altruism—see Kennedy, 1976).

Consider, first, formalism and market-individualism. As we have seen, market-individualist realists will not shrink from putting the rule-book to one side where it obstructs commercial convenience (*e.g.* in *Williams v Roffey*, p.78, and in *The Eurymedon*, p.89).

Nevertheless, they cannot encourage unbridled realism, for this would be to invite the destruction of certainty and predictability so essential to market-individualism. Market-individualist realists, therefore, must exercise their realism with restraint, departing from the rule-book only where it is judged that the market needs change more than it needs continuity. Now, formalist judges seek a rule-book which has just the sort of clear rules generally favoured by market-individualists. It follows that formalists must find it easier to work with market-individualism than with consumer-welfarism. There is, therefore, a natural affinity between formalism and market-individualism for, irrespective of the content of the rule-book, both ideologies favour a particular form of rule-book (comprising clear, general, non-discretionary rules) and a particular style of judging (basically directed towards the routine application of general rules).

Converse considerations suggest a natural affinity between realism and consumer-welfarism. Both ideologies favour a flexible rule-book giving judges discretion to accommodate the particular circumstances surrounding a dispute. Naturally, this militates against setting down rules which will settle disputes irrespective of their particular characteristics. In a sense, the whole thrust of consumer-welfarism is to point judges in a realist direction, by insisting that decisions should be fair and reasonable in the particular circumstances.

(iv) Synthesis

To sum up, the relationships between the ideologies are conditioned by the natural affinities and by the contingent content of the rule-book. Formalism and market-individualism have a common concern with clarity, certainty, and predictability in the rule-book and its application, realism and consumer-welfarism a common concern with the availability of judicial discretion, doctrinal flexibility and with the importance of getting the right result in particular cases.

Where the rule-book embodies market-individualist values, *formalists* will unintentionally, as it were, implement market-individualism; *market-individualist realists* will generally find it prudent and natural to ape a formalist approach, but, where the rule-book is judged to be in need of revision, they must be careful not to encourage realism backed by consumer-welfarism; and *consumer-welfarist realists*, although working across the grain of the rule-book, will often be able to ape formalism.

Where the rule-book shifts from market-individualism to consumer-welfarism, *formalists* will apply the clear rules (thereby aiding market-individualism or consumer-welfarism as the case may be), will attempt to "formalise" consumer-welfarist discretions, and, where the rule-book is equivocal, will prefer the traditional (market-individualist) rules.

Market-individualist realists will attempt to defend their traditional doctrines, to infiltrate encroaching consumer-welfarist doctrines, and to revise the rule-book in the interests of commerce without encouraging further consumer-welfarist realism. *Consumer-welfarist realists* will support and develop the consumer-welfarist features of the rule-book, and, with increasing legitimacy, they will be able to apply consumer-welfarism more openly.

For those who wish to take the temperature of contract in the early years of the twenty-first century, these ideological patterns suggest that the advance of consumer-welfarism will be retarded, both by formalist caution and by market-individualist cunning. However, as we shall see in Part III, there is more to the modern transformation of contract than the incremental progress of consumer-welfarism in the courts.

PART III

THE RULE-BOOK AND THE TRANSFORMATION OF CONTRACT

9

CONTRACT TRANSFORMED

If contract were the type of phenomenon which could be photographed, and if we had a photographic record of contract running back over the last two hundred years or so, what changes, if any, would we see? Many commentators believe that, like the London skyline, contract has changed significantly in this period. In this chapter, we examine the views of some of these commentators.

There is a preliminary problem, however, which we must confront. How are we to specify the field of contract for the purpose of recording change? We could continue to take the rule-book as traditionally conceived as our focus, in which case it would be the transformation of the rule-book which would set the bounds of our enquiry. But this would not assist the enquiry which we have in mind. It would be somewhat analogous to regarding the London skyline as consisting only of the skyline to be found within the square mile of the City. Just as we suppose that the skyline outside the City is important in considering the transformation of the London skyline as a whole, so we must suppose that developments beyond the covers of the rule-book are a vital part of the transformation of contract. Therefore, to facilitate our enquiry, we must abandon the traditional concept of contract. We must consider the general enterprise of regulating agreements together with its concomitant practice and institutional apparatus. It is the transformation of contract in this broader sense which is our focus. It is, however, pertinent to ask in relation to some of the writers covered in this section whether or not they are according unjustified primacy to the law as defined in the rule-book, and are therefore in a sense intellectual casualties of it.

This chapter has modest ambitions. At this stage, we do not attempt to relate the movements described to the development of the political economy as a whole, nor to consider how they might be theorised. Questions of this order are reserved for the next chapter.

1. THE TRANSFORMATION OF CONTRACT: A PASTICHE

There is no shortage of opinion about the nature of the transformation undergone by contract over the last two centuries or so (see, *e.g.* Collins, 1993; Wilhelmsson, 1993). Quite apart from a large body of American writing, two Oxford professors (Atiyah, 1978; Treitel, 1981) focused on this topic in their respective inaugural lectures. In this section, we put together a pastiche of views as a way of forming a general impression of the character of the alleged changes. Our starting point is a theory which has enjoyed considerable vogue, that of the American jurist Morton Horwitz (1977).

Horwitz's thesis runs roughly as follows. In the eighteenth century private law was "benign", reflecting the assumptions of a premarket economy. Its function was to impose a natural, objectively just order upon society. By a variety of mechanisms, the law was adapted in the nineteenth century to legitimate and facilitate the inequalities of a market economy in which entrepreneurs flourished, and the weak suffered. Before the change, the justification of contracts was the inherent justice and fairness of the exchange. It was assumed that things had a proper price or value, which did not depend solely upon market forces. Contract was primarily a mechanism for transferring property, not a mechanism for securing expectation. However, in the last quarter of the eighteenth century, the idea took hold that the source of contractual obligation was not the justice of the bargain, but the convergence of the wills of the parties. A humane body of law was thereby converted into a weapon of oppression. This process was assisted by "formalism", which arose *circa* 1825–30, gathered momentum in the 1840s, and developed strongly after 1850. The concept of "formalism" adopted by Horwitz seems more or less to correspond to our own ideal type outlined earlier (pp.185–187).

By contrast to what emerged in the nineteenth century, the eighteenth-century "equitable" theory of contract was essentially antagonistic to the interests of the commercial classes. The courts did not fully recognise executory contracts, did not award expectation damages, and accepted the inadequacy of consideration as a ground for refusing specific performance. There was a "substantive doctrine of consideration" under which juries were instructed to reduce damages where consideration was deemed to be inadequate. There was an implied warranty of quality where the price was at least the normal one for goods. Moreover, counts in express and implied contract could be joined.

We may gloss this thesis with a quotation from another American jurist, Lawrence Friedman (1965, pp.20–1):

"[Classical] contract law is abstraction—what is left in the law relating to agreements when all particularities of person and subject-matter are removed . . . The abstraction of classical contract law is not unrealistic; it is a deliberate renunciation of the particular, a deliberate relinquishment of the temptation to restrict untrammeled individual autonomy or the completely free market in the name of social policy. The law of contract is, therefore, roughly coextensive with the free market. Liberal nineteenth-century economics fits in neatly with the law of contracts so viewed . . . In fact, there was never any point at which the law of contract corresponded exactly with such an economic theory. But in a rough way, the rise and fall of the law of contract paralleled the rise and fall of liberal economics as a working philosophy."

This passage reflects the view of another American jurist, Willard Hurst (1956), likening nineteenth-century contract law to a releaser of individual energy, and we may recall Sir Henry Maine's famous dictum that "the movement of the progressive societies has hitherto been a movement from Status to Contract" (1861), which is to be understood in the context of his optimistic view of contract as a mechanism of social improvement.

The Horwitz thesis takes the story no further than the nineteenth century. For a continuation of the tale we can draw on the views of Wolfgang Friedmann (1972, Chapter 4). According to Friedmann, the movement from status to contract persists up to a point, but the overall trend of the twentieth century is a reversal from contract to status. The reduction of an individual to a status position can be seen particularly where collective bargaining takes place in industry and where contracts are standardised. This reversal, however, is not the only significant development in the recent history of contract. Friedmann also notes the moves made by governments to regulate contracts, for example the protection of consumers and employees. One of the hallmarks of the twentieth century, according to Friedmann, is the legislative erosion of freedom of contract, and a dawning recognition of the falsity of the assumption of equality between the parties which underpinned the classical law. For Friedmann, however, more significant even than these major developments is the burgeoning of public sector contracting. Government emerged in the twentieth century as a major contracting party in its own right. Instead of the state acting simply as an umpire arbitrating disputes arising between contractors in the private sector, government itself became a major contractor with parties in the private sector. Subsequently, of course, the "contractualisation" of the public sector itself was to blur the line between the public and the private (see further, below at p.223).

To this broad picture of transformation we will now add a few further ideas.

Lawrence Friedman (1965) suggested that the role of contract declined in the twentieth century, and that as the role of the courts and contract declined, the courts became less initiators of economic policy and more adjusters of private disputes arising on the periphery of commercial exchange, *i.e.* more consumer-welfarist, in our terminology. The courts sought to achieve fairness on the particular facts of those cases fortuitously presented to them for decision.

Friedman's view that modern courts are less concerned with policy-setting than with the adjustment of individual disputes corresponds very closely with the thesis of one of the leading English commentators, Patrick Atiyah (1978b). According to Atiyah, whereas the courts of the nineteenth century were concerned with laying down general rules which would serve to encourage or discourage particular forms of behaviour, the courts of the twentieth century narrowed their function to producing what they regarded as just results to particular cases (given the particular circumstances of individual disputes). In this sense, there was a marked shift from "principle" to "pragmatism". Moreover, this shift can to some extent be put down to a changing perception of the relationship between Parliament and the courts. The trend is not, however, confined to judicial decisions, for statutes too reflect the move away from principle.

Atiyah's acccount is supplemented by his Oxford colleague, Guenter Treitel (1981), who argues that from mid-century there was a significant move from "doctrine" to "discretion" in the law of contract. By this he means that reasonably precise dispositive rules gave way to judicial discretion (understood broadly as embracing vague, open-textured legal materials). According to Treitel, the courts contributed to this change in a number of ways. For instance, judges modified the rigid distinction between conditions and warranties, extended the principle of duress, and recognised "exceptional case" escape clauses. A number of precise rules were generalised under a broad principle, such as frustration, and Lord Denning's principle of equitable relief in mistake cases. The legislature contributed to this development by enacting various measures which allowed the courts to act as it appeared to them to be just and reasonable.

Another gloss on the essential transformation outlined by Friedman, Atiyah, and Treitel is offered by the Finnish scholar Thomas Wilhelmsson (1992). As Wilhelmsson astutely observes, the "contracting parties" of the classical law of contract take on a more particular specification in the modern law. In the modern law, it is a matter of some importance whether one is dealing as a "consumer" or as a "commercial" contractor; equally, one's ability as a "layman" or as an "expert" in relation to a particular contract may be significant. Indeed, in what Wilhelmsson characterises as a movement towards a need-oriented regime, the individual circumstances and biographies of disputants (as distinct from their membership of a particular class, *e.g.* consumers) increasingly feature in the rhetoric of the law of contract. Hence, for example, the dispute in *Lloyd's Bank v Bundy* (p.117) was no mere dispute between contracting parties—it was a dispute between a bank and one of its customers, old Mr Bundy, who was in danger of losing his farmhouse.

Whilst few doubt that contract has undergone some kind of transformation, the American writer, Grant Gilmore (1974), has gone one step further by advancing the provocative view that "contract is dead". According to the "death of contract" school of thinking, the classical law was something of a myth—in fact, a precarious formalist edifice constructed on the cornerstone idea of consideration in the sense of a "bargained-for exchange". With the growth of reliance enforcement, the centrality of exchange has been undermined and the classical myth has been destroyed.

To complete this pastiche, we can note the views of two more American writers, Peter Gabel and Jay Feinman (1982). For Gabel and Feinman, the crucial function of contract law is not to enforce bargains, or to resolve disputes arising under agreements, rather it is to project a series of utopian images of the social world, which serve to divert attention from the oppressive nature of social relations. To this extent, contract has not changed. However, its utopian imagery has been transformed. Very much in line with the Horwitz-Friedmann picture, Gabel and Feinman suggest that the prevailing imagery in the eighteenth century was of a hierarchical social order in which a person's particular position was governed by "nature", custom and religion. In the "classical" period of contract in the nineteenth century, contract projected an order of free and equal citizens pursuing their interests by voluntarily entering into contractual transactions. Moving into the twentieth century, however, the image changes once more. Now, contract portrays the social order as a co-operative alliance between various interest groups, in which the state regulates transactions, redistributes wealth, and generally co-ordinates the common goal of building a fair society. And, if we were to extend this kind of analysis into the coming century, as we have already remarked, the emerging image seems to be one of global markets and consumer rights, but with a hard edge emphasising individual responsibility.

2. ANALYSING THE TRANSFORMATION

The advantage of a pastiche is that it quickly conveys the sense of changes supposed to have been taking place in contract. Its weakness, however, is that the image it presents is impressionistic. We must therefore attempt to sharpen the picture.

Three aspects of the transformation appear to be central. These concern: (1) changes in the rule-book itself; (2) changes in institutional role; and (3) changes in the relationship between the state, the individual and the institution of contract. If we can focus more clearly on these ingredients, we should have a better view of the transformation.

(i) Changes in the rule-book

Rule-book transformations seem to be central for several commentators, but the perceived changes do not uniformly relate to a single feature of the rule-book. For Horwitz and Gilmore, for example, it is the substantive doctrines of the rule-book which are the focus of attention; for Treitel (and to some extent Atiyah and Wilhelmsson), however, it is more the style of the rule-book which is their concern. For writers who emphasise the increasing statutory regulation of agreements it is the balance or composition of the rule-book which is the critical feature. So the transformation thesis is not simply that the rule-book has changed, but that it has changed in a number of specific and distinct respects.

Subject to two qualifications, one general, one specific, we can accept the general thrust of the suggested rule-book transformations as being in principle applicable to England, assuming they are applicable at all. The general qualification is that statements of broad trends of the above kind are inevitably vulnerable to the objection that they do not fit with particular historical detail. Thus Horwitz's characterisation of English contract law in the eighteenth century is to this extent suspect (see Simpson, 1979), as is the status-to-contract characterisation of the nineteenth century (see MacDonagh, 1980). Therefore, if we are to accept the general picture, we must not look too carefully at some of the details. The specific *caveat* concerns Gilmore's thesis that the traditional exchange model of consideration has given way to a reliance model of enforcement. As we will see, this thesis can only be applied in England with some considerable reservation.

Gilmore's views are generated by exploring the tensions between para. 75 of the American *Restatement of Contracts 2d*, which defines consideration in the traditional exchange (or bargain) terms, and para. 90 which provides:

> "A promise which the promisor should reasonably expect to induce action or forbearance on the part of the promisee . . . and which does induce such action or forbearance is binding if injustice can be avoided only by enforcement of the promise. The remedy granted for breach may be limited as justice requires."

Gilmore's thesis is that para. 75 has yielded to para. 90. Two well-known American cases will suffice to indicate the sort of change Gilmore has in mind. In *Hoffman v Red Owl Stores* (1965) the Hoffmans, who were small town bakers, sold their business and moved to a new town on the strength of a representation by a Red Owl supermarket chain representative that if they fulfilled certain conditions they would be granted a franchise. Negotiations for the franchise broke down when Red Owl unexpectedly increased the amount of capital that the Hoffmans were required to put into the store. In line with para. 90, the court ruled that injustice could only be avoided if the Hoffmans were awarded their reliance losses as compensation for the defendants' failure to keep their promise. Similarly, in *Drennan v Star Paving Company* (1958), the California Supreme Court held that a sub-contractor's quotation to a main contractor was binding where the latter had reasonably relied upon the bid in computing his own tender.

Although, as we have said, a principle of reasonable reliance can be detected in the consumer-welfarist approach, it would be misleading to suggest that English contract doctrine embodies as explicit a notion of reliance enforcement as that represented by para. 90. The simplest way of taking stock of English law in this respect is to recall its treatment of: (a) reliance on agreed variations to contracts, and (b) pre-contractual reliance.

In relation to the former, the most significant developments in the modern law are the doctrine of promissory estoppel (seminally in *High Trees*) and the weakening of the consideration requirement (notably in *Williams v Roffey*). Whilst the similarities between the text of para. 90 and the standard formulations of the promissory estoppel principle are undeniable, it must not be forgotten that English judges often display a formalist nervousness about extending the range of the principle, preferring to deal with variation problems in terms of consideration. Of course, now that *Williams v Roffey* has redefined the traditional understanding of consideration (and, with it, the notion of exchange), the need to put the protection of the promisee on the ground of reasonable reliance might have passed.

In relation to questions of pre-contractual reliance, the position is a little more complex. Consumer-welfarists obviously have sympathy for parties who reasonably rely on expected contracts (see, *e.g.* the approach of the Court of Appeal in *Gibson v Manchester City Council*) and, in principle, there are a number of protective resources available—for instance, the English courts might follow the Australian example (see *Walton's Stores (Interstate) Ltd. v Maher* (1988)) and extend the application of the doctrine of equitable estoppel to situations of pre-contractual reliance. The simplest response, however, is to employ collateral contracts in a flexible way. For example, if a client sends a "letter of intent" to a party, P, who has tendered for some work, indicating in the letter that the client's intention is to award the contract to P and encouraging P to proceed with the work, it is easy enough to imply a collateral contract to protect P's reasonable reliance on the letter of intent (should the main contract, in fact, fail to materialise) (*cf. British Steel Corpn. v Cleveland Bridge and Engineering Co Ltd.* (1984)). The potential of this kind of response is nicely illustrated by *Blackpool and Fylde Aero Club v Blackpool Borough Council* (1990), where the defendant council had invited tenders for an airport concession, the tenders having to be submitted by a particular date. The plaintiff club submitted a tender in due time. However, due to an error on the part of the defendant, the plaintiff's tender was incorrectly marked as having being received late and, in consequence, it did not get considered. The airport concession was duly awarded to another bidder. Although it was unclear whether the plaintiff's tender would have been successful had it been considered, the very fact that it had not been considered was seen by the Court of Appeal as an injustice in itself:

> "[W]here, as here, tenders are solicited from selected parties all of them known to the invitor, and where a local authority's invitation prescribes a clear, orderly and familiar procedure ... the invitee is in my judgment protected at least to this extent: if he submits a conforming tender before the deadline he is entitled, not as a matter of mere expectation but of contractual right, to be sure that his tender will after the deadline be opened and considered in conjunction with all other conforming tenders or at least that his tender will be considered if others are." (*per* Bingham L.J. at p.30)

In short, the council, by failing to comply with its own tendering rules, was in breach of contract. Clearly, if the English courts were prepared to follow the lead given in the *Blackpool* case, they would have no difficulty in protecting the promisees in a case like *Hoffman v Red Owl Stores*. Nevertheless, some caution must be exercised here, for it is not clear that the English courts' occasional protective interventions in pre-contractual dealings can be put on precisely the same footing as the para. 90 jurisdiction—it is arguable, for example, that intervention in the *Blackpool* case was aimed at protecting legitimate or reasonable expectation rather than detrimental reasonable reliance (see Adams and Brownsword, 1991).

It is important to note that what Gilmore and the other writers are seeking to provide is not a chronicle of change in the sense of a bare list of rules which have come and gone in the rule-book, but rather what they regard as systematic rule-book changes. Thus, if we look at the various doctrinal changes occurring between the eighteenth and nineteenth century, particularly the decline of any doctrine of substantive fairness, the Horwitz-Gabel and Feinman thesis is that these doctrinal changes were required for the furtherance of commercial enterprise. For Atiyah, the decline of the equitable discretions was simply the decline of pragmatism in the face of rising principle. Or again, if we move on to consider the changes in the rule-book over the last hundred years, no one supposes that they are unpatterned. In terms of our discussion in Part II of this book, we might characterise such developments as a shift from market-individualism to consumer-welfarism; or, following Atiyah, as a recovery for pragmatism at the expense of principle; or, following Treitel, as a move from doctrine to discretion, and so on. Faced with such various interpretations of the transformation of contract, we are driven on to the question addressed in the next chapter: "How are we to describe and explain legal and social change?"

(ii) Changes in institutional role

For some commentators, the most striking feature of the transformation of contract lies in changes in institutional role as much as in changes in the rule-book. It is interesting in this respect to compare the views of Atiyah with those of Gabel and Feinman.

Atiyah's "principles to pragmatism" thesis makes a presupposition and a claim. The presupposition is that legal institutions (like legislatures and courts) primarily play one or both of two roles: they are concerned either with dispute settlement or with what Atiyah calls the "hortatory" function, namely the provision of incentives and disincentives for various types of behaviour. This presupposition underlies Atiyah's claim about the shift, first, from pragmatism to principle, and then back again. At both levels, Atiyah's views are plausible. First, his presupposition about the functions of legal institutions fits neatly with the widely accepted "law jobs" theory propounded by Karl Llewellyn (1940). According to Llewellyn's theory, the two principal functions for legal institutions are the disposition of the "trouble case" (compare Atiyah's dispute settlement function), and the preventive channelling of behaviour (compare Atiyah's hortatory function). Secondly, there is plenty of evidence to support Atiyah's claim that in the superior English courts the pendulum has indeed swung from pragmatism to principle and back again. To confirm the latter swing, it is necessary only to refer back to Part II of this book. Quite how far Atiyah's claim holds for legislation in England is rather more questionable. Making certain contractual provisions void and unenforceable (see, *e.g.* the Unfair Contract Terms Act 1977) or certain trading practices illegal as criminal offences (see, *e.g.* the Trade Descriptions Act 1968 and orders made under s.22 of the Fair Trading Act 1973 (prior to its repeal by the Enterprise Act 2002)) look more like attempts at deterrence *per se*. Nevertheless, in general Atiyah's thesis has a great deal to be said for it.

In contrast, the thesis presented by Gabel and Feinman rests on rather different presuppositions. Whilst these writers do not quite repudiate the conventional wisdom about the functions of legal institutions, they imply that such institutions are not really in the business of dispute settlement and general regulation. Their assumption is that legal institutions principally have the function of projecting a favourable image of the social order (which image conceals the reality of the unjust ordering of social relations). In other words, the fundamental function of legal institutions is to "legitimate" the existing social order. The implication of this appears to be that we might accept the validity of both Atiyah's and Gabel and Feinman's theses, but that if we are with Gabel and Feinman, we must regard Atiyah's observations as in some sense missing the point.

Some readers may be tempted to reject out of hand Gabel and Feinman's views as fanciful. However, this would be a mistake. The point is that both Atiyah and Gabel and Feinman employ a theoretical framework which *inter alia* makes certain assumptions about the functions of legal institutions. The fact that we may be more receptive to one set of assumptions than another is irrelevant, and indeed dangerous. If we are to have a critical understanding of the transformation of contract, we cannot afford to reject the views of either Atiyah or Gabel and Feinman until we have reflected a little on the problems of theorising about legal and social change discussed in the next chapter.

(iii) Changes in the relationship between the state, the individual and the institution of contract

The transformations so far described, whilst major, at least seem to be confined to the traditional realm of contract. Wolfgang Friedmann's account of modern government's participation in contract, however, points to a different order of change. It is not simply that legislatures have taken a greater responsibility for the regulation of agreements; government's involvement as a contracting party and the institutional apparatus which goes with the new regulation indicate a shift in the whole framework of contract. Moreover, Friedmann was not to foresee that in Thatcherite England the contractualisation of the public sector (along with privatisation and marketisation) was to become an article of New Right political faith.

To take account of government acting as a contractor, we need a new focusing typology of contracts. At a minimum, we must discriminate between non-government and government contracts as follows:

    (a) "non-government" contracts, *i.e.* where neither party makes the contract as an agent of government (that is, neither

party acts on behalf of a central government department, a local authority, or a public corporation, or the like);
and,

(b) "government" contracts, *i.e.* where one party makes the
contract as an agent of government, and the other does not.

This scheme is minimal because it makes no provision for
intra-governmental contracts (*i.e.* contracts wholly within the
public sector, where both parties contract as agents of government). Accordingly, before we deal with cross-sector government contracts (*i.e.* contracts between public sector and private
sector contractors) we need to speak briefly to the idea of intra-
governmental contracts.

In principle, there is no reason why one agency within the public sector should not purchase goods or services from another
agency within the public sector (nor why one department of a public sector organisation should not trade with another department
of the same organisation). Thus, for many years, local authorities
have procured goods and services in-house or from other local
authorities. Moreover, even with the introduction of Compulsory
Competitive Tendering, and its successor, Best Value, local authority direct labour organisations may succeed in winning local
authority contracts. Similarly, the internal market for health services could be viewed as an attempt to mimic private sector contracting within the public sector (although it should be noted that
s.4(3) of the National Health Service and Community Care Act,
1990, provides that NHS contracts "shall not be regarded for any
purpose as giving rise to contractual rights and liabilities").
Elsewhere in the public sector, contract has been put to a rather different use. For example, although the Framework Documents
associated with the Next Steps initiative, which represent a com-
pact between central Government Departments and agencies serv-
icing those Ministries, have been described as quasi-contractual,
their essential function is to enhance the quality of public management. Clearly, the contractualisation of the public sector is an idea
whose time has come, but the implications of this multi-faceted
development remain uncertain (see Harden, 1992; Campbell and
Vincent-Jones, 1996; Deakin and Michie, 1997).

To return to our distinction between non-government and government contracts, and combining this with our original threefold
classification of private, consumer, and commercial contracts, our
new focusing typology is thus:

non-government contracts	*government contracts*
(i) private	(i) consumer
(ii) consumer	(ii) commercial
(iii) commercial	

Within this typology, there would be no instance of a private government contract. This would be precluded by the implication that a party acting as an agent of government acts in the course of a business. We can, however, consider the case of consumer and commercial government contracts.

By a *consumer government* contract, we mean a contract under which private sector consumers procure goods or services supplied by a public sector agency. Prior to the privatisation programme of modern governments, a good deal of private consumption, particularly of the utilities, fitted the description of consumer government contracting. In many respects, the consumer experience of such contracting was little different to the experience of dealing with monopolistic enterprises in the private sector. Consumers could no more negotiate the terms with Electricity, Gas, or Water Authorities, or with British Rail, than they could with private sector equivalents. Predictably, privatisation has made little difference. Tariffs, for example, are imposed and standardised; and, in general, regulation in the interests of the consumer is catered for, not by private law mechanisms such as the law of contract, but by public regulatory agencies (Ofwat, Offer, Ofgas, etc.). Given that the privatised utilities have a statutory duty to supply, and given the nature of the regulatory regime surrounding the operation of the utility companies, the break with government contracting is less than complete. Indeed, privatisation notwithstanding, we might well treat the utility companies as agents of government and continue to characterise domestic consumption of the utilities as pursuant to consumer government contracts.

Although routine consumer dealing with large enterprises in the private sector bears some resemblance to routine consumer dealing with large public sector or privatised enterprises, there is one important difference. If, say, a private sector removal company fails to collect or deliver a customer's goods as agreed, in principle at least, there is a contractual remedy. However, in the case of public authorities, there may be special provisions, even to the point of removing the transaction altogether from the sphere of contract. The Post Office, for example, enjoyed a special immunity. As Lord Diplock explained in *Gouriet v Union of Post Office Workers* (1978):

> "The Post Office, its officers and servants enjoy a special immunity from liability in private law. So long as the Post Office continued to be a department of government [*i.e.* before it became a separate public authority in 1969], carriage by post of packets entrusted to the Post Office by subjects was not undertaken pursuant to any contract. Acceptance for transmission to the addressee gave rise to no contractual rights . . . This exclusion of contractual liability is preserved by s.9(4) of the Post Office Act 1969." (p.497)

Consider also, for instance, the case of *Willmore and Willmore (Trading as Lissenden Poultry) v South Eastern Electricity Board* (1957). Here, the plaintiffs applied to the defendants for electricity to be supplied to their poultry farm, explaining that the supply was needed to operate infra-red lamps, under which chicks would be reared, and emphasising the importance of there being a regular flow of electricity. Due to voltage fluctuations an abnormal number of the chicks were lost. The plaintiffs sued the defendants for breach of contract. With some regret, however, Glyn-Jones J. held that the plaintiffs' application for electricity was not contractual at all; rather, it was simply a case of the Board carrying out its "statutory duty to give a supply to a customer who, being entitled, demands it" (p.380). In principle, it seems, the defendants could have made a special contract outside their statutory duty, but to have proved this would have taken some extraordinarily strong evidence. In this respect, the Willmores' application for connection, albeit unusual, was still essentially a routine application to which the Board responded in the routine way. The moral of *Willmore*—that, where consumers routinely deal with government in what are superficially contractual situations, they do so in a special (status-like) capacity rather than as free contractors—is borne out by the later case-law. In the important case of *Pfizer Corp. v Ministry of Health* (1965), one of the questions that arose for decision before the House of Lords was how to characterise the supply of drugs under NHS prescription for (what was then) a nominal charge of two shillings. In a not entirely dissimilar context, we can assume that when Mrs Carlill bought her smoke-balls from the chemist, there was a contract; and (recalling the *Boots* case, above p.50) we can assume, too, that when Boots Cash Chemists supplied products under the supervision of the pharmacist, there was a contract. However, within the framework of the NHS scheme, was there a contract between the supplying pharmacist and the patient who paid the statutory charge? Giving the leading speech in *Pfizer*, Lord Reid, having identified "agreement" as essential for a contract, said that there was no room (nor need) for agreement where, on the one side, there was a statutory right to demand the drug on payment of the standard charge and, on the other side, a statutory obligation to supply. Lord Reid also pointed out that there was no scope for bargaining and that the charge was in no sense a market price. If, then, the transaction was not contractual, and neither was it a gift (because a charge was made), what precisely was it? According to Lord Upjohn, the transaction was one that was *sui generis*: it was, said his Lordship, simply "the creature of statute" (at p.552).

Their Lordships' remarks in *Pfizer* take us back to basics by suggesting that contracts are to be distinguished *inter alia* by a threshold level of voluntariness and agreement (in the sense that the parties at least have some control over the substance of the transaction). More recently, these fundamental elements of voluntariness and control were treated as critical in both *Norweb plc v Dixon* (1995) and *W v Essex CC* (1998). In the former, the Divisional Court applied *Pfizer* in ruling that the relationship between a public electricity supplier and a tariff customer was not contractual. As Dyson J. put it, "the legal compulsion both as to the creation of the relationship and the fixing of its terms is inconsistent with the existence of a contract" (at p.959). With regard to the former (compulsion as to the creation of the relationship), the electricity company was under a statutory obligation to supply if so requested; and, with regard to the latter (compulsion as to the fixing of the terms of supply), the principal terms, including the tariff, were set in accordance with the statutory scheme. Moreover, the statutory scheme, by allowing for special supply agreements—where what "is contemplated is a negotiated agreement to meet the particular requirements of a consumer" (*ibid.*)—only served to confirm the view that the relationship between public electricity suppliers and their tariff customers is to be characterised as statutory rather than contractual. Similarly, in the *Essex* case, the argument that a specialist foster care agreement (made between a council and foster parents) should be treated as contractual was rejected. Following *Norweb*, Stuart Smith L.J. said: "A contract is essentially an agreement that is freely entered into on terms that are freely negotiated. If there is a statutory obligation to enter into a form of agreement the terms of which are laid down, at any rate in their most important respects, there is no contract" (at p.128).

Accordingly, where consumers deal with government or privatised suppliers of public goods and services, they deal largely as status-holders rather than as contracting customers in the ordinary sense. This does not mean that they deal without any protection. At minimum, they can expect a degree of integrity on the other side (fortified, no doubt, by various kinds of customer charters (*cf.* Barron and Scott, 1992)). However, their ability to pursue *contractual* remedies may well be thwarted by our general conception of a contractual relationship as well as by special rule-book provisions—quite apart, that is, from the usual deterrents to private litigation (*cf.* Harvey and Parry, 1992, Chapter 4).

When we turn to *commercial government* contracts, the first thing to say is that government is an extremely big spender. The principal procuring departments of central government (*e.g.* Defence, Environment, Health and Social Security), with responsibilities for military equipment, weaponry, motorways, trunk roads, hospitals, etc. have colossal budgets for buying goods and services. Add to this, procurement by local authorities and by the nationalised industries (such as they are), and it will be evident that government is a major customer of the private sector.

According to Colin Turpin (1989), who is a leading authority on government contracts, the general principles of the law of contract have only a subsidiary or contingent application to public procurement from the private sector:

> "The classical law of contract which was formulated by nineteenth-century judges was a 'law of the market' . . . This law in general did not, and does not, make provision for the peculiar circumstances of government procurement, the unique relationship between the Government and its principal contractors, or the specific issues of the public interest that arise in government contracting. The need for particular legal rules adapted to the requirements of government procurement has been met in the United Kingdom by the regular use of appropriate standard conditions of contract."
> (p.105)

When problems arise in connection with government contracts, the preferred method of dispute resolution is informal negotiation and compromise rather than litigation. This is hardly surprising for, as Turpin reports, despite the radical changes in the aims and procedures of government contracting since 1979, "there still exists a 'procurement community' of purchasing departments and their major suppliers" (p.259). It must be remembered, too, that governments have various extra-legal sanctions to which they can resort (*e.g.* striking a contractor off the approved lists, or disallowing or reducing a contractor's agreed profit).

In the 1972 version of his book, Turpin characterised the relationship between the Government and its contractors as a kind of partnership. Perhaps the most striking aspect of this partnership was the convention of the fair and reasonable price.

There had been some particularly notorious cases of private companies making unjustifiable profits at the public expense. Friedmann, for example, cites the American case of *US v Bethlehem Steel Corporation* (1942) in which the majority of the Supreme Court applied classic contractual principles to reject the United States government's claim that Bethlehem had taken an unconscionable profit from shipbuilding contracts made during the First World War. More recently, in England, the Ferranti case (concerning the profits made by Ferranti on contracts for the production of electronic equipment for the Mark I Bloodhound missile) had achieved similar notoriety. This led to the setting up of the Review Board for Government Contracts, whose functions include reviewing the profit formula in government contracts and handling claims concerning excessive profits and unconscionable losses under certain individual contracts (see Turpin, 1989, Ch. 6). However, with the emphasis now on competitive tendering, the notion of the "fair and reasonable price" has had to yield to that of the price which promises the Government the best value for money (see Turpin, 1989, p.154). Moreover, a developing E.C. law of public procurement increasingly impinges on government commercial contracts (see Harden, 1992, Chapter 6).

We can sharpen these observations about government contracting by recalling that the classical law of contract was designed to regulate dealing within civil society. Granted, the state supplied the sanctioning apparatus that stood behind private sector transacting, but the line between public and private was tolerably clear. Now, the contractualisation of the public sector, public procurement and privatisation not only threaten to break the private sector's monopoly on contract, they tend to blur the line between public and private. Such a blurring has also arisen as a result of the recognition, in England and elsewhere, that private law remedial techniques simply are not adequate to the task of protecting consumers. Accordingly, we find agencies, like the Office of Fair

Trading, being given a special responsibility for the supervision of consumer contracting—nowhere more strikingly than in relation to the Unfair Terms in Consumer Contracts Regulations, where enforcement action by the OFT's Unfair Contract Terms Unit has already led to a great many standard contract terms being abandoned or amended (OFT, 1999) (and, for the Director General's first reported attempt to obtain injunctive relief under the Regulations, see *Director General of Fair Trading v First National Bank plc*, above at p.114). Although it is a very difficult calculation to make, one might at least wonder whether 10 years of concerted action by the OFT has achieved more in cleaning up unfair terms than nearly 30 years of sporadic individual consumer action under the Unfair Contract Terms Act.

Even before this latest flurry of activity by the OFT, Hugh Collins (1986), reflecting on developments of this kind, detected a "corporatist pattern of regulation" (p.204), comprising: the negotiation of agreed standards (in codes of practice and the like); state support for, and recognition of, such agreed practices (through agencies such as the OFT); dispute settlement through arbitration; and the use of the judiciary to monitor the conduct of the negotiating groups and the bureaucratic administrators. Whatever one makes of this, and of Collins' view that corporatism "offers a practical reconciliation between a successful market order and demands for distributive justice and an emancipating concept of freedom" (p.209), there can be little doubt that the extension of the state into the domain of consumer contracting further confounds the traditional simple model of contract law and polity.

The institutional transformation of contract leaves many matters unclear. It is unclear how far the private law of contract reaches into the public sphere and, in the light of the recently enacted Human Rights Act 1998, how far public law bills of rights impinge on private law (see above at p.120); it is unclear how far new public institutions are to take over the functions of the private law of contract; and it is unclear how the running tensions between the ideologies of market-individualism and consumer-welfarism are to be resolved. With so much unclear, there is a danger that we turn the transformation of contract into a "crisis" of one kind another (*cf.* Brownsword, 1993). However, even as we strive to get to grips with the modernisation of contract law, we find it being overtaken by another major development (namely, the "globalisation" of contract) and this is something that we must consider before traversing the difficult ground waiting for us in our final chapter.

3. THE GLOBALISATION OF CONTRACT

Globalisation as a charter for free trade and the lowering of barriers to commerce implies some significant changes for contract, both for the rules governing contracting and for the practice itself. If global markets are to be coherently regulated, there will need to be some doctrinal adjustment; contract law can no longer be quite so local. And, if global contractors are operating at a distance in electronic markets, regulation must be geared for environments of this kind. At one level, globalisation refers to the development of technologies that make it feasible for contractors to simulate face-to-face dealing even though they are physically separated by great distances (*e.g.* by using telephones and fax machines). Thinking about globalisation in such terms, it is the bringing together of sophisticated computer, telecommunications, and information technology to put in place a world-wide electronic marketplace that has most dramatically caught the imagination. As a recent report from the World Trade Organization (1998) has put it:

> "These modern technologies are being combined, especially through the Internet, to link millions of people in every corner of the world. Communications are increasingly unburdened from the constraints of geography and time. Information spreads more widely and more rapidly than ever before. Deals are struck, transactions completed, and decisions taken in a time-frame that would have seemed simply inconceivable a few years ago." (p.1)

At another level, globalisation refers to the various moves taken to harmonise the law regulating international commerce (see Schmitthoff, 1981; and, on the UNIDROIT Principles for International Commercial Contracts, see Furmston, 1996) and, in a shrinking world of contract, there is every prospect of such measures spreading to consumer dealings. Viewing such developments and initiatives, we might surmise that, as we stand at the cusp of the information society, contract law is liable to undergo a further (globalising) transformation.

Even if we think that such talk of a post-industrial transformation of contract is premature and speculative, there is no denying that, for over a quarter of a century, there has been a sustained attempt to harmonise contract law in Europe. A number of teams are now engaged in comparative studies of European contract law, including the Trento group's project on a "Common Core of European Private Law", where the strategy is to focus on agreement as to outcomes (so-called "result convergence") rather than an identity as to the doctrinal resources employed. However, the outstanding example of the attempt to articulate harmonised principles for a European law of contract is found in the work of the Lando Commission. Having begun its deliberations in the mid-1970s, the Commission published Part I of the *Principles of European Contract Law* in 1995 (Lando and Beale, 1995), with Part II being published some five years later. According to the Commission:

> "[The Principles] are available for immediate use by parties making contracts, by courts and arbitrators in deciding contract disputes and by legislators in drafting contract rules whether at the European or the national level. Their longer-term objective is to help bring about the harmonisation of general contract law within the European Community." (1995, p.xix)

As Lando deliberated, the European Parliament and Commission acted. We have already encountered the Directive on Unfair Terms in Consumer Contracts (above p.113) but this is just one of a raft measures designed to achieve the free movement of goods between the states constituting the European Economic Area and to standardise consumer protection law in the single European market. Thus, Directives have been issued on such various matters as doorstep selling (85/577), consumer credit (87/102, amended by 90/88), product liability (85/374), and package holidays (90/314). We can give a few further illustrations of the impact of European legislation on the domestic law of contract.

Europe, as elsewhere, needs a regional law to regulate electronic commerce, to facilitate contracting in electronic environments and to protect consumers. To some extent, the protection of consumers can be achieved by the Distance Contracts Directive (97/7, [1997] O.J. L144), which applies to contracts which make exclusive use of one or more means of "distance communication", that is, any means which, without the simultaneous physical presence of the supplier and the consumer, may be used for the conclusion of a contract between those parties. Amongst other things, the Directive requires (in Art. 4) that, prior to the conclusion of the contract, the consumer is to be supplied with information including the identity and address of the supplier, the main characteristics of the goods or services, the price, delivery costs, and the existence of a right to withdraw. Moreover, under Art. 4(2), such information is to be "provided in a clear and comprehensible manner in any way appropriate to the means of distance communication used, with due regard, in particular, to the principles of good faith in commercial transactions . . ." These requirements are underpinned by Art. 5(1) which stipulates that the consumer must receive written confirmation or "confirmation in another durable medium available and accessible to him" of the principal points referred to in Art. 4. If the information has not been given in this form prior to the conclusion of the contract, it must be given "in good time" during performance or, at the latest, at the time of delivery.

Whether or not the Distance Contracts Directive is wholly fit for the purpose of consumer protection in the context of Internet contracting is a moot point (see Brownsword and Howells, 1999). The Directive, it will be appreciated, was not specifically aimed at the latest forms of electronic commerce. At all events, the Community, recognising the importance of putting in place a regulatory framework that squarely addresses electronic commerce, soon adopted Directive 2000/31/EC (the "Directive on electronic commerce"). Broadly speaking, this Directive, which actually deals with a number of matters concerning the provision of "information society services", seeks to ensure (in Art. 9) that the local law of contract in Member States does not impede the development of electronic commerce and (in Arts 10 and 11) that consumers in particular are properly informed about the applicable on-line contracting procedure. In the UK, these requirements are reflected in the Electronic Communications Act 2000 (with regard to the removal of impediments) and in the implementing Regulations, the Electronic Commerce (EC Directive) Regulations 2002 (SI 2002/2013). Until on-line contracting becomes as familiar as off-line contracting, we can readily imagine how consumers might inadvertently place an order, clicking by accident or clicking several times without realising that each click signals a further order. In order to safeguard against this risk, Art. 10 of the Directive aims to ensure that, prior to placing an order, customers are informed as to the technical steps to be followed to conclude the contract as well as being told how to identify and correct input errors. Article 11.2 places an obligation on Member States to ensure that service providers make available to customers "appropriate, effective and accessible technical means allowing [them] to identify and correct input errors, prior to the placing of the order". Hence, the common reference to this legislation as the "double click Directive".

In its draft form (which we discussed in the previous edition of this book), the double click Directive aspired not only to regulate the placing of the order but also to determine at which point in the procedure the contract was formed. It will be recalled that, in English law, there is room for debate about the precise time at which an e-mailed or an on-line clicked acceptance will be effective to conclude a contract. With different default rules concerning the time of effective acceptance in different legal regimes in Europe, the attractions of establishing a settled rule are obvious. However, this proved one harmonising step too far and the Directive, as finally adopted, omitted the relevant proposals (and, in fact, where contracts are concluded exclusively by exchange of electronic mail, much of Arts 10 and 11 is not applicable anyway).

Had these draft proposals gone through, it seems that the contract would have been formed at the seller's place of business. Within the European Economic Area, this would not affect questions of jurisdiction, these being determined by applying the principles of the Brussels and Lugano Conventions (now enacted with certain changes by Regulation 44/2001); nor would this affect issues concerning the applicable law, these being governed by the rules laid down in the Rome Convention ([1980] O.J. L266) which was given effect to in the UK by the Contracts (Applicable Law) Act 1990. Briefly, the general rule is that a contract is to be governed by: (a) the law chosen by the parties, or; (b) in the absence of choice, the law of the country with which the contract is most closely connected. Given the presumption that the country with which the contract is most closely connected is that where the party who is to effect the performance which is characteristic of the contract has at the time of conclusion of the contract his habitual residence (or, in the case of a corporation, its central administration), the Convention accords with the common law in holding that it is the law of the seller's place of business that will be applicable. There are, however, special rules for consumer contracts. In particular:

(i) if in [the country in which the consumer has his habitual residence] conclusion of the contract was preceded by a specific invitation addressed to him or by advertising, and he had taken in that country all the steps necessary on his part for the conclusion of the contract; or

(ii) if the other party or his agent received the consumer's order in that country then, according to Art. 5, a choice of law clause shall not have the effect of depriving the consumer of the protection afforded to him by mandatory rules of the country in which he has his habitual residence; and, in the absence of choice, the contract is governed by the law of the consumer's country anyway.

A further important example of the impact of EC legislation is the Directive on Sale of Goods and Associated Guarantees (99/44 [1999] O.J. L171, p.12) which has been implemented by the Sale and Supply of Goods to Consumers Regulations (SI 2002/3045). Where a Directive slices into a local legal regime, its impact can be positive or negative, or sometimes neutral. In the case of the Sales Directive, we can see the full range of impacts.

First, as we remarked in Chapter 2, there has been a long-running debate about how the formation requirements of the common law rule-book are best deployed so that consumer guarantees of the kind offered, for example, by manufacturers of electrical goods can be treated as contractually enforceable (see Twigg-Flesner, 2003a). Cases such as *Carlill*, *Bowerman*, and *Shanklin Pier v Detel* (1951) indicate that, where there is a strong enough will, there is probably a common law way. However, this is hardly the mark of transparent regulation. Accordingly, those parts of the Directive and the implementing Regulations which declare that, where consumer guarantees of this kind are offered, then they are to be treated as contractually binding are to be welcomed—as, indeed, are the requirements for the use of plain and intelligible language in the terms of the guarantee. To this extent, the impact of the Directive is positive.

Secondly, under Art. 2(1) of the Directive, "[t]he seller must deliver goods to the consumer which are in conformity with the contract of sale." Consumer goods are presumed to be "in conformity with the contract" if they satisfy certain requirements relating to description (including correspondence with the characteristics of goods held out by way of a sample or model), fitness for purpose, and quality. On the face of it, these requirements are effectively equivalent to the terms already implied by ss.13–15 of the Sale of Goods Act. In line with this analysis, the implementing Regulations confirm that goods will be non-conforming if they involve a breach relative to the express terms of the contract or the statutory terms implied by ss.13–15. On this matter, therefore, the impact of the Directive seems to be neutral.

Thirdly, the Directive introduces a complex scheme of remedies that are to be available to consumers where goods are non-conforming. Essentially, this is a two-tiered scheme, consumer buyers first being restricted to repair or replacement before reduction of the price or rescission become available. Recital 10 captures the performance spirit of the scheme, declaring that, in the event of non-conformity, "consumers should be entitled to have the goods restored to conformity with the contract free of charge, choosing either repair or replacement, or, failing this, to have the price reduced or the contract rescinded." However, the devil is in the detail, access to the second tier remedies hinging on the possibility and/or proportionality of the consumer's preferred remedy. On both points, the implementing Regulations seek to avoid sellers being required to respond in a way that is "unreasonable"—consumer-welfarism, as it were, turned around for the protection of business contractors. Not surprisingly, therefore, commentators have questioned just how far the Regulations represent a remedial charter for consumers (see, *e.g.* Twigg-Flesner, 2003b). To some extent, such concerns are assuaged by the important point that Art. 8(2) permits Member States to maintain in force more stringent provisions for consumer protection than those required (as a minimum) by the Directive—further to which, the remedial regime introduced by the Regulations is supplementary to the remedies already available in English law to consumer buyers. In other words, where non-Regulation law is more favourable to consumers in its remedial provisions (as arguably it is in some respects), buyers may rely on it. This consideration, however, highlights a deeper negative impact—namely, that the remedies of consumer buyers are now governed by two bodies of law, the new law implemented by the Regulations and the general body of consumer sales law outwith the Regulations. The resulting messiness of legal provision for consumer remedies is matched by that relating to unfair terms in consumer contracts where UCTA sits alongside the Regulations on Unfair Terms in Consumer Contracts. In an attempt to tidy up the latter, the Law Commission (2002) has been working on a consolidation of the overlapping regimes; and it would not be altogether surprising if, in due course, calls were made for a cleaner consolidation of the law providing for the remedies available to consumer buyers.

The longer-term logic of these developments is that, in place of ad hoc Directives targeting particular aspects of the consumer law of contract, there will be larger legislative measures offering more consolidated and co-ordinated regulation. That the (European) Commission is already thinking along these lines is evident in its much-debated Communication to the Council and the European Parliament, formally launching a consultation on the question of whether the absence of a convergent, or unified, European contract law is an inhibition to the development of the single market (see COM (2001) 398 final, Brussels, 11.07.2001; and for a comprehensive response, see Von Bar and Lando (2002)). It is also evident in the draft Directive on Unfair Commercial Practices (Brussels, June 17, 2003), Art. 5.1 of which sets out a general duty designed to control unfair commercial practices, especially such practices as are misleading or aggressive.

In the light of such Europeanising measures, we might conclude that the English transformation theorists now need to look in more than one direction—for, if a sea change in English contract law is taking place, it is being brought about by the impact of European legislation as much as by the common law jurisprudence elaborated across the Atlantic.

10

UNDERSTANDING CONTRACT AS A SOCIAL PHENOMENON

As we indicated in the previous chapter, there are some difficult questions underlying the apparently simple story of the transformation of contract. By treating contract as a social and historical phenomenon we have embarked on a challenging enquiry. We cannot avoid asking questions either about how we are to "do" history or sociology, or about the status to be accorded to historical or sociological statements and theories. Is it the case that the practitioners of history and sociology simply "do their own thing", producing statements and theories which, in the final analysis, are neither true nor false? If not, how in practice are we to measure such statements and theories for their truth or falsity?

The aim of this chapter is to pose some of the methodological questions raised by the transformation theses. In the first part of the chapter, we consider some aspects of historiography, incorporating an introduction to some of the ideas associated with two of the great names of sociology, Karl Marx and Max Weber. In the second part of the chapter, we draw together the threads in an attempt to provide readers with the basis for developing a critique not only of the transformation theses, but also of our own account of the ideologies of contract in Part II of this book.

1. UNDERSTANDING SOCIAL CHANGE: PITFALLS AND PROBLEMS

One of the primary tasks of the historian is no doubt retrieving, and giving an accurate account of, the *minutiae* of the past. However, this *minutiae* of itself is meaningless. Sense is made of it by the concepts the historian employs in interpreting it. Those concepts, of necessity, are of the present. Some writers have argued indeed that each age writes history afresh, which is a relativist position. Others have argued that an objective view of the past is in principle attainable (for an introduction to this difficult area, see Marwick, 1989). Without confronting directly such complexities, it is pertinent to make some general observations about the pitfalls into which it is possible to fall if we fail to be critically aware of the concepts we are using to analyse the past, and about the related problems of historiography.

One of the foremost difficulties about interpreting the past is that we *must* look back through modern eyes. It is essential therefore that we should take a critical view of the conventions and assumptions which structure modern thinking. In particular, we should not take it for granted that linguistic conventions hold constant throughout time, nor should we assume that a modern phenomenon has no functional equivalent in an earlier period simply because some of the modern trappings are absent. It is possible, for example, that Horwitz, by looking at the past through modern eyes, has missed the possibility that there may have been homologues for the modern institution of contract in the eighteenth century, which in fact performed as he suggests the rule-book performed in the nineteenth century, but that they were not identified as contracts (this example is purely hypothetical).

One important point we are trying to make is that a principal problem to be confronted by anyone undertaking the task of identifying social change is to identify the units through which change is to be studied. At the most basic level, it is obviously no use simply relying on the designation given to units at any point in time. What is called "contract" in the nineteenth century does not necessarily correspond to what is called "contract" in the eighteenth century. For example, Blackstone's Commentaries (1765–9) deal with contract in the section of that work dealing with Property (Book II). That should not, however, mislead us into supposing that the equivalents of contracts at that time were viewed primarily as conveyances of property rather than as mechanisms for securing future performances. Failure to perform by one party is in fact dealt with under "private wrongs" in Book III (pp.153-66). Fitting what we would now think of as "contract" into Hale's scheme as adopted by Blackstone no doubt looks strange to modern eyes, and it is easy therefore to read into it some wider significance. That is largely, however, because we have become used to viewing the matter through concepts derived from the "rule-book". It is not relevant for present purposes to pursue this example further, and in particular to speculate as to whether or not eighteenth-century law protected the expectation interest. The main point we wish to make is that we must always be alert to the danger of looking at the past using present-day linguistic and conceptual conventions (*cf.* Scheiber, 1998).

A related danger is to approach the past with problems in mind generated by a body of received knowledge, such as the rule-book. For this reason it is necessary to generate new problematics. A way of doing this is to move to a more general overview of the society to which the institution being studied belongs, and then to come back to earth, as it were, and try to see from the perspectives provided by the overview what institutions at one period are the equivalents in function of those at another. It could be the case, for example, that by looking at reported cases and textbooks written for eighteenth-century lawyers we are missing the point that an equivalent of Horwitz's "oppressive" nineteenth-century contract law existed, but that it was a product of *social* relations and the ideology involved in them, rather than a product of *legal* relations and the ideology involved in them. The relationship of the agricultural worker, living in a tied cottage, to his employer might perhaps be an example.

We are now bordering on the edge of rather a large field (to put it mildly). We will venture into that field as a way of highlighting differences between two well known schools of historiography, the Marxist and the Weberian. We do not intend to present the perspectives of these schools as a step in expounding any particular view of the relationship between contract and society, but rather as a way of exposing to view the mechanics of historiography. We do this because we believe that many lawyers, when they try to write history, fail to realise the extent to which the rule-book colours the way in which they look at the past.

(i) Marx

The general overview of the social and economic development of society with which we propose to begin is that of Karl Marx. Marx makes a good starting point, both because his theories are well known and have been fruitful in throwing up lines of historical enquiry in the way we are suggesting, and because he provides a fairly accessible gloss to Horwitz-type theses. Unfortunately, Marx can be interpreted in a number of very different ways. He was not the most systematic of writers, and like many great thinkers, he changed his mind. In consequence, what we describe here does not purport to be definitive of Marx's thought, but rather a version of Marxism (see, *e.g.* Anderson, 1974).

Marx proposed a theory of development in the political economy. In Western Europe, the slave mode of production which prevailed in classical times gave way to the feudal mode of production, which gave way to the capitalist mode of production which in turn would give way to the final phase which would be the socialist mode of production. Crucially, each mode of production, except the last, had within it theseeds of its own destruction. There were "levels of over-determination" reflecting the contradictions in the material circumstances—the famous materialist dialectic which Marx substituted for Hegel's dialectic theory of the development of human thought. For example, the Roman slave economy required a regular supply of slaves, and conquest of new territories provided this. However, the frontiers of the Empire could not be expanded for ever, and there would come a point at which the expansion would in any event destabilize the political economy, resulting in its collapse. In each mode of production except the last there are two classes, the exploiters who expropriate the surplus value, and the exploited who provide the surplus value. It is the conflict between these two classes which provides the motor of historical change.

Although many Marxists would dispute this, there is very little doubt that Marx regarded his theory as a scientific law for the development of human societies in general, of the same order as, for example, the laws of thermo-dynamics. The source and impetus for historical change is men who have become conscious of their situation in history and whom that situation, coupled with their "species-being", impels to seek revolutionary change in their condition (revolution should not be understood here as necessarily involving violent conflict).

A key feature of this theory is the hierarchy of levels in society, with production relations being primary. In any given mode of production except the final one, both exploited and exploiters are prevented from seeing the true nature of their relations by ideological "spectacles" which distort their view of the world; these "spectacles" are in turn a product of the production relations. The removal of the "spectacles" is the mechanism of change. The state is a part of this ideological superstructure, and the law too (see, *e.g.* Gabel and Feinman, 1982) in as much as the law and the state are two sides of the same coin. We can see from this how some Marxists might regard contract law as a mechanism of expropriation of surplus value of central importance, and changes in contract law as a reflection of the changes in the production relations in the economic base. One could gloss the Horwitz thesis by suggesting that the change he asserts represented changes in the superstructure reflecting the triumph of capitalism over earlier forms. In feudal society, by contrast, the expropriation of surplus value took place through status relations, and the feudal dues which each person on a lower rung of the feudal "ladder" owed to the person on the next higher rung. The role of any equivalent of contract in such a society would necessarily be more limited. By contrast, as capitalism developed through the course of the eighteenth century, we would expect a proliferation of mechanisms by which this expropriation was effected in place of the status relations. These mechanisms might or might not correspond to contract in the rule-book sense, and by looking for them as such we should have avoided the trap of being overconcerned with the rule-book.

However, we may have avoided one historiographical pitfall, only to fall into another, at least if we believe we have finally encapsulated the truth. There are many problems with the Marxist view. The one we wish to focus on here is its "reductionism" (*i.e.* reducing analysis of social change to just one factor). The periodisation of history into slave, feudal and capitalist modes of production which it entails, notwithstanding its very abstract formulation, is problematic to the extent that societies possessing the institutions of slavery, feudalism and capitalism in the Marxist sense have shown marked variations historically. Even starting with the primacy of the economic, it is possible to present a very different picture from that of Marx of the development of Western European societies. For example Fernand Braudel (1986) gives us a detailed account of wide cultural divergencies existing in the different societies around the Mediterranean, based on the exigencies of their economic existence. The base-superstructure model outlined above is in any case only one of a number of possible starting points for analysis. Obviously, other starting points may yield very different characterisations of the same societies in the same period. Indeed, it can be argued that there is a necessity for a plurality of starting points in order to progress towards historical understanding.

(ii) Weber

The sociologist Max Weber (Bendix, 1959) recognised this, and suggested that it was important not to submerge the differences between societies, but on the contrary to evaluate them in the light not only of economic criteria, but also of sociological and jurisprudential criteria. Weber in fact hardly permits a unified theory of historical change at all. Instead, he provides a set of conceptual tools for analysing social change. Weber argued that man is productive not merely in his material production, but in his creation of values. Every decision an individual makes affirms one set of values, and denies another. The decisions taken are, however, explicable in the light of the individual's general image of existence (which will generate particular reasons for action).

One of Weber's foremost concerns was to understand how an individual's image of existence could ground different types of relations of domination (and, with them, different notions of legitimacy and different attitudes of leadership and obedience). To this end, Weber formulated his celebrated typology of "charismatic", "traditional" and "legal" domination. Charisma, which is the primitive sense of the sacredness of an object, but which is equally applicable to offices and institutions, cannot be explained in terms of either material or ideal factors entirely. It always exists within a historical situation. It is exhibited in certain types of government, notably theocracies, where characteristically the priestly function and the law-making function merge. Fundamentalist Moslem states at the present day provide examples of this kind of charismatic domination, as did many societies historically. Such charismatic authority can be seen to varying degrees in all modern societies, where, however, other forms of legitimation are more dominant. English society for most of modern history has had two other types of domination in greater prominence: namely traditional domination, the legitimacy accorded to an authority which is perceived always to have existed, *e.g.* the Crown; and legal domination, the obedience to a system of rules applied judicially and administratively in accordance with established principles which are valid for all members of the society (*i.e.* unlike charismatic and traditional domination, people obey the law *as such* rather than by virtue of the persons implementing it).

These types are merely conceptual devices for analysing societies. It is not necessary that any society actually possesses them in their pure form. Unlike Marx, Weber examined a range of non-European societies, and his typologies have proved rewarding when applied to these. For our purpose two aspects of Weber's thought need to be examined: the emergence of legal rationality and legal domination in Western Europe, and the position of contract in that scheme. Weber (1968, 1978) suggested that law had passed through four stages (which are not, however, to be understood as necessarily consequential one upon another in any evolutionary sense): charismatic legal revelation; empirical creation and finding of law by notables; the imposition of law by secular or theocratic powers; and finally the systematic elaboration of law and the professional administration of justice. Weber stressed the importance of the Church in this last development, because the Church as an institution was a child of Roman law and always had, side by side, the charismatic, the traditional and the legal forms of domination. Ultimately, as we have seen, the influence of the Church and the canon law on the growth of legal rationality was to be profound (*cf.* Gordley, 1991).

In contrast to older law, Weber suggested, the most essential feature of modern substantive law, especially private law, is the the the greatly increased significance of legal transactions, particularly contracts, as a source of claims reinforced by legal coercion. So very characteristic is this feature of private law that one can *a posteriori* designate the contemporary type of society, to the extent that private law obtains, as a "contractual" one (we will recall here Sir Henry Maine's thesis, p.209). The juridico-economic position of the individual, *i.e.* the totality of his legitimately acquired rights and valid obligations, is determined on the one hand by inheritance, and on the other by contracts concluded by him in his name.

In public law, too, Weber suggested, the role of contractual transactions is of some importance. Every official is appointed by contract, and some important phenomena of constitutional government, especially the determination of the budget, presuppose in substance, if not formally, a free agreement among a number of independent organs of the state, none of which can legally coerce the other. However, neither the officials' obligations to the state, nor the freely reached agreements preceding the budget, are treated as "contracts" in the legal sense. This is because the state is sovereign, and the acts of its organs are regarded as instances of the exercise of public duties. In public law, the domain of free contract is essentially found in international law.

By contrast, in former times the position of a public official was less based upon a free contract, but rather upon his submission to the personal, quasi-familial authority of a lord. However, in such societies, political acts, such as the raising of means for wars and other public purposes, were nothing but contracts between the prince and the estates. Similarly, the feudal bond was in essence based upon contract. The collection of customary laws such as the *leges barbarorum* were referred to as "*pactus*", and innovations in the law could be brought about only by freely made agreement between the official authorities and the community. Indeed, in Anglo-Saxon political theory at any rate, there was a tradition that the relationship of the king with his subjects was contractual.

The concept of contract is also met with in primitive political associations which were based on freely concluded agreements between autonomous groups.

"Contract" in the sense of a voluntary agreement constituting the legal foundation of claims and obligations has thus been widely diffused even in the earliest periods and stages of legal history. On the other hand, the further we go back in legal history, the less significant becomes contract as a device of economic acquisition in fields other than the law of the family and inheritance. The situation at the present day is very different. The present-day significance of contract is primarily the result of the high degree to which our economic system is market orientated and of the role played by money. Contracts propagated by the market society are completely different from those contracts which in the spheres of public and family law once played a greater role than they do today. In accordance with this fundamental transformation of the general character of the voluntary agreement, the more primitive type is called "status contract" and that which is peculiar to the exchange or market economy "purposive contract" (*Zweck-Kontraki*—again recall Sir Henry Maine, p.209). The distinction is based on the fact that all those primitive contracts by which political or other personal associations are created involve a change in what may be called the total legal situation, and the social status of the persons involved. To have this effect, these contracts were originally either straightforward magical acts or at least acts having a magical significance. By means of such contracts persons could become somebody's child, father, wife, brother, master, slave, kin, comrade-in-arms, protector, client, follower, vassal, subject, friend, or, quite generally, comrade (*Genosse*). The contract meant that a person would become something different in quality (or status) from the quality he possessed before. People whose thinking is embedded in magic cannot imagine any other than a magical guarantee of the parties' conformity to their new roles. Characteristically, such contracts are accompanied by symbolic rituals such as (at a later stage) the mixing of blood (the reader may recall Tom Sawyer and Huckleberry Finn emulating such rites to become blood brothers), or the creation of a new "soul" by some animistic process or other magical rite.

As the notion of divinity replaces animism, these rituals are replaced by other rituals placing each party under the dominion of a supernatural power which both protects them and threatens them in the event of non-conformity. The oath assumes the character of a conditional self-curse calling for divine wrath to strike in the event of non-conformity. In this form it survives in our society to the present day in the swearing of witnesses and juries. The oath has uses from an early period outside the field of status contracts. It could also be used to guarantee the performance of purposive contracts.

Economic barter, which is the characteristic form of purposive contract common to even the most primitive societies, is characteristically confined to transactions with persons who are not members of the parties' own houses, *i.e.* non-kinsmen, non-brothers, etc. Barter enjoyed no guarantee, and the concept that it could mean the assumption of an obligation was non-existent. Barter usually, in fact, involved the simultaneous transfer of possession. Possession was protected; thus the legal protection accorded to barter was not of an obligation but of possession newly acquired. Formal legal construction of barter does not begin until certain goods, especially gold and silver, have acquired a monetary function, *i.e.* barter becomes sale. However, just as the simultaneous transfer of possession of goods requires no legal protection, so the simultaneous transfer of goods for money does not either.

One of the earliest situations in which an obligation arising from a purposive contract (as opposed to *ex delictu*) was recognised to exist was the debt arising out of a loan. Loans within a kinship group were not perceived of as actionable, since no action would be admissible among brothers, and similarly loans between other persons in a relationship involving personal loyalty. The characteristic enforcement, apart from peer pressure, was magical. Thus in China the creditor would threaten suicide in the expectation of pursuing his debtor after death, and in India he would sit in front of the debtor's door and either starve himself or hang himself, in order to compel his sib to avenge him. By contrast, the debt contracted outside the kinship group, or similar, did carry with it a sense of obligation. Characteristically, the obligation was marked by some symbolic act such as in Roman law *nexum*, the debt contracted *per aes et libram*, and *stipulatio*, the debt contracted by symbolic pledge. We have seen how English law similarly required a deed for the action of debt on an obligation.

At a later period, the law evolved the possibility of making purposive contracts legally enforceable by creating new actions out of actions arising *ex delictu*. The economic rationalisation of law favoured the rise of the idea that liability arose not so much out of a buying off of vengeance, but rather out of a duty to make compensation for harm suffered. At this point, non-performance of a contract becomes a harm requiring compensation. Thus the Romans extended the sphere of legal protection first through the extensive application of delictual action and then through the concept of *dolus*.

In Weber's thesis the growth of a rational legal order, and the predominance of purposive contracts, was an essential precondition to the growth of capitalism. However, England, which in modern times was the first and most highly developed capitalist country, retained a less rational and less bureaucratic judicature than did Germany. The reason for this was that the guild structure of the profession had raised English law to the status of a technology based on apprenticeship. Crucially, the common law by these means provided a secure system for the accumulation of landed wealth, and the accumulation of landed wealth primed the pump which set off the industrial revolution.

It should be noted that Weber uses his typology of legal domination to explain certain stages in the development of institutions which would not be regarded as "legal" in the man in the street's understanding. Thus he suggests that the survival of irrational modes of thought in Germanic law promoted the acceptance of the negotiable instrument there. The instrument appeared as a sort of fetish, by the formal delivery of which, at first before witnesses, specific legal effects were produced, as by other quasi-magic symbols. Originally, the parchment was delivered blank, the writing being entered up later. By contrast, in Italy, even in the early Middle Ages, the development of documentary evidence *per se* was greatly favoured. In England, as we have seen, great difficulty was experienced in coming to terms with negotiable instruments, partly because of the procedural difficulties inherent in the forms of action at common law. The deed, however, has at times seemed to possess a somewhat equivalent quasi-magical power.

(iii) Overview

Although as far as contract is concerned there may appear to be some similarity between a Weberian and a Marxist analysis, there is a fundamental difference between the two. By contrast with Marxism, which is a theory *of* social change, Weber is primarily concerned to provide a *methodology* to identify social change. His technique in doing so is to construct models, *e.g.* of types of domination, which are empirically derived but which do not necessarily correspond exactly to any institution in the real world. These are not definitional in the legal sense. They are basic tools for the understanding of social phenomena, historical or otherwise. The models are, as it were, necessary lenses to enable us to perceive the landscape. The models are of value to the extent that they further our understanding, but it is important to emphasize that it may be possible to view the same social phenomenon through a variety of lenses or models. These lenses or models we call "ideal types". Of course, it is a complex question whether some ideal types have better credentials than others (see pp.243 *et seq.*).

It is interesting to note that Weber's own view of contract is in the rule-book tradition. In short, his ideal type of contract seems to owe its origin rather to theoretical than to empirical derivation.

Consciously, or unconsciously, our understanding of the world is mediated through ideal types. A realisation of this is not an absolute precondition to an attempt to spell out any aspect of social change—many historians do it intuitively. However, as we have suggested, lawyers by their training tend to be conditioned into a particular view of the past. The common law method of tracing the evolution of doctrine through decided cases is, after all, a method of "doing history" with blinkers on. It is no bad thing, therefore, for lawyers to think consciously about what others may do unconsciously.

There is a final cluster of problems to which we should now draw attention. It is sometimes claimed that theories of social development such as Marxism are "scientific" But can such theories legitimately be described in those terms? Of course, historical and sociological explanations take the laws of the natural world for granted. For example, the statement "X was hanged on the orders of Y" will presuppose that the force of gravity was instrumental in precipitating X's departure from this world. To this extent, at least, historical and sociological statements are scientific. Yet can historians and sociologists, in their own practice, emulate the methods and "law-like" statements of science?

If scientific method consists in the formulation and testing of hypotheses running in the form "Where A, then B", then this is not a method which can always be adopted by historians and sociologists. There are obvious practical difficulties about "turning the clock back" and about controlled testing of the social world. Moreover, given that the object of the enquiry is animate, as opposed to inanimate, there are ethical problems for researchers. For instance, there would be obvious moral objections to testing out the hypothesis that capital punishment would deter drunken driving.

There is also a question about the possibility of historians and sociologists generating law-like statements analogous to scientific laws. Consider the following three statements:

(i) "Capitalism is part of an evolutionary sequence. When capitalism reaches crisis point, it will give way to socialism";

(ii) "Where there is an increase in the division of labour within a society, that society's penal code will favour restitutive rather than repressive sanctions"; and

(iii) "The crime rate varies inversely relative to the level of enforcement".

Each of these statements seems to fall short of what we take to be a paradigmatic scientific law. Thus: (i) is both vague and circular; (ii) is vague too, and it is unclear what sort of relationship is contemplated between the degree of division of labour and the form of penal sanction; and (iii), while coming close to the target, lacks universality, because it does not claim that all members of the class (*i.e.* all human beings) will respond in the same manner to varying degrees of enforcement. In the final analysis, however, these worries may be irrelevant. If historical and sociological statements are true, does it really matter whether they are "scientific"?

This question leads into the second phase of our enquiry. How are we to construct a critique of theories such as the transformation theses?

2. DEVELOPING A CRITIQUE: OFF TO THE RACES!

Suppose that we asked four experts to offer their thoughts on the transformation of horse racing in England since the Second World War. They might point to very different developments. Ms Ascot might report that oil-rich Arabs have taken over from the English aristocracy as the principal owners of racehorses; Ms Brighton might point to an increase in commercial sponsorship of races; Mr Chester might make something of the movement of punters away from the racecourses to off-course betting shops; and Mr Doncaster might suggest that nothing has changed, with rich owners and trainers exploiting cheap stable labour, wealthy bookmakers exploiting the working man, and the Jockey Club continuing to legitimate the racing industry by presenting it as a sport. What are we to make of these views?

The first point is that each of these views is offered as a description of the practice of horse racing. We take it that, in principle, each statement has a truth value (*i.e.* is either true or false). In practice, of course, some descriptive claims may be easier to check than others. For example, it may be relatively easy to check Ascot's claim about the pattern of horse ownership, but less easy to check Doncaster's view.

The fact that we have been offered more than one descriptive statement does not in itself affect any of this. If, say, Ascot's claim had been denied by Brighton (*e.g.* by suggesting that the English aristocracy remained the principal owners) we could not, of course, accept both statements as true. But the statements in our hypothetical set do not contradict each other in this way. In principle, all four statements could be true, all four could be false, or some could be true and others false. For practical purposes, assessment of the truth or falsity of a particular statement will depend upon the grounds we have for believing the statement to be true. We shall return to this question in a moment.

Next, suppose that we asked a fifth expert, Ms Epsom, to identify the "most significant" statement in the set, and suppose that Epsom replied in the following terms: "No one statement is 'most significant' in an absolute sense. It depends upon whether you are thinking about practical or theoretical significance. If the former is your measure, then Ascot's statement is perhaps the most practically significant because the changing pattern of ownership has affected lots of people in the racing world. On the other hand, if you take theoretical significance as your standard, then Doncaster's observations are potentially the most significant because they purport to describe the 'essence' of the racing enterprise."

This, we might think, seems plausible, but what does Epsom mean by the "essence" of some practice? If we ask Epsom to clarify, she may advise us that the essence of an enterprise is constituted by what it really amounts to. Accordingly, a descriptive statement is theoretically significant to the extent that it goes to the heart of the phenomenon. However, she may warn us that if we broach such matters we will find ourselves well and truly "off to the races"!

Let us, therefore, move on from the question of significance to the question of explanation. Suppose that we ask our experts to explain some specific development, say the growth in commercial sponsorship. We might get various suggestions purporting to explain this development, for example that commercial sponsorship of sport was growing and that those associated with horse racing saw it as a good idea; that some enterprises had used sponsorship in racing as an alternative to television advertising; that it "facilitated capital accumulation, and so promoted the interests of the ruling class", and so on.

Now if we asked Epsom for guidance (because she seemed to know more about the philosophy of social science than horse racing), she might advise us that explanation is fraught with difficulties.

First, Epsom might warn us that there are rival conceptions of explanation. There is an "interpretive" idea of explanation according to which an explanation consists in putting oneself in the relevant agent's position, understanding his view of the situation, and understanding his reasons for action (notice how we sometimes say "That explains it" when we are able to see an otherwise puzzling action from the agent's own point of view, particularly in the light of his purposes). However, there is also a "causative" conception of explanation, according to which an explanation consists in identifying the relevant causal sequence which brought about a particular event. Moreover, within the causative camp there is not necessarily agreement about which causal factors (*e.g.* human biology, the material circumstances of an individual or group, the ideas or attitudes of an individual or group, and the like) are, in principle, relevant for the purposes of constructing a chain of causation. Neither conception, Epsom might conclude, seems free from difficulty. If we take the interpretive approach, we seem to be dodging the problem of giving real explanation. On the other hand, if we take the causative line, it seems rash to leave human ideas out of account, yet do an individual's reasons for action "cause" an event in quite the same way as, say, a snooker cue causes a ball to move (see generally Unger, 1976, especially pp.245-62)?

If we accept that either conception of explanation may be employed, then explanatory statements within both modes seem, in principle, to have truth value. Statements purporting to explain the commercial sponsors' view of the situation, or attempting to build up the causal sequence which led to commercial sponsorship, are either true or false. In practice, the assessment of explanatory statements will turn on whether there are grounds for particular explanatory beliefs. It is of fundamental importance, however, that we should not confuse belief with truth. A professional gambler may know the form book inside out, and place his bets on the basis of that information, whereas the average punter may place bets by sticking a pin in the race card. One punter has grounds, the other does not, but neither may back the winner. In the same way, some explanatory beliefs may be better grounded than others, but which explanations are true is quite a different matter. For example, we may judge that there is little ground for supposing that the (until recently) declining attendances on Derby Day at Epsom are to be accounted for by the weather (because, a fortnight or so later, crowds flock to Royal Ascot in even the most appalling June weather). We might think that the more likely explanation is to do with switching Derby Day from Wednesday to Saturday, with traffic congestion in the area, with the attractions of off-course betting, with improved televised coverage, with below-par entries for the race, with the retirement of leading jockeys who were household names, and so on. Yet, the explanation that cites the weather factor, however improbable, might in fact be correct.

Before we leave the races, there is another important point to make. We have suggested that both descriptive and explanatory statements have, in principle, a truth value, but that in practice assessment of such statements must concentrate on the grounds for belief. What, however, might constitute "grounds for belief"? The obvious answer is that grounds are constituted by the facts or the evidence. If, for example, the register of horse ownership does not bear out Ascot's claim, then we must conclude that her belief is unfounded, and treat it for practical purposes as false. Some commentators, however, may not suppose that grounds are to be found by such direct and narrow attention to the evidence. For them grounds are constituted by a general theory supporting their particular claim. Thus, Doncaster might say that the grounds for his description (at least where the description is in general terms of exploitation and legitimation) are provided by the theoretical soundness of Marxism, which (he asserts) correctly describes the fundamental nature of the social world, including the world of horse racing. If one takes the former line, the evidence and counter-examples and so on are relevant to the assessment of a claim. If one takes the latter, they are not: the basic claim cannot be repudiated by empirical means, but only by repudiating the underpinning general theory.

If we substitute "the transformation of contract" for "the transformation of horse racing", we should be able to see how a critique of the transformation theses might be developed. Three aspects of such a thesis appear to be open to question: namely, the truth of its descriptive statements, the significance of its descriptive statements, and the truth of its *explanatory* statements (for the sake of simplicity, we do not consider disputes concerning the significance of explanatory statements, but, in principle, the issues raised are the same as those concerning the significance of *descriptive* statements).

Starting with descriptive statements, it will be apparent that the number of such statements offered has no bearing on the truth or falsity of any particular statement. Admittedly, we cannot accept that two contradictory statements are both true (they may, of course, both be false), but, in general, descriptions of the transformation of contract do not raise this problem. The main critique seems to hinge on assessing the grounds for believing individual descriptive statements to be true.

It will be evident in the light of our discussion in the first section of this chapter that scouring the historical record is no straightforward task. Moreover, the problem is compounded where there is a switch from grounds-constituted-by-evidence to grounds-constituted-by-theory. For example, suppose that we reject the Horwitz thesis because, say, we think it falls into the trap of reading history through modern eyes, and in consequence misreads the facts of the eighteenth century. Now, if the thesis is given a Marxist gloss, the apparent failure of the thesis to fit the facts may be treated as immaterial. For dogmatic Marxists, the relevant facts are the irrefutable facts supplied by Marxist theory. This entails a sort of "heads we win, tails you lose" position, for, to the extent that Horwitz's particular descriptive examples are accepted, this is grist to the mill; to the extent that they are rejected, it scarcely matters, for Horwitz must be essentially right in presenting the law of contract as an instrument of class oppression.

Our encounter with dogmatic Marxism leads us on to the distinction between "immanent" and "external" critique. In the former case, the critique does not challenge the general theoretical framework within which the statements under review are presented; in the latter case it does. As regards the dogmatic Marxist, this puts us in something of a difficulty. Immanent critique has little impact (because whatever the particular facts, Marxism can offer a general description of the situation), and our dogmatic Marxist is not interested in external critique.

A second area for critique concerns the significance of descriptive statements. This takes us back to a problem we encountered in the last chapter. There, it will be recalled, we did not know quite what to make of the idea that Gabel and Feinman's (1982) descriptive thesis might be of greater significance than Atiyah's (1978). If we recall our earlier discussion in this section of this chapter, the argument that Gabel and Feinman's thesis is more theoretically significant would be that, by virtue of its being locked into a Marxist theoretical framework, it highlights the essence of adjudication in contract disputes. Against this, however, Atiyah's supporters might argue that the very idea of an essence of adjudication is absurd, or that Marxism mislocates the essence (which is to be found instead in Atiyah's background law-jobs theory). It will be appreciated that we are here confronting competing theoretical paradigms, each with its own views about essences, about the essence of law, and about the theoretical significance of particular descriptive statements. To carry the argument forward, it would be necessary, therefore, to develop an external critique of the underlying theoretical paradigms—no wonder Epsom warned us that we were off to the races!

Let us, therefore, turn to the possibility of developing a critique of explanatory statements. Here, it is important to distinguish between those explanatory statements which are underpinned by general preformed explanatory models and those which are not. As representative models of these two types we can take respectively a Marxist explanatory statement, and Atiyah's (1978) explanation of the shift between principle and pragmatism.

The most striking features of the Marxist explanatory scheme are its simplicity and all-embracing nature. Marxists evince both omniscience and prescience in appealing to their ready-made explanatory model (comprising class dynamics, base and superstructure, ideology, and so on). Gabel and Feinman, for example, need not explain why judges attempt to legitimate the existing class relations—such judicial behaviour is explained by general Marxist theory. Similarly, Marxists need not explain why, in the early years of the twentieth century, American judges appealed to the idea of "freedom of contract" in order to resist legislative attempts to regulate working conditions and to facilitate union organisation (see, *e.g. Lochner v New York*, 1905; *Coppage v Kansas*, 1915). Nor need they explain how employers are able to use the concept of breach of contract to justify the dismissal of striking workers.

The implications of a position such as Marxism are that the general explanatory scheme (together with its general descriptions) has already been identified, and the only explanatory puzzles really concern the subtleties of the scheme. Accordingly, unless one is able to mount an external critique, one can aspire to little more than an immanent critique, effectively restricted to an exercise in fine-tuning.

With this we can contrast Atiyah's approach. In the descriptive phase of his account of the fluctuation between principle and pragmatism, Atiyah implicitly employs an ideal-typical framework, constituted by the hortatory and dispute-resolving functions. His ideal types, however, have no pre-formed explanatory theory to which he can appeal. Therefore, the explanatory phase of his enquiry involves a fresh start. He says:

> "The change appears to have been largely an unconscious one, but if it has taken place in the broad way I have argued, then its causes must be sought in general trends rather than in specific ideas, events, or personalities." (Atiyah, 1978: 15)

Atiyah then proceeds to speculate as to the general trends, focusing on the intellectual milieu of the period. Thus, he argues that the change from pragmatism to principle largely coincided with the general rise in fashion of the idea of principle, and longer-term calculation. The change back from principle to pragmatism coincided with a declining faith in deterrence, and with a growing division of moral beliefs. The characteristics of this explanatory strategy are as follows: explanation presupposes identifying the causes of things; there are neither simple answers, nor pre-formed general answers; each explanatory enquiry calls for an empirical sifting of the evidence. Atiyah would be the first to admit that his explanatory account could be wrong, and that it would be quite in order for us to attempt to develop a critique of his views by an examination of the evidence. Accordingly, explanatory statements of the type advanced by Atiyah are open, in principle, to serious review as a matter of both internal and external critique.

It is time to take stock. Descriptive and explanatory statements, in principle, are true or false. In practice, the plausibility of such statements must be tested by examining the grounds for believing them to be true or false. Belief (even justifiable belief) is not, however, to be confused with the truth. Grounds for belief may reside in some general theoretical axioms from which the particular descriptions or explanations are derived; alternatively, grounds for belief may be constituted by an appeal to the evidence (which, of course, presupposes a background theoretical framework endorsing such an empirical strategy). If we accept the theoretical framework within which descriptive and explanatory statements are offered, critique must be of an immanent nature. If we dispute the theoretical framework, critique is external. Where rival theoretical paradigms are in contention, each side may claim that its own descriptive statements have special theoretical significance. Such a claim is tenable only if the supporting theoretical paradigm itself is tenable, which, in turn, raises questions of external critique.

Finally, how do these methodological remarks bear on the ideological framework which we employed in Part II of the book? We would characterize our framework as adopting an idealtypical approach, constructed for descriptive purposes, but also having explanatory potential.

In presenting our ideological framework as ideal-typical for descriptive purposes, our strategy was basically Weberian. We suggested that decisions made around the traditional rule-book could be plotted within our descriptive framework. Any particular decision could be located somewhere within the typology (but *cf.* Wightman, 1989). Of course, we did not leave the plotting of particular cases as an abstract possibility; we cited many cases as instances of our particular ideal types. The limitations of this descriptive exercise, however, should be noted. As a vehicle for description, our scheme did not purport to explain why particular cases were decided in a particular way. It merely purported to indicate where particular cases fell in relation to certain ideas and values represented by the ideologies. Thus understood, a critique of our descriptive framework could be mounted along the following two fronts.

First, as a matter of external critique, it might be contended that our theoretical framework is misconceived. At worst, the contention would be that we fundamentally misdescribe judicial employment of the rule-book, at best that our picture of a field of competing ideologies fails to strike at the heart of things. Accordingly, even if it were allowed that we make certain true statements about the relationship between particular decisions and doctrines, and their corresponding ideologies, our descriptions would be discarded as lacking any real theoretical significance. Secondly, as a matter of internal critique, it might be contended that whilst our general picture of a field of competing ideologies is on the right track, our ideal-typical construction of the field needs some revision (*e.g.* because our ideal types are too crudely drawn). (Readers who entertain such critical thoughts might care to look at Brownsword, 1994, for some furthers models of "welfarism" and Brownsword, 1996 and 1997, for a distinction between two types of market individualism). Our kindest critics would limit themselves to saying that everything is fine except that we sometimes err in our interpretation of particular cases.

Although our analysis in Part II is largely descriptive, it also has, in our contention, explanatory potential. This means that the ideological framework is a resource not only for describing where particular decisions stand in respect of certain values, it is a resource too for explaining why judges decide cases the way they do. The ideologies, so viewed, are more than descriptive reference points: to some extent they tell us what moves judges to decide cases the way they do. This does not imply that judges consistently follow a particular approach, or that a judge must whilst deciding a case remember that he is, say, a formalist, before formalism can explain his decision—of course not! If a judge believes that precedents should be followed and the rule-book respected, then he displays formalist traits, and the ideology may account for his decisions. Like Atiyah, however, we do not think that explanation is a simple matter. We accept, therefore, that particular cases may have to be explained by appealing to factors which lie outside the bounds of our ideological framework. For example, some decisions may have to be explained in terms of administrative considerations (*e.g.* where a judge is particularly busy and needs a quick decision—virtually any decision), or, indeed, in terms of promoting the interests of the ruling class, or "teaching insurance companies a lesson", or something of that sort. A limited amount of explanation in such different terms does not undercut our claim that the ideological framework is a resource with explanatory potential. However, if a critique showed that our framework was of no explanatory relevance at all, this would be damaging, not simply because it would destroy our explanatory claim, but also because the descriptive interest of the scheme would be devalued. We trust that this is one critique at least which readers will attempt without success.

3. SHOULD MACHIAVELLI HAVE THE LAST WORD?

The theories we have discussed assume in one form or another the development of human societies. Well, obviously things do change, but do individuals? Everyone working with basic historical source materials, duly alert to the dangers of viewing the past through the eyes of the present, nevertheless experiences from time to time a sense of *déjà vu*. On these occasions, Machiavelli's view (1513) of human life as a play in which the actors and scenery may change, but the drama does not, seems to offer a real insight. If we were to go behind the dry record of the law reports etc. (and readers are strongly recommended to look at some recent attempts to research the background to famous cases—see, *e.g.* Danzig on *Hadley v Baxendale*, 1975; Simpson on *Carlill*, 1985), we might well find the same scenes acted out, for example between the "Young Turks" and the "Old Guard", in the fourteenth century as in the modern era. Only the props are different. As Bertholt Brecht says at the end of *The Good Woman of Szechwan*, "You can't change human nature, but you can change the world!" Well, maybe that is only changing the set! Indeed, an assumption of constancy, if we think about it, is an essential underpinning of much historical explanation.

EPILOGUE

In this book we have attempted to pave the way for a critical understanding of contract. For much of the time we have concentrated on contract as it is traditionally presented, putting it into perspective and attempting to identify its tensions. Put in perspective, the black-letter approach can be seen to make only a narrow enquiry into the phenomenon of contract. Moreover, even this narrow section of contract will be misunderstood unless the rule-book is viewed as a battleground of competing ideologies.

To advance our understanding of contract, enquiry must be pursued on a number of fronts. In this book, we have tended to work along conceptual, descriptive and explanatory lines, scarcely touching on evaluative questions. To avoid any misunderstanding, therefore, it is appropriate for us to finish by at least indicating why evaluative enquiry is a no less important dimension of any attempt to understand contract (*cf.* Brownsword, 1989, 1993).

Particular aspects of contract (its rules or associated institutions) may be evaluated either for their instrumental efficiency and effectiveness or for their intrinsic moral legitimacy. Where we focus on instrumental efficiency and effectiveness, our concern is to assess how well some contractual item serves a particular end or purpose, but the moral legitimacy of the end or purpose itself is not yet in question. Where our focus is on intrinsic moral legitimacy, our concern is precisely to evaluate which ends or purposes are right for contract.

The relevance of evaluating contract for its instrumental efficiency and effectiveness is almost self-evident. After all, such evaluative enquiry involves nothing less than an understanding of whether contract "works"—for example whether its rules actually facilitate or hinder commerce, whether they actually protect consumers, whether its institutions facilitate the settlement and avoidance of disputes, and so on. Indeed, questions of this type are already implicit in the drive towards understanding more about the practical operation of contract. The more we understand practice, the clearer our appreciation of which legal devices do and do not work (and how they work), and the better informed and more effective our reforming proposals.

The case for the relevance of enquiry focused on the moral legitimacy of contract (in general or in its particular manifestations), however, is, if anything, even more compelling. To say that one understood contract without enquiring into this aspect would be rather like saying that one understood slavery without realising that it was immoral. Similarly, we cannot understand contract without calling into question its moral legitimacy, without questioning, for example, whether the transformations in contract are morally progressive or regressive (which is not necessarily equivalent to evaluating it in terms of the concepts entailed in the judicial ideologies we employed, which were purely descriptive). Contract is one of our enduring social institutions and we are accountable for its legitimacy. To neglect our moral responsibility for contract is not simply to undermine our understanding, it is to neglect our civic responsibility.

Cynics, of course, may protest that we cannot really attach much importance to evaluative enquiries, otherwise we surely would have paid more attention to such matters. This, however, overlooks our prefatory remarks in which we explained that our intention was to provide a rough map of the area, which would, as it were, familiarise the reader with the lie of the land. Our map suggests that understanding contract calls for the pursuit of various lines of enquiry, including evaluative enquiry. Equally, though, it presupposes that some sequences of enquiry are more rational than others. In particular, we take it that someone who wished to evaluate a practice would do well first to have an accurate description of the practice. Accordingly, we have devoted considerable space to description rather than evaluation of judicial employment of the rule-book, not because we think evaluation is unimportant, but because we think that it is important for evaluation to have some purchase on practice as it is, rather than on practice as it is mistakenly supposed to be.

To these concluding comments, we can add a postscript. Readers may wonder if it would not take something of a Renaissance man to understand contract. After all, the thrust of our presentation is that a critical understanding of contract involves tangling with philosophy, sociology, history, and economics, quite apart from mastering traditional legal skills. Is this not rather a tall order? To this we can only confess and avoid. Understanding contract certainly is a tall order, but whoever suggested that it would be easy?

BIBLIOGRAPHY

References in text

Adams, John N. (1978a), "Consideration for Requirements Contracts", 94 *Law Quarterly Review* 73.

Adams, John N. (1978b), "The Standardisation of Commercial Contracts or the Contractualisation of Standard Forms" 7 *Anglo-American Law Review* 136.

Adams, John N. (1979), *"Hadley v Baxendale* and the Contract/Tort Dichotomy", 8 *Anglo-American Law Review* 147.

Adams, John N. (1983), "The Battle of the Forms", *Journal of Business Law* 297.

Adams, John N., Beyleveld, Deryck and Brownsword, Roger, (1997) "Privity of Contract—the Benefits and Burdens of Law Reform" 60 *Moden Law Review* 238.

Adams, John N. and Brownsword, Roger (1982) "Contractual Indemnity Clauses", *Journal of Business Law* 200.

Adams, John N. and Brownsword, Roger (1988a), "The Unfair Contract Terms Act: A Decade of Discretion" 104 *Law Quarterly Review* 94.

Adams, John N. and Brownsword, Roger (1988b), "Double Indemnity—Contractual Indemnity Clauses Revisited" *Journal of Business Law* 146.

Adams, John N. and Brownsword, Roger (1990a), "Contract, Consideration and the Critical Path" 53 *Modern Law Review* 536.

Adams, John N. and Brownsword, Roger (1990b), "Privity & the Concept of a Network Contract" 10 *Legal Studies* 12.

Adams, John N. and Brownsword, Roger (1991), "More in Expectation than Hope: The Blackpool Airport Case" 54 *Modern Law Review* 281.

Adams, John N. and Brownsword, Roger (1993), "Privity of Contract—That Pestilential Nuisance" 56 *Modern Law Review* 722.

Adams, John N. and Brownsword, Roger (2003) *Understanding Law*, 3rd ed., London: Sweet & Maxwell.

American Law Institute (1981), *Restatement of the Law Second Contracts 2d*, St Paul, Minn.: American Law Institute Publishers.

Anderson, Perry (1974), *Passages from Antiquity to Feudalism*, London: New Left Books.

Atiyah, Patrick S. (1978a) "Promises, Oligations and the Law of Contract" 94 *Law Quarterly Review* 193.

Atiyah, Patrick S. (1978b), "From Principles to Pragmatism", Oxford: Clarendon Press.

Atiyah, Patrick S. (1989), *An Introduction to the Law of Contract*, 4th ed., Oxford: Clarendon Press.

Bacchetta, Marc; Low, Patrick; Mattoo, Aaditya; Schuknecht, Ludger; Wager, Hannu and Wehrens, Madelon (1998), *Electronic Commerce and the Role of the WTO*, World Trade Organisation, Geneva.

Barron, Anne and Scott, Colin (1992), "The Citizen's Charter Programme" 55 *Modern Law Review* 526.

Barton, J.L. (1969), "The Early History of Consideration", 85 *Law Quarterly Review* 372.

Beale, Hugh and Dugdale, Tony (1975), "Contracts between Businessmen: Planning and the Use of Contractual Remedies", 2 *British Journal of Law and Society* 45.

Beatson, J (2002) *Anson's Law of Contract*, 28th ed., Oxford: Oxford University Press.

Beatson, Jack and Friedmann, Daniel (eds) (1995), *Good Faith and Fault in Contract Law*, Oxford: Clarendon Press.

Bendix, Reinhard (1959), *Max Weber: an Intellectual Portrait*, London: Methuen.

Blackstone, Sir William (1825), *Commentaries on the Laws of England*, 16th ed., London: Cadell and Butterworth.

Blegvad, Britt-Mari (1990), "Contract and Litigation in Denmark: A Discussion of Macaulay's Theories" 24 *Law and Society Review* 397.

Braudel, Fernand (1986), *The Mediterranean and the Mediterranean World in the Age of Phillip II*, London: Fontana/Collins.

Bright, Susan, "Winning the Battle Against Unfair Contract Terms" (2000) 20 *Legal Studies* 331.

Brownsword, Roger (1977), "Remedy-Stipulation in the English Law of Contract: Freedom or Paternalism?", 9 *Ottawa Law Review* 95.

Brownsword, Roger (1985), "Henry's Lost Spectacle and Hutton's Lost Speculation: a Classic Riddle Solved?", 129 *Solicitors' Journal* 860.

Brownsword, Roger (1989), "Liberalism and the Law of Contract" in Richard Bellamy (ed.) *Liberalism and Recent Legal and Social Philosophy*, Stuttgart: Franz Steiner 86.

Brownsword, Roger (1992), "Retrieving Reasons, Retrieving Rationality? A New Look at the Right to Withdraw for Breach of Contract" 5 *Journal of Contract Law* 83.

Brownsword, Roger (1993), "Towards a Rational Law of Contract" in Thomas Wilhelmsson (ed.) *Perspectives of Critical Contract Law*, Aldershot: Dartmouth, 241.

Brownsword, Roger (1994), "The Philosophy of Welfarism and its Emergence in the Modern English Law of Contract" in Brownsword, Roger; Howells, Geraint and Wilhelmsson, Thomas (eds), *Welfarism in Contract Law*, Aldershot: Dartmouth, 21.

Brownsword, Roger (1996), "Static and Dynamic Market-Individualism" in Halson, Roger (ed.), *Exploring the Boundaries of Contract*, Aldershot: Dartmouth, 48.

Brownsword, Roger (1997), "Contract Law, Co-operation, and Good Faith: The Movement from Static to Dynamic Market-Individualism" in Deakin, Simon and Michie, Jonathan (eds) (1997), *Contracts, Co-operation and Competition*, Oxford: Oxford University Press, 255.

Brownsword, Roger (1998), "Copyright Assignment, Fair Dealing, and Unconscionable Contracts" *Intellectual Property Quarterly* 311.

Brownsword, Roger; Hird, Norma and Howells, Geraint (eds) (1999), *Good Faith in Contract, Concept and Context*, Aldershot: Ashgate.

Brownsword, Roger and Howells, Geraint (1999), "When Surfers Start to Shop: Internet Commerce and Contract Law" 19 *Legal Studies* 287.

Brownsword, Roger and Hutchinson, Dale (2000), "Privity of Contract: Beyond Promissory Principle and Protective Pragmatism", *Theoretical Approaches to Privity* (ed. Peter Kincaid) Aldershot: Ashgate, 126.

Brownsword, Roger (2001a), "Freedom of Contract, Human Rights and Human Dignity" in Daniel Friedmann and Daphne Barak-Erez (eds) *Human Rights in Private Law*, Oxford: Hart Publishing, 181.

Brownsword, Roger (2001b),"Individualism, Co-operativism and an Ethic for European Contract Law" 64 *Modern Law Review* 628.

Brownsword, Roger (2003a), "After *Investors*: Interpretation, Expectation and the Implicit Dimension of the 'New Contextualism'" in David Campbell, Hugh Collins, and John Wightman (eds), *Implicit Dimensions of Contract*, Oxford: Hart Publishing, 103.

Brownsword, Roger (2003b), "General Considerations" in M.P. Furmston (ed), *The Law of Contract* 2nd ed, London: Butterworths.

Burrows, Andrew (1993), *The Law of Restitution*, London: Butterworths.

Campbell, David and Harris, Donald (1993), "Flexibility in Long-Term Contractual Relationships: The Role of Co-operation" 20 *Journal of Law and Society* 166.

Campbell, David and Vincent-Jones, Peter (eds) (1997), *Contract and Economic Organisation*, Aldershot: Dartmouth.

Clapham, Andrew (1993), *Human Rights in the Private Sphere*, Oxford: Clarendon Press.

Collins, Hugh (1986), *The Law of Contract*, London: Weidenfeld and Nicholson.

Collins, Hugh (1992), "Implied Duty to Give Information During Performance of Contracts" 55 *Modern Law Review* 556.

Collins, Hugh (1993), "The Transformation Thesis and the Ascription of Contractual Responsibility" in Thomas Wilhelmsson (ed.) *Perspectives of Critical Contract Law*, Aldershot: Dartmouth, 293.

Coote, Brian (1964), *Exception Clauses*, London: Sweet and Maxwell.

Cross, Rupert (1991), *Precedent in English Law*, 4th ed., Oxford: Clarendon Press.

Danzig, Richard (1975), "*Hadley v Baxendale*: a Study in the Industrialization of the Law", 4 *Journal of Legal Studies* 249.

Deakin, Simon and Michie, Jonathan (eds) (1997), *Contracts, Co-operation and Competition*, Oxford: Oxford University Press.

Dworkin, Ronald (1986), *Law's Empire*, London: Fontana.

Farnsworth, E.A. (1987), "Pre-contractual Liability and Preliminary Agreements: Fair Dealing and Failed Negotiations" 87 *Columbia Law Review* 217.

Forte, A (ed.) (1999), *Good Faith in Contract and Property Law*, Oxford: Hart Publishing.

Friedman, Lawrence M. (1965), *Contract Law in America: a Social and Economic Case Study*, Madison, Wisc: University of Wisconsin Press.

Friedmann, Wolfgang (1972), *Law in a Changing Society*, 2nd ed., Harmondsworth: Penguin.

Fuller, Lon L. and Perdue, William R. (1936), "The Reliance Interest in Contract Damages", 46 *Yale Law Journal* 52 and 373.

Furmston, M.P. (2001), *Cheshire, Fifoot and Furmston's Law of Contract*, 14th ed., London: Butterworth.

Furmston, Michael (1996), "Unidroit General Principles for International Commercial Contracts" 10 *Journal of Contract Law* 11.

Furmston, Michael (2000), "How Modern is English Contract Law?" 39 *Saggi, Conferenze e Seminari*, Rome.

Gabel, Peter and Feinman, Jay M. (1982), "Contract Law as Ideology" in D. Kairys (ed.), *The Politics of Law*, New York: Pantheon Books.

Galanter, Marc and Rogers, Joel (1988). "The Transformation of American Business Disputing? Some Preliminary Observations" (paper presented at the 1988 Annual Meeting of the Law and Society Association, Vail, Colorado).

Gilmore, Grant (1974), *The Death of Contract*, Colombus, Ohio: Ohio State University Press.

Gordley, James (1991), *The Philosophical Origins of Modern Contract Doctrine* Oxford: Clarendon Press.

Gordley, James (ed.) (2001), *The Enforceability of Promises in European Contract Law*, Cambridge: Cambridge University Press.

Harden, Ian (1992), *The Contracting State*, Buckingham: Open University Press.

Harvey, Brian W. and Parry, Deborah (1992), *The Law of Consumer Protection and Fair Trading*, 4th edn., London: Butterworth.

Havighurst, Harold C. (1961), *The Nature of Private Contract*, Evanston: Northwestern University Press.

Heldrich, Andreas and Rehm, Gebhard M (2001), "Importing Constitutional Values through Blanket Clauses", in Daniel Friedmann and Daphne Barak-Erez (eds), *Human Rights in Private Law*, Oxford: Hart Publishing, 113.

Holdsworth, Sir William, *History of English Law*.

Holmes, Oliver Wendell (1881), *The Common Law*, Boston: Little, Brown.

Holmes, Oliver Wendell (1899), "The Theory of Legal Interpretation", 12 *Harvard Law Review* 417.

Horwitz, Morton J. (1977), *The Transformation of American Law 1780–1860*, Cambridge, Mass.: Harvard University Press.

Hurst, James Willard (1956), *Law and the Conditions of Freedom in the Nineteenth-Century United States*, Madison, Wisc.: University of Wisconsin Press.

Kennedy, Duncan (1976), "Form and Substance in Private Law Adjudication" 89 *Harvard Law Review* 1685.

Lando, Ole and Beale, Hugh (eds) (1995), *The Principles of European Contract Law* (Part 1: Performance, Non-Performance and Remedies) Dordrecht: Martinus Nijhoff.

Law Commission (1991), _Privity of Contract: Contracts for the Benefit of Third Parties_ (Consultation Paper No. 121).

Law Commission (1996), _Privity of Contract: Contracts for the Benefit of Third Parties_ (Law Com. No. 242) (Cm. 3329, July 1996).

Law Commission (2002), _Unfair Terms in Contracts_ (Consultation Paper No. 166).

Law Revision Committee (1937), Sixth Interim Report, _Statute of Frauds and the Doctrine of Consideration_, (Cmd 5449).

Levack, Brian P. (1973), _The Civil Lawyers in England 1603–1641_, Oxford: Clarendon Press.

Llewellyn, Karl N. (1940), "The Normative, the Legal, and the Law-Jobs: the Problem of Juristic Method", 49 _Yale Law Journal_ 1355.

Llewellyn, Karl N. (1960), _The Common Law Tradition: Deciding Appeals_, Boston: Little, Brown.

McLauchlan, D.W. (2000), "The New Law of Contract Interpretation" 19 _New Zealand Universities Law Review_ 147.

Macaulay, Stewart (1963), "Non-Contractual Relations in Business", 28 _American Sociological Review_ 55.

Macaulay, Stewart (1966), _Law and the Balance of Power: the Automobile Manufacturers and their Dealers_, New York: Russell Sage Foundation.

Macaulay, Stewart (1977), "Elegant Models, Empirical Patterns, and the Complexities of Contract", 11 _Law and Society Review_ 507.

Macdonagh, Oliver (1980), "Pre-transformations: Victorian Britain", in E. Kamenka and A.E.-S. Tay (eds.), _Law and Social Control_, London: Edward Arnold.

Machiavelli, N. (1961), _The Prince_, Harmondsworth: Penguin.

Macneil, Ian R. (1974), "The Many Futures of Contract", 47 _Southern California Law Review_ 691.

Macneil, Ian R. (1978), "Contracts: Adjustments of Long-Term Economic Relations under Classical, Neo-Classical and Relational Contract Law", 72 _Northwestern University Law Review_ 854.

Maine, Sir Henry Sumner (1861), _Ancient Law_, originally published 1861, London: Dent 1917.

Marwick, Arthur (1989), _The Nature of History_, 3rd ed. London: Macmillan.

Mocatta, Sir A.A., Mustill, Sir M.J. and Boyd, S.C. (1996), _Scrutton on Charterparties_, 20th ed., London: Sweet and Maxwell.

Murray, Andrew D. (2000), "Entering into Contracts Electronically: The Real W.W.W." in Lilian Edwards and

Charlotte Waelde (eds), *Law and the Internet* 2d ed., Oxford: Hart Publishing, 17.

Office of Fair Trading (1999), *Unfair Contract Terms*, (Bulletin No. 6) April, 1999.

Paley, William (1809), *The Principles of Moral and Political Philosophy*, 1809 ed. (London, first published 1758).

Peel, Edwin (1993), "Making More Use of the Unfair Contract Terms Act 1977: *Stewart Gill Ltd v Horatio Myer and Co Ltd*" 56 *Modern Law Review* 98.

Phillipson, Gavin (1999), "The Human Rights Act, 'Horizontal Effect' and the Common Law: a Bang or a Whimper?" 62 *Modern Law Review* 824.

Poole, Jill (1996), "Damages for Breach of Contract— Compensation and 'Personal Preferences'" 59 *Modern Law Review* 272.

Posner, Richard A. (1992), *Economic Analysis of Law* 4th ed. Boston: Little, Brown.

Powell, John Joseph (1790), *Essay Upon the Law of Contracts and Agreements* (first published Dublin; later editions 1796 and 1802).

Powell, Raphael (1956) "Good Faith in Contracts" 9 *Current Legal Problems* 16.

Rubinstein, W.D. (1993) *Capitalism, Culture and Decline in Britain*, London: Routledge.

Schmitthoff, C. (1981), *Commercial Law in a Changing Economic Climate* (2nd ed.), London: Sweet and Maxwell.

Scheiber, Harry N. (ed.) (1998), *The State and Freedom of Contract*, Stanford: Stanford University Press.

Simpson, A.W.B. (1966), "The Penal Bond with Conditional Defeasence", 82 *Law Quarterly Review* 392.

Simpson, A.W.B. (1975), "Innovation in Nineteenth Century Contract Law", 91 *Law Quarterly Review* 247.

Simpson, A.W.B. (1979), "The Horwitz Thesis and the History of Contracts", 46 *University of Chicago Law Review* 533.

Simpson, A.W.B., ed. (1984), *Biographical Dictionary of the Common Law*, London: Butterworth.

Simpson, A.W.B. (1985), "Quackery and Contract Law: the Case of the Carbolic Smoke Ball", 14 *Journal of Legal Studies* 345.

Staughton, Sir Christopher (1999), "How Do the Courts Interpret Commercial Contracts?" *Cambridge Law Journal* 303.

Steyn, Johan (1996), "Does Legal Formalism Hold Sway in England?" 49 *Current Legal Problems* 43.

Steyn, Johan (1997), "Contract Law: Fulfilling the Reasonable Expectations of Honest Men" 113 *Law Quarterly Review* 433.

Summers, Robert S. (1968), "Good Faith in General Contract Law and the Sales Provisions of the Uniform Commercial Code", 54 *Virginia Law Review* 195.

Treitel, G.H. (1981), "Doctrine and Discretion in the Law of Contract", Oxford: Clarendon Press.

Treitel, G.H. (2003), *The Law of Contract*, 11th ed., London: Sweet & Maxwell.

Trubek, David M. (1975), "Notes on the Comparative Study of Processes of Handling Disputes Between Economic Enterprises" (paper presented at the US-Hungarian Conference on Contract Law and the Problems of Large Scale Economic Enterprise, New York).

Turpin, Colin C. (1989), *Government Procurement and Contracts*, Harlow: Longman.

Twigg-Flesner, Christian (2003a), *Consumer Product Guarantees*, Aldershot: Ashgate .

Twigg-Flesner, Christian (2003b), "New Remedies for Consumer Sales Transactions: A Change for the Worse?" 2 *Journal of Obligations and Remedies* 5.

Twining, William (1973), *Karl Llewellyn and the Realist Movement*, London: Weidenfeld and Nicolson.

Ullmann, Walter (1975), *Medieval Political Thought*, Harmondsworth: Penguin.

Unger, Roberto M. (1976), *Law in Modern Society*, New York: Free Press.

Vincent-Jones, Peter (1989), "Contract and Business Transactions: A Socio-Legal Analysis" 16 *Journal of Law and Society* 166.

Von Bar, Christian, and Lando, Ole (2002), "Communication on European Contract Law: Joint Response of the Commission on European Contract Law and the Study Group on a European Civil Code" 10 *European Review of Private Law* 183.

Waddams, S.M. (1976), "Unconscionability in Contracts" 39 *Modern Law Review* 369.

Wade, Sir William (2000), "Horizons of Horizontality" 16 *Law Quarterly Review*, 217.

Weber, Max (1968), *On Charisma and Institution Building* (ed. by S.N. Eisenstadt), Chicago: University of Chicago Press.

Weber, Max (1978), *Economy and Society*, Berkeley: University of California Press.

White, James J. and Summers, Robert S. (1995), *Uniform Commercial Code*, 4th ed., St Paul, Minn.: West Publishing Co.

Wiener, Martin J. (1985), *English Culture and the Decline of the Industrial Spirit, 1850–1980*, Harmondsworth: Penguin.

Wightman, John (1989), "Reviving Contract" 52 *Modern Law Review* 115.

Wilhelmsson, Thomas (1992), *Critical Studies in Private Law*, Dordrecht: Kluwer.

Wilhelmsson, Thomas (1993), "Questions for a Critical Contract Law and a Contradictory Answer: Contract as Social Cooperation" in Thomas Wilhelmsson (ed.) *Perspectives of Critical Contract Law*, Aldershot: Dartmouth, 9.

Williamson, Oliver (1979), "Transaction-Cost Economics. The Governance of Contractual Relations" 22 *Journal of Law and Economics* 233.

Winfield, P.H. (1939), "Some Aspects of Offer and Acceptance", 55 *Law Quarterly Review* 499.

Further Reading

Atiyah, Patrick S. (1979), *The Rise and Fall of Freedom of Contract*, Oxford: Oxford University Press.

Atiyah, Patrick S. (1986), *Essays on Contract*, Oxford: Clarendon Press.

Beale, Hugh G. (1980), *Remedies for Breach of Contract*, London: Sweet and Maxwell.

Beale, H.G., Bishop, W.D. and Furmston, M.P. (1990), *Contract, Cases and Materials*, 2nd ed. London: Butterworth.

Fried, Charles (1981), *Contract as Promise*, Cambridge, Mass.: Harvard University Press.

Macneil, Ian R. (1981), *The New Social Contract*, New Haven: Yale University Press.

Tillotson, John (1985), *Contract Law in Perspective*, 2nd ed., London: Butterworth.

Wightman, John (1996), *Contract: A Critical Commentary*, London: Pluto Press.

Yates, David (1982), *Exclusion Clauses in Contracts*, 2nd ed., London: Sweet and Maxwell.

TABLE OF CASES

INDEX

[all references are to page number]